Unheard Voices

Farah Naz • Dieter Bögenhold

Unheard Voices

Women, Work and Political Economy of Global Production

palgrave
macmillan

Farah Naz
Department of Sociology
University of Sargodha
Sargodha, Pakistan

Dieter Bögenhold
Faculty of Management and
Economics, Department of Sociology
University of Klagenfurt
Klagenfurt, Austria

ISBN 978-3-030-54362-4 ISBN 978-3-030-54363-1 (eBook)
https://doi.org/10.1007/978-3-030-54363-1

This Palgrave Macmillan imprint is published by the registered company Springer Nature Switzerland AG.
The registered company address is: Gewerbestrasse 11, 6330 Cham, Switzerland

Preface

As the title of the book *Unheard Voices: Women, Work and Political Economy of Global Production* itself suggests, there are agents in business and society who are weak and who have no or just very small voices to articulate their interests and to fight for their rights in global production system. In particular, authors are dealing with the question of how and under what conditions female home-based workers contribute to global supply chains. The *Unheard Voices* bring together the work and experience of authors having diverse background. The author, Farah Naz, works at a university in Pakistan, where many production places in that region employ female home-based workers who work on (final) commission of the world-known brands engaged in the industry of sports articles. The other author, Dieter Bögenhold, works in Austria, where all those seemingly European products and companies are located and shops and supermarkets are flooded with those nice brands which we all know and particularly wear, Adidas or Nike being among the most known ones.

The book builds on different elements and includes many intensive research pieces, accomplished by Farah Naz through her empirical investigation in global football industry. This research was carried out in the course of her PhD thesis that she submitted at Klagenfurt University in 2016, but the working parts are integrated with several others and still ongoing research results. Dieter Bögenhold is undertaking research, partly with Farah Naz, partly in different other contexts, on global inequalities, work and political economy. The book reflects that behind the two seemingly different worlds with sometimes very diverse forms of economy, business and culture, in which the authors are currently residing, some of the same procedures coexist. Behind the international scenery of different national states, one common logic governs, that is, the logic of global capitalism, which is the universal bracket of social and economic life world-wide, determining careers and family destinies, fostering social and economic prosperity but also resulting in diverse forms of specific ecological, social and economic problems.

Narrowly, the book is about living conditions of female workers in home-based working locations in Pakistan, mostly—at the end of global supply chains—on commission of Western companies with established international brands whose voices are never heard, whose working and living situations are mostly overlooked, whose dreams and zones of aspiration are unknown and who belong, from a Western point of view, to a seemingly very distant and very different social sphere of the globe. Western contemporaries acknowledge very rarely *the fact* that conditions under which people sell their labour around the world are far from uniform. Rather, labour market choices are in fact shaped by geographically and culturally specific circumstances.

The profits of one side are the missing or damaged profit processes of the other side. This book puts forward the case of football industry of Pakistan to illustrate the tensions and contradictions between dominant globalized views about industrial home-based work and lived realities of these workers in developing countries like Pakistan. The attempts to look at the home-based work from the analytical perspective of Western development and moral frameworks have had a significant impact on the effectiveness of policies introduced to improve labour conditions in developing countries. Most of these tensions stem from the divergence in views on what constitutes, moral framework, well-being and quality of life. The *Unheard Voices* places this embedded tension in global production organization within a context, by drawing attention to various social, economic, structural and moral issues that surround the existing debate about corporate responsibility, ethical standards and informal home-based work.

Over the past 30 years or more, there has been a growing body of literature examining how especially multinational Western corporations try to adapt to ethical standards in the working process but also in the perception of the ecological environment. Especially obvious are those firm strategies in developing countries where often less institutionalized regulations exist so that Western firms find themselves forced by expectations from their home countries to implement higher ethical standards to govern corporate strategies. However, independently of possible serious intentions,

CSR strategies also serve as drug to make economic ambitions cleaner, and they are used for purposes of corporate self-promotion or ecological alibi. Football industry provides an interesting context in which to study the relationship between CSR and working conditions in global supply chains.

Empirical evidence presented in the book shows that female homeworkers, stitching footballs for international brands, are paid so little that it is impossible to secure the family's income, despite full working days and hard labour. Many of them earn considerably less than men who do the same jobs. At the end, work and income situations are so precarious that further sources of income have to be sought for the time after a full regular working day. Through the narrative life story interviews, the study lets people speak, and it is concluded that the evaluation of individual experiences is highly dependent upon the stories of life-courses which have to be seen as stories of individual generations and related age cohorts. Memories are highly selective and always based on those constructions of life careers. Analysing the real perception and well-being of those football stitchers, the book distinguishes between economic, individual and social and psychological well-being. The result is a multi-complex social relativity theory, which is far beyond binary black-and-white schemes, but which shows a variety of shades of grey. People's attitudes and behaviour must be studied within the institutional framework of space, culture, history, economy and society and cannot be defined ex cathedra from theory.

The topic and messages of the *Unheard Voices: Women, Work and Political Economy of Global Production* are truly interdisciplinary. In a narrow sense, the authors are asking how female homeworkers work and survive in Sialkot, Pakistan, where they are engaged as homeworkers stitching together leather footballs for international brands. In a wider sense, the authors follow a much more general question by taking all the local observations and evaluations as an example of general mechanisms of one and the same global world system of capitalism. The book will show broadly why it is so necessary to conduct a study on homeworkers. Homework appears to be very traditional but it isn't. The opposite is true, homework is analysed as being ultimately incorporated in the flux of global capitalism. In the case of this investigation, homeworkers are producers of sports equipment, which is taken on Wednesdays and Saturdays by soccer players from Madrid, Barcelona, Manchester, Turin or Munich, fascinating the masses in European societies. The reader will get the message that the football champions league and football production in a district in the Pakistan are two sides of the same medal.

The discussion we wish to engender is whether the twenty-first century shall be the century where debate on social phenomena shall be referenced primarily to individual nation states and their very limited framework or to the social universe of a global world society. Too often we rationalize and act only in categories of individual states in which we are living as point of reference. If we say that somebody is poor or rich, we mean implicitly our national context as reference scale. Of course, this procedure is very simple-minded and narrow from an enlightened academic perspective. Instead, this book and all the related questions must be read with a perspective that *all* human beings are living in one interconnected but *unequal* world.

Sargodha, Pakistan — Farah Naz
Klagenfurt, Austria — Dieter Bögenhold

Contents

1 Introduction: Political Economy of Globalization 1

2 Transformation of Labour Market and Gender Patterns of Work 19

3 Homeworkers in Global Supply Chains: Issues and Controversies 45

4 CSR and Home-Based Work: Conceptualizing Social Responsibility in Global Market Economy 75

5 Dilemmas of Corporate Responsibility in a Globalized World: Empirical Evidences from Global Football Industry 97

6 Home-Based Work and Political Economy of Global Football Production Organization 123

7 Unheard Voices: Globalization Stories from Invisible Margins 157

8 What Lessons Did We Learn? 181

Index 195

Abbreviations

BWI	Bretton Woods Institutions
CA	Capability Approach
CBS	Columbia Broadcasting System
CSR	Corporate Social Responsibility
EOBI	Employees' Old-Age Benefits Institution
EPZ	Export Promotion Zones
EU	European Union
FDI	Foreign Direct Investment
FGD	Focus Group Discussion
GCC	Global Commodity Chain
GPN	Global Production Networks
GSP	Global Supply Chain
GVC	Global Value Chain
ICSE	International Classification of Status in Employment
IFIs	International Financial Institutions
ILO	International Labour Organization
IMAC	Independent Monitoring Association for Child Labour
IMF	International Monetary Fund
IPEC	International Programme on the Elimination of Child Labour
LDCs	Less-Developed Countries
LPT	Labour Process Theory
MNCs	Multinational Corporations
MNEs	Multinational Enterprises
NAFTA	North American Free Trade Agreement
NGOs	Non-Governmental Organizations
OEM	Original Equipment Manufacturers

SAPs	Structural Adjustment Programmes
TNC	Transnational Companies
UEFA	Union of European Football Associations
UN	United Nations
UNICEF	United Nations International Children Emergency Fund
USA	Unites States of America
WB	World Bank

List of Figures

Fig. 2.1	Women in production. (Source: Authors elaboration based on literature review)	27
Fig. 3.1	Quorom flowchart of literature review. (Source: Authors elaboration. Petticrew and Roberts (2006))	46
Fig. 3.2	Summary chart of literature review. (Source: Author's elaboration)	52
Fig. 4.1	CSR and network of actors in GPNs. (Source: Authors elaboration)	86
Fig. 5.1	Impact of and responses to ban on home-based stitching in Sialkot, Pakistan. (Source: Authors elaboration)	108
Fig. 5.2	Causal flow of responses to a fall in earnings by homeworking household. (Source: Focus Group Discussions)	117
Fig. 6.1	Football production organization Sialkot, Pakistan. (Source: Author's elaboration)	129
Fig. 6.2	Integration of football stitchers into the global football supply chain. (Source: Naz and Boegenhold (2020))	131

List of Tables

Table 3.1	Summary of the Literature	48
Table 6.1	Earnings in Football Stitching in Pakistan, December 2014	132
Table 6.2	Estimate of Living Wages	135
Table 7.1	Operationalisation of well-being of female homeworkers	171

CHAPTER 1

Introduction: Political Economy of Globalization

World Society and Inequalities

The Covid-19 virus pandemic, which evolved in early 2020 and had started in the city Wuhan in People's Republic of China, demonstrates very well how fragile and interdependent the global word system is. The virus spread across the globe, ignoring national borders and reaching almost all countries, and infected a tremendous number of people, tens of thousands of whom died. The virus brought the whole world society and economy to a standstill, causing a lockdown of a scale that has never happened in before. No single country proved to be immune against the evolution of the disease, and no country was successfully prepared and armed against the upcoming developments. People became ill and were dying everywhere, and the whole system of previous reasonable forecasting proved to be full of scientific flaws. The task of modelling economic, social and environmental developments is always dependent upon the axiomatic input of model constructers.[1] If applicants of those econometric models create their ideas in a sterile world of assumptions, it is a clean world of certainty where all external variables are known and calculable or where those external variables are just ignored, and surprising effects, non-intended consequences and interdisciplinary problems will not occur. Instead, we are living in a dynamic world which includes different dimensions of uncertainties which comprises different degrees of complexity

[1] For different models in the history of economics and econometrics, see Morgan (2012).

F. Naz, D. Bögenhold, *Unheard Voices*,
https://doi.org/10.1007/978-3-030-54363-1_1

leading permanently to effects which are not forecasted (Merton, 1936). However, the real world is not (always) clean but (sometimes) dirty when further phenomena and consequences exist which are not included in the initial assumptions. Opposed to a model world, in a real world many shades between black and white exist.

The same issue applies for our topic of globalization. Firstly, the sharp battle about the advantages and disadvantages of globalization processes, which we have been observing for a few decades at least, has seemingly become less controversial during the past few years because people started to think that there are no visible alternatives to an increased internationalization called globalization. Anthony Giddens has defined globalization as a social process of "intensification of worldwide social relations which link distant localities in such a way that local happenings are shaped by events occurring many miles away and vice versa" (Giddens, 1990: 64). Of course, according to this definition, we are living in an increasingly globalized world where forms of economic, social, cultural and environmental exchange or interplay are more visible and influential than in earlier times. Apparently, the globe has turned into a "world society", a term that was introduced, independently of each other, by Wallerstein (1983, 2011), N. Luhmann (1971) and John W. Meyer (Meyer, Boli, Thomas, & Ramirez, 1981). The idea of world society claims that debate on social phenomena shall not only be referenced to individual nation states and their very limited framework but to a social universe of a global world society.

Numerous studies have found a close relationship between economic globalization and trade liberalization (Barrientos, 2019; Kurian, 2003; Staples, 2006). How global and universal trade do not automatically interact with an increase of wealth and sustainability, at least not for the Third World countries, has been shown in numerous studies. Especially in the case of the food industries, such as bananas and other well-known fruits, we know that these fruits travel from poor to rich countries and their consumers do not bring reasonable profit to those people living in producer countries, who do not always have enough food and water. Similarly, for the produce of tomato one can reconstruct working principles of global capitalism where individual products are crossing many borders (Barndt, 2008). Trade liberalization has been increasing the global lottery of world capitalism where winners and losers emerge newly and simultaneously. Long-term observations show that globalization processes have existed since a long time (Gills & Thomson, 2006).

Looking at the multiplication of entrepreneurial billionaires in the world (Bögenhold, 2019) shows that one reason for the enormous accumulation of such wealth is that globalization, understood as the increased economic, political, social and cultural interconnectedness of the world, has produced many more opportunities in different parts of the world, which have enabled some people to increase their wealth vastly (Giddens, 2009: 525), while on the other hand we find a lot of poverty all over the world, including people suffering from hunger, homeless people without even a roof over their heads and working migrants who are pushed around the world in order to raise income to try to feed their families (Case & Deaton, 2020). The bottom billion (Collier, 2007) often has no access to gas and electricity for cooking, drinking water and water in the toilets, education in schools and sufficient medical care; therefore, life expectancies are comparatively short (World Bank, 2002). Social stratification research deals with inequalities, and, vice versa, inequality is the indicator of the degree of social stratification, in individual countries and between countries.

Unheard Voices is mainly about the topic of social stratification in a global world economy. The evolution of the richest and the poorest people in contemporary societies is almost buffered by people being between those strata. It may make sharp contrasts less visible. These are the middle classes. The middle classes are of interest for multiple reasons: (1) through the lenses of social order, integration and political conflict, the middle classes serve as a buffer between the strata; (2) the middle classes are defined as household groups in middle-income ranges between poverty and richness. They are open to new consumer markets, new fields to study lifestyles and, in relation to this, new consumer behaviour; (3) the middle classes are of interest for investigating patterns of inequality and social mobility. This last point is of particular relevance in view of the proposed decline in the middle classes in a globalized world. An important research question is whether there is an ongoing "de-middledization", a term coined by Bögenhold and Permana (2018). The question matters since all discussion on growing (or declining) inequality refers directly to the existence of the middle classes.

The concept of stratification refers to the idea of vertical segmentation in a sense of having more or less resources. There is apparently an analogy to the field of geology, where different forms of material stratification are investigated. The term "social stratification" is used to describe the system of social order in a vertical perspective. Degrees of stratification are always relational, and they express degrees of social inequality. Science is not primarily interested in the fate of individual actors but in social categories of humans as statistical categories.

The classic idea in Marx's categorization was that access to means of production serves as the pivot point of all sociological and economic analysis. This view was universal and dominant for decades. The positioning of actors in the stratification system was located in relation to the system of industrial relations and ownership. Being wage or salary dependent implied belonging to the class of proletarians, whereas all others belonged to the class of the bourgeoisie, the class of capitalists. Marx never produced a systematic treatise of the class topic; at the end of the third volume of his famous Capital (Marx, 1977), the text ends abruptly and remains unfinished after the introduction. All that we have is a collection and interpretation of Marx's ideas from various other places in his many written works. The principal view in the materialist Marxist perspective is that relations to the system of production govern the system of stratification. Accordingly, all other dimensions of life are subordinate to or consequences of the principal material position in society.

This programme was relevant for many academics for a long time, but has declined in its relevance and attraction during the last 40–50 years. Recent neo-Marxist approaches, especially the international world-system view by Wallerstein (2011), try to incorporate former analyses and modify the analysis process by adding global perspectives. An early programme contrasting to the dominant Marxist view was elaborated by Max Weber (1972 [1921]), who stressed the fact of differentiation (Giddens, 1973). Although he shared Marx's view that issues of property or non-property are fundamental concerns in society, Weber concluded that, within those two categories, manifold further steps of separation can be found according to qualification and related labour market chances. He said that different individual market chances correspond with different life chances, and, consequently, he talked about many further classes within the two main categories. As far as we identify specific market chances, we can talk about specific classes. However, Weber also introduced the concept of status as the subjective feeling and orientation of people in terms of lifestyles and cultural expressions. The concept of lifestyle within the framework of his *Protestant Ethics* (Weber, 1988) is mostly used as a caricature of the modern and "*standardized free*" way of living.

Another interesting research lens is whether globalization can and must be seen as a process of increasing Americanization in a sense of McDonaldization, as George Ritzer (1993) suggested in his often quoted book *The McDonaldization of Society* (Bögenhold & Naz, 2018; Ritzer, 1993). McDonaldization reminds us of plastic cutlery, turbo capitalism and mass production of food as new ways of practising consumption. Of course, his book deals directly with the development and success of the well-known fast-food restaurant chain, but on a second look McDonaldization implicates a process of globalization that creates similarities between countries. The term may also be used as proxy in order to explain capitalistic developments. Different forms of organizing economy and society apply the process of McDonaldization: grocery stores, the textile industry, the tourism and entertainment industries as well as credit cards. In all, globalization and McDonaldization are different lenses to look at the same processes of integrating different units into a more and more universal world society. The world society always experiences the same universal consumption goods which standardize and harmonize the cultural face and experience of daily life, at least in terms of goods such as Levi Strauss jeans, Samsung or Apple mobile phones, British pop music or Hollywood movie. We come across all these different items across the world when visiting different cities in different countries and looking at different generations.

Sociology of social stratification asks for the position of groups of humans in relation to others based upon income, wealth, education and further variables. Forms of social stratification can be described by objective measures of indicators. Being located higher up in the vertical social stratification of income has several serious implications since more available financial resources imply better food, living and housing, better education, health and further life chances. Human beings operate their activities in a social space within complex societies by socially constructed sense and cognitive mechanisms. In other words, social stratification implies a social logic of inclusion and exclusion, which means income, education and related scales of prestige create borders between different circles of people which integrate some and—vice versa—exclude others. All this reasoning shows our conceptual framework as to how and why to invest research on home-based female workers. We see them as part of the *team world society*, and we like to find out how they are relatively disadvantaged and because of whose advantages they are disadvantaged. The relative distance from a satisfying life of those who suffer near poverty or who are captured in poverty is sometimes mirrored as profit at the other hierarchical end of society. We try to analyse those interrelations between nations, social strata groups, income groups, labour force members and gender in order to provoke questions of social justice and fairness in the world, not more, not less. There are considerable discontents among scholars about the history, meaning, outcomes and processes of *globalization*. However, despite existing confusions and controversies that surround the concept, it generally refers to increasing interconnectedness among people, economies and cultures at the global level, which is facilitated through the massive reduction of costs of transportation and communication, and the breaking down of artificial barriers of cross-border flows of goods, services, capital, knowledge and people as well. However, this assumption about the inevitability of integration as essential component of globalization has been often challenged (Ritzer & Dean, 2015).

Existing literature (Bauman, 1998; Chirico, 2014; Stiglitz, 2002) supports the notion that globalization is not a uniform and neutral process, but rather that it is lacking in commonly assumed uniform effects and has multifaceted social causes and consequences. Due to diversity and complexity of the phenomenon, existing debates on globalization are polarized. The *great globalization debate* is between the *sceptics* and the *globalists* (Ritzer & Dean, 2015). For an individual human being, it makes a crucial difference where one is born. As a member of a rich(er) country, people have a *citizen premium* where—vice versa—those from poor(er) countries suffer a *citizen penalty*. "Citizenship premium (or citizenship rent; the terms are used interchangeably) … refers to the boost in income one receives simply from being a citizen of a rich country, while citizenship penalty is the reduction in income from being a citizen of a poor country" (Milanovic, 2019: 129). Milanovic (2019) talks about the bright and the dark sides of capitalism which belong ultimately together; he coins it an "inevitable amorality of hyper-commercialized capitalism" (Milanovic (2019: 176 ff.). This really opens up for a principal question as to what is legal and what is ethical or legitimate (Cohen, 2012).

Globalization and the Notion of Free Markets: Sceptics and Globalists

Scholars who adopt *globalist perspective* consider globalization as an irreversible process and the intractable fate of the world (Altman, 2007; Chanda, 2007). According to Bauman (2003), it is the most important change in human history that has become an omnipresent reality and is evident in various domains. Martin Wolf, a prominent neoliberal, in his book *Why Globalization Works* (Wolf, 2005), has argued that criticism of globalization is not just wrong but entirely misguided and almost, if not entirely, ungrounded. According to Wolf (2005), fragmentation of the economy into the isolated national economies would result in precipitous decline in standard of life. Some argue that globalization is such an important part of our lives that current era should undoubtedly be labelled as *global age* (Ritzer & Dean, 2015: 2). Globalists argue that globalization has led to the decline of nation state and market has greatly, if not entirely, supplanted state control especially in cross-border flow of goods and services (Yergin & Stanislaw, 1998: 396). However, the very notion of flow is attacked on the grounds that metaphor flow communicates a distorted sense of globalization. In words of Ferguson (2006: 47), globalization does not *flow*; it *hops*, instead, at least in some parts of the world. Existing inequalities between global North and South make a point that globalization flows swiftly in more advanced countries and outskirt many less developed regions of the world. Globalization is thus an uncomfortable combination of flow and hops.

The globalists highlight the role of economic structures such as multinational corporations (MNCs), the transnational economy and the emergence of a new global division of labour, whereas sceptics have turned this argument on its head and claim that the whole idea of free-market control has been exaggerated and the state has gained new control by use of more high-tech surveillance equipment for border control. Nowadays, states and various regional blocks are in a position to exert greater control on global economy. Most MNCs are maintaining close ties with nation states from which they originated. Sceptics expressed their genuine and understandable dismay about mass poverty and inequality that effectively exclude a wider portion of global population from the process that are generally associated with globalization. They argue that nation states and other regional groups largely restrict global flows. Thus, considering the diversity of processes and outcomes, it is hard to claim that there is a single process of globalization; rather, it can be safely concluded that there are multiple globalizations (economic, political, social and cultural). It is quite important to tease out the difference between economic, political and cultural globalization for conceptual clarity. Economic globalization is based on the principle of free market that demands opening of the market for cross-border flow of goods and services.

Political globalization refers to interstate relations that are largely but not entirely shaped by economic interests (So, 2012). Political globalization also encompasses other political relations, for example global organizations like United Nations are part of this global political arena. Globalization has also generated wider cultural flows in form of literature, performing arts, sports, education and so on between and among various nations. Although it is hard to divorce cultural globalization from other forms of globalization, it has a unique character and cannot be simply reduced to political or economic globalization. Globalists also acknowledge the merit of using term the *globalizations*, but they consider it just a terminological difference that eventually refers to same phenomenon.

Considering the plausibility of variety of globalizations, it is hard to trace a single specific driver of globalizations. One way to deal with this complex problem is to look for a general materialistic or ideological explanation. The classical examples of materialistic and ideological explanations can be traced in works of Karl Marx. Materialistic view led us to think about globalization in terms of material aspects and economic factors as the main drivers of the globalization. However, ideological explanations inspired by Hegel and, later on, young Hegelians rest on belief that changes in thinking and ideas are drivers of globalization. Max Weber has provided an intellectual middle ground in history of social theory by recognizing the significance of both ideal and material factors (Weber, [1927] 1981). In his work *Protestant Ethics and Spirit of Capitalism*, he emphasized the role of religious ideology in setting the scene for origin and growth of capitalism in the West.

It is evident from an overview of theoretical hinterlands of globalization that taking extreme positions like *globaphilia* or *globaphobia* though has some ground but is not entirely justified. What scholars from both camps ignore is the fact that globalization is neither a source of unlimited blessing as it is cherished by globaphilia, nor the mother of all evils that needs to be abolished as it is perceived by those closely associated with globaphobia.

Although from perspective of social sciences it is problematic to claim inexorability or inevitability of any social phenomenon, considering the existing conditions it could be concluded with a level of certainty that globalization trends, especially in economic sphere, are most likely to continue, even may accelerate, in years to come. Need for finding some middle ground is already fairly established in scholarly traditions.

Does Rising Sea Raises all Boats?

Although globalization has been explored from a variety of theoretical perspectives, the debate over globalization on ground is still unsettled. Globalization, on the one hand, has provided opportunities of integration and a reduced sense of isolation among the global population by providing access to knowledge that was previously denied to a wide majority. On the other hand, alongside the global opening of the space by means of economic globalization facilitated through finance, trade and information flow, there is also the localizing and space-fixing dimension of the process of globalization. Jagdish Bhagwati (2004), a prominent economist, in his influential work *In Defense of Globalization* (2004), reluctantly acknowledged some downsides of globalization. For some people, globalization means a new freedom and mobility, whereas for others globalization means localization, a new means of control and an uninvited fate. These closely connected but divergent processes have a differentiating impact on existential conditions of different segments of the global population. Regardless of repeated promises of development and poverty reduction, the actual number of poor increased to an estimated level of 100 million during last decade of the twentieth century, though there is an increase in overall world income (Stiglitz, 2002). The increasing disparity within and between countries points to the fact that globalization is not able to completely deliver on its promises, though there are some positive aspects like the increase in overall life expectancy that cannot be overlooked as well.

Eminent economist and Nobel Laureate Joseph Stiglitz,[2] in his book *Globalization and its Discontents* (2002), has rejected the deterministic view that globalization is all good or all bad. He effectively altered the terms of debate over globalization and associated controversies (Koechlin,

[2] The American economist Joseph E. Stiglitz was born in 1943. He was awarded the Nobel Prize for Economics in 2001 (jointly with George A. Akerlof and Michael Spence) for his work on markets and information, especially on the asymmetry of information.

2006). It is important to acknowledge at this point that Stiglitz is not anti-globalist and has not argued against globalization; rather, he made a case against globalization from above. Globalization from above is based on the premise that globalization is imposed by minority of powerful states, multinational companies (MNCs), and wealthy individuals. Stiglitz demanded improvement and better coordination of supranational organizations like WB and IMF (Bögenhold, 2015). *Globalization and its Discontents* (Stiglitz, 2002) is a scathing criticism on the role of International Monetary Fund (IMF) and its neoliberal[3] vision of globalization.

Although argument that globalization is mostly directed from above holds water, its power is far-fetched. People, in the words of Ritzer (2008: 387), are not ***judgmental dopes*** unconditionally following the dictates of powerful segments of the society. Rather, they are powerful agents (Giddens, 1984) who under certain conditions have at least some agency to swim against tide. There are many grass-roots movements protesting against the negative impacts of globalization. Such counter-reactions against globalization from marginalized groups are manifestation of the power of people and is commonly referred as globalization from below.

Preceding discussion shows that subject matter of the studies on globalization ranges from political, economic, geographic, ecological, religious and historical processes to increased complexities of inter-societal links and the growth of the sizes of social system (Sheffield, Korotayev, & Grinin, 2013). However, despite extensive existing literature on globalization, sheer magnitude, growing complexity and recurrent economic and political crisis today, there are demands for a more nuanced and contextualized understanding of the globalization processes. Globalization is not just limited to the actions of big players like giant corporations and state bodies but is also initiated at bottom by the actions of marginalized individuals and groups. The role and the impact that the economic reasoning of the market economy has on social life, and vice versa, is of immense significance and is gaining ground in current debates (Douglass, 1991).

This book embraces the need for empirical exploration of the local sociocultural manifestation of global political and economic processes.

[3] Neoliberalism as an economic theory is based on fundamental premise that free markets provide best possible economic outcome and any state intervention is detrimental for economic growth.

This chapter in particular deals with the interplay of global economic and political structures.

Political Economy of Globalization: An Overview

Economics as we know it today has a clear origin in political economy. One of the complex issues in a globalized world is to unpack various dimensions of these intertwined polar processes. Semantic of political economy is rather confusing as it means different things to different people depending on their respective worldview. Miller (2008) has articulated three different political-economic worldviews on capitalism: namely, free market, institutional, and Marxist. The history of political economy can be traced back to Scottish moral philosopher Adam Smith, whose book *The Wealth of Nations* (1776/1953) is considered the originating treatise of classical political economy. The field of political economy has gained a new resonance since 1980s due to the increasing evidence of comprehensive global economic interdependences. According to Miller (2008),

> International Political Economy is an interdisciplinary social science field of study that investigates, analyzes, and proposes changes in the processes of economic flows and political governance that cross over and/or transcend national boundaries. These flows include the exchange of goods and services (trade), funds (capital), technology, labor, natural resources, environmental pollution, and so on. (p. 2)

The subject matter of the field of political economy is combined with interacting effects of economic and political structures. Consequently, the interaction of the nation state, the all-pervasive market, complex financial systems, newly emerging forms of business organization (especially the corporation) and capitalism itself is core of the discipline. In order to fully comprehend the political economy of globalization, it is important to unfold how capitalist economic structures and market processes influenced and are influenced by political power at local, national and international levels. Political fragmentation and economic globalization go hand in hand, resulting in worldwide restratification, where local livelihoods are fading. The rapid change of pace due to economic globalization without placing proper safety nets and ensuring the due provision of time for cultural adaptation in many developing countries has often backfired, even in the case of well-intentioned efforts. Due to these contradictory outcomes, the phenomenon of globalization has been subject to both praise and vilification at the same time.

As capital has no fixed abode and state authorities are declining, the nation states are playing the role of security providers for transnational firms. The economy is gradually exempted from political control due to free trade rules and free-floating capital and finances, deregulation, liberalization, flexibility, and ever-increasing fluidity. The narrow focus on neoliberal version of economic globalization, through the forced liberalization of the markets by international financial institutions like the IMF, is subject to the greatest controversy in existing debates on globalization.

Neoliberal Economic Globalization

Cheerleaders (Friedman, 2005, 2007) for neoliberal globalization put their faith in assumption that global economic filed has been largely, if not entirely, levelled out for all people. Despite having some vociferous critics, *Neoliberalism* as a theory of globalization has profoundly influenced global economics and politics. Neoliberalism that has emerged in the 1930s has drawn its philosophical inspiration from *Liberalism*. Intellectual pursuit of neoliberalism is a combination of classical liberalism's commitment to individual liberty with neoclassical economics that favour laissez-faire system (Harvey, 2005, 2011).

In the field of economics, neoliberalism is swiftly translated into the mantra of free-market capitalism that is based on principles of deregulation of economy and privatization of industry. Many ideas associated with neoliberalism were promoted mainly by creation of Bretton Woods System in 1944, which has led to the creation of global economic structures like World Bank (WB) and International Monetary Fund (IMF). IMF and WB used conditional aid to developing countries as a coercive mechanism to force recipient countries to restructure their economies in line with neoliberal theory through structural adjustment programmes.

These policies along with the reduction in welfare expenditure by the states open up these sectors for private profit-making and had differential outcome for various segments of the societies across the globe. Undergirded faith of neoliberal theory is market fundamentalism, that is, free market governed by open completion and individual's self-interests will take care of all our needs.[4] This line of argument echoes Adam Smith's (1976) widely quoted passage:

> It is not from the benevolence of the butcher, the brewer, or the baker that we expect our dinner, but from their regard to their own interest. We address ourselves not to their humanity but to their self-love. (pp. 26–27)

Trade occupies a central place in any discussion about the neoliberal economy. Under auspice of neoliberal economic globalization, trade and production processes across the world have undergone immense transformations over the last few decades.

This book takes the singularity of a case of football production in one Asian country to show universal principles of global divisions of work. Although the location of this empirical study is seemingly rather distant to Western countries, the study questions the spatial relevance, at least in its consequences because our findings minimize spatial distances. The objects of empirical inquiry are increasingly part of our life and our organization of life. We will draw the attention to global independencies of different stakeholders in a commonly shared world society. Watching football games, for example at the level of the world championships, reveals that football production is not restricted just to one region in Pakistan, but the majority of (high-quality leather) footballs of all the major brands like Nike or Adidas and so on are produced within this area of local production in Pakistan, based upon the working conditions of the labour market there. As soccer players or as football TV spectators, we are ultimately part of the same game, in which different actors are producing, trading, consuming reciprocally and globally with, however, different sources of power at the individual level. Taken together, this discussion delivers a portrait of modern capitalism by focusing an intensive spotlight at particular phenomena of recent economic societies in order to highlight very general mechanisms behind those phenomena. As a consequence, the study is a story about the political economy and a critique of the political economy simultaneously.

The following chapters discuss further conceptual elements by referring to the division of labour, and especially to female labour, in contemporary

[4] However, there are also those (for detailed discussions, see Polanyi, 1944) who are highly sceptical about these neoliberal claims. Neoliberalism is often criticized for being a *one-size-fits-all* ideological model.

capitalism. (Female) homeworkers are a subcategory of female work on which the research is focusing. Then, we continue doing conceptual reflections on well-being and inner worldviews by working actors, which may show their own rationality. If somebody feels bad or happy is always a very relative emotional status, which is dependent upon prior biographical experiences, personal alternatives and collectively shared interpretations to act with a situation (Bögenhold, 2018; Sent, 2018). In this understanding, we draw upon Sen's capability approach (Sen, 1993) to get an adequate understanding of modes of life organization, dreams and strategies of people to cope with an individual future which must always be read as being in relation to social and historical comparisons (Naz, 2016). Based upon that fundament, the study does empirical research by doing interviews with actors at the far end of global production chains—the female stitchers of footballs in Pakistan—who work, lastly, on commission of some famous Western brands. One of the final conclusions of our journey is that homework is almost qualified as being a negative issue, a kind of precarious employment being a relic of pre-modern societies, which is worse than salary- or wage-dependent work of regular employees. Our way to treat the research is by the attempt to lets the actors speak and to speak through and with the actors. Our message is that the conventional view of homework as traditional and precarious work is somehow misguided, since this is a distant and poorly informed view by Western academics who are just trained to think in clean models of black and white, respectively bad or good. Asking for well-being, our treatment is much more in line with the participants; we try to get into their life stories, and we really want to make sense of what people deliver in terms of information regarding their family histories, their current personal situation, dreams and hazards. Result of our study is that modern statements on quality of living and working conditions are just produced at the desks of academics who are far away from the daily practice of (home)workers.

References

Altman, D. (2007). *Connected: 24 Hours in the Global Economy.* New York: Farrar, Straus and Giroux.

Barndt, D. (2008). *Tangled Routes: Women, Work and Globalization on the Tomato Trail.* Lanham: Rowman and Littlefield Publishers.

Barrientos, S. (2019). *Gender and Work in Global Value Chains: Capturing the Gains?* Cambridge: Cambridge University Press.

Bauman, Z. (1998). *Globalization: The Human Consequences*. New York: Columbia University Press.

Bauman, Z. (2003). *Liquid Love*. Cambridge: Polity.

Bhagwati, J. (2004). *In Defense of Globalization*. New York: Oxford University Press.

Bögenhold, D. (2015). Globalization and Its Discontents. In F. F. Wherry & J. B. Schor (Eds.), *The SAGE Encyclopedia of Economics and Society* (pp. 795–797). Thousand Oaks: Sage.

Bögenhold, D. (2018). Bounded Rationality, Emotions and How Sociology May Take Profit: Towards an Interdisciplinary Opening. In H. Staubmann & V. M. Lidz (Eds.), *Rationality in the Social Sciences. The Schumpeter/Parsons Seminar 1939/40 and Current Perspectives* (pp. 105–120). Heidelberg, New York et al.: Springer.

Bögenhold, D. (2019). From Hybrid Entrepreneurs to Entrepreneurial Billionaires: Observations on the Socioeconomic Heterogeneity of Self-Employment. *American Behavioral Scientist, 3*(2), 129–146.

Bögenhold, D., & Naz, F. (2018). *Consumption and Life-Styles. A Short Introduction*. London: Palgrave.

Bögenhold, D., & Permana, Y. (2018). *End of Middle Classes? Social Inequalities in Digital Age*. Discussion Paper 04-2018. Department of Sociology, Klagenfurt University.

Case, A., & Deaton, A. (2020). *Deaths of Despair and the Future of Capitalism*. Princeton: Princeton University Press.

Chanda, N. (2007). *Bound Together: How Traders, Preachers, Adventurers, and Warriors Shaped Globalization*. New Haven: Yale University Press.

Chirico, J. (2014). *Globalization: Prospects and Problems*. Thousand Oaks, CA: Sage Publications.

Cohen, J. L. (2012). *Globalization and Sovereignty. Rethinking Legality, Legitimacy, and Constitutionalism*. Cambridge: Cambridge University Press.

Collier, P. (2007). *The Bottom Billion: Why the Poorest Countries Are Failing and What Can Be Done About It*. Oxford: Oxford University Press.

Douglass, N. (1991). *Institutions, Institutional Change, and Economic Performance*. Cambridge: Cambridge University Press.

Ferguson, J. (2006). *Global Shadows: Africa in the Neoliberal World*. Durham: Duke University Press.

Friedman, T. (2005). *The World Is Flat: A Brief History of the Twenty-first Century*. New York: Farrar, Strauss, Giroux.

Friedman, T. (2007). *The World Is Flat: A Brief History of the Twenty-First Century*. New York: Picador.

Giddens, A. (1973). *The Class Structures of the Advanced Societies*. London: Hutchinson.

Giddens, A. (1984). *The Constitution of Society: Outline of the Theory of Structuration*. Berkeley, CA: University of California Press.

Giddens, A. (1990). *The Consequences of Modernity*. Cambridge: Polity Press.
Giddens, S. (2009). *Sociology*. Cambridge: Polity Press.
Gills, B. K., & Thomson, W. R. (Eds.). (2006). *Globalization and Global History*. New York: Routledge.
Harvey, D. (2005). *A Brief History of Neoliberalism*. Oxford: Oxford University Press.
Harvey, D. (2011). The Rise of Neoliberalism and the Riddle of Capital. In S. Lilley (Ed.), *Capital and Its Discontents: Conversations with Radical Thinkers in a Time of Tumult*. Oakland: Fernwood Publishing.
Koechlin, T. (2006). Stiglitz and His Discontent. *Review of Political Economy, 18*(2), 253–264.
Kurian, R. (2003). *Vulnerabilities and Opportunities in Gendered Labour Markets: Women Workers in Global Economy and Challenges for Trade Unions*. Working Paper No. 384. The Hague: Institute of Social Studies.
Luhmann, N. (1971). Die Weltgesellschaft. *Archiv für Rechts- und Sozialphilosophie, 57*(1), 1–35.
Marx, K. (1977). *Capital: A Critique of Political Economy* (Vol. 3). Moscow: Progress Publishers.
Merton, R. K. (1936). The Unanticipated Consequences of Purposive Social Action. *American Sociological Review, 1*(6), 894–904.
Meyer, J. W., Boli, J., Thomas, G. M., & Ramirez, F. O. (1981). World Society and the Nation-State. *American Journal of Sociology, 103*(1), 144–181.
Milanovic, B. (2019). *Capitalism Alone: The Future of the System that Rules the World*. Cambridge: Belknap Press at Harvard University Press.
Miller, R. C. (2008). *International Political Economy: Contrasting World Views*. Routledge, Lonodon.
Morgan, M. (2012). *The World in the Model: How Economists Work and Think*. Cambridge: Cambridge University Press.
Naz, F. (2016). Understanding Human Well-Being: How Could Sen's Capabilities Approach Contribute?. *Forum for Social Economics*. https://doi.org/10.1080/07360932.2016.1222947
Polanyi, K. (1944). *The Great transformation*. New York: Rinehart.
Ritzer, G. (1993). *The McDonaldization of Society: An Investigation into the Changing Character of Contemporary Social Life*. Thousand Oaks: Pine Forge Press.
Ritzer, G. (2008). *Classical Sociological Theory* (5th ed.). New York: McGraw-Hill.
Ritzer, G., & Dean, P. (Eds.). (2015). *Globalization*. Oxford: Blackwell Publishing Ltd.
Sen, A. (1993). Capability and Wellbeing. In M. Nussbaum & A. K. Sen (Eds.), *The Quality of Life* (pp. 30–53). Oxford: Oxford University Press.

Sent, E. M. (2018). Rationality and Bounded Rationality: You Can't Have One Without the Other. *The European Journal of the History of Economic Thought, 25*(6), 1370–1386.

Sheffield, J., Korotayev, A., & Grinin, L. (Eds.). (2013). *Globalization: Yesterday, Today, and Tomorrow*. Littlefield Park: Emergent Publications.

Smith, A. (1976). In R. H. Campbell, A. S. Skinner, & W. B. Todd (Eds.), *An Inquiry into the Nature and Causes of the Wealth of Nations*. Oxford: Clarendon Press.

So, A. (2012). Political Globalization. In G. Ritzer (Ed.), *Wiley-Blackwell Encyclopedia of Globalization*. Oxford: Wiley-Blackwell.

Staples, D. E. (2006). *No Place Like Home: Organizing Home-Based Labor in the Era of Structural Adjustment*. New York and London: Routledge.

Stiglitz, J. E. (2002). *Globalization and Its Discontents*. New York: W.W. Norton and Co.

Wallerstein, I. (1983). *Historical Capitalism*. London: Verso.

Wallerstein, I. (2011). *The Modern World System* (4 vols.). Berkeley, CA: University of California Press.

Weber, M. (1972 [1921]). *Wirtschaft und Gesellschaft*. Tübingen: J.C.B. Mohr.

Weber, M. (1981 [1927]). *General Economic History*. New Brunswick, NJ: Transaction Books.

Weber, M. (1988). Die protestantische Ethik und der Geist des Kapitalismus. In M. Weber (Ed.), *Gesammelte Aufsätze zur Religionssoziologie* (pp. 17–206). Tübingen: J.C.B. Mohr.

Wolf, M. (2005). *Why Globalization Works*. New Haven: Yale University Press.

World Bank. (2002). *Globalization, Growth, and Poverty. Building an Inclusive World Economy*. Oxford: Oxford University Press.

Yergin, D., & Stanislaw, J. (1998). *The Commanding Heights: The Battle for the World Economy*. New York: Touchstone.

CHAPTER 2

Transformation of Labour Market and Gender Patterns of Work

Introduction

> The restructuring of work does not simply 'happen to' people—either as a result of an unstoppable techno-economic process, or as a strategic and calculated project. Rather, it is always experienced, reflected upon, interpreted and lived in the context of historically specific spaces. (Amoore, 2002: 61)

Over the past few decades, labour markets have undergone profound transformations. These changes are cumulative effects of recent as well as historical trends in social, economic and political processes. During 1980s and 1990s, the liberalization process in many economies around the world had facilitated the creation of a new integrated global economic system. The revolution in transport and the information technology, formation of a single international financial market and the active role of the transnational corporations make this new economic system possible. The new global economy concerns all the core processes and elements of an economic system and has the capacity to operate as a single unit on world scale (Jimenez, 2000). These transformations have been experienced by all the societies of world, though there are variations in the nature and extent of the experience. During this era, money, goods, information and services have moved across borders on unprecedented pace and scale. This has brought noticeable changes in the configuration of the world order and reinforced neoliberal discourse. Emergence of global economy has also led to important transformation in the management of production and

F. Naz, D. Bögenhold, *Unheard Voices*,
https://doi.org/10.1007/978-3-030-54363-1_2

distribution process. In global production organization, the production process is broken down into constituent tasks and distributed across the globe depending on the comparative advantages of a particular region. These changes have created possibilities to integrate developing countries in global production networks. This in turn has generated opportunities for paid work for hundreds of millions of workers in emerging and low-income countries, drawing in a substantial number of women with limited previous labour market access. This paradigmatic shift in industrial organization has extended the scope of analysis beyond the traditional dynamics of the production process that was mainly focused on the production site. Existing research on global production organization (Barrientos, 2008, 2013, 2019; Barrientos, Kabeer, & Hossain, 2004; Carswell & De Neve, 2013; Kabeer, 2003; Lund & Srinivas, 2000; Lund-Thomsen, Lindgreen, & Vanhamme, 2016) has documented a rapid process of transformation that has affected work and employment conditions in numerous ways. These transformations in key societal sites like household, workplace and urban space are linked with the reproduction of inequality of powers in modern capitalist societies (Bruff & Tansel, 2019). From contemporary literature on the organization of work in a global capitalist system of production organization (Benería, 2001; Benería & Floro, 2005; Burchielli, Delaney, & Coventry, 2013; Burchielli, Delaney, & Goren, 2014; Delaney, Burchielli, Marshall, & Connor, 2019; Islam, 2008; Mehrotra & Biggeri, 2005, 2007, 2010), at least two major patterns in the workforce can be discerned: firstly, a feminization of the labour force characterized by increased female participation in the workforce; and secondly, the more flexible nature of work signalled by an increasingly large number of people employed as casual, temporary and part-time workers under precarious and unstable conditions (Naz & Bögenhold, 2020). This chapter provides an overview of labour market transformation and changing gender patterns of work associated with new global production system, and it is guided by two principal questions: How has new global production system shaped the gender pattern of work? What are the outcomes of these transformations for workers, especially for female home-based workers in Global South? The major aim of this chapter is to provide background information and an analytical framework needed to examine the gender patterns of work in global production organization explored in subsequent chapters.

Ideological Foundation of Economic Globalization

Globalization also has an ideological dimension, which is variously described as neoliberalism, market fundamentalism and Washington Consensus. Although these terms are often used interchangeably, their distinct nuances are acknowledged too. Neoliberalism is the revival of nineteenth-century ideas associated with laissez-faire economic liberalism and free market capitalism.

Freedom and democracy are the fundamental values of liberalism. Two major and widely recognized classifications of liberalism are classical and modern liberalism. Classical liberalism, associated with earlier liberals such as John Locke, Adam Smith, Alexis de Tocqueville and Friedrich von Hayek from the twentieth century, is based on the fundamental premise that the role of the state ought to be minimal. In contrast, modern liberalism is associated with theorists such as Benjamin Constant and John Stuart Mill, John Dewey, William Beveridge and John Rawls, and, so, it is situated politically to the left of classical liberalism.

Modern liberalism is willing to provide space to state as an instrument to redistribute wealth and welfare (Beveridge, 1944, 1945; Rawls, 1993). On the contrary, classical liberals favour economic liberalism and advocate for laissez-faire economic policies. This provides a whole new paradigm for economic theory that has laid the foundation of modern capitalist society. However, "liberalism" has become a nebulous concept over the years as this is mostly used as a generic term of denunciation that is used to describe almost any economic and political development deemed incorrect or undesirable.

According to Ryan (1993),

> Anyone trying to give a brief account of liberalism is immediately faced with an embarrassing question: are we dealing with liberalism or liberalisms? It is easy to list famous liberals; it is harder to say what they have in common. John Locke, Adam Smith, Montesquieu, Thomas Jefferson, John Stuart Mill, Lord Acton, T. H. Green, John Dewey and contemporaries such as Isaiah Berlin and John Rawls are certainly liberals—but they do not agree about the boundaries of toleration, the legitimacy of the welfare state, and the virtues of democracy, to take three rather central political issues. (p. 291)

Neoliberalism is a revival of liberalism in a reincarnated form. Under this interpretation of neoliberalism, it is somewhat similar to liberalism and yet different from much conventional conservative discourse. Most of the critical literature on neoliberalism argues that it is a revival of one specific aspect of the liberal tradition, namely economic liberalism. Economic liberalism is based on the presumption that self-regulating markets are the most efficient way to allocate resources. Any intervention from state in the form of regulation is considered undesirable. According to this line of argument, state intervention can undermine the finely tuned logic of the market economy, and thus reduce economic efficiency (Munck, 2005). Neoliberal ideology places more emphasis on free markets, deregulation and privatization to set up a free-enterprise system. Assertion of this ideology in developing countries through the Bretton Woods Institutions (BWI) demand integration into the world market through strict fiscal discipline, reordering of public expenditure priorities, tax reform, liberalization of the financial sector, exchange rate management, trade liberalization and free flow of foreign direct investment. This led to marked shift in the general orientation of economic policy across the globe. However, despite continuous efforts, promised benefits of new policies have not yet materialized (Irfan-ul-Haque, 2004). The critical literature on neoliberalism (Chomsky, 1999; Giddens, 1998; Harvey, 2005) has questioned the purportedly overshadowing importance of the concept.

Advocates of neoliberal economic globalization suggest Structural Adjustment Programs (SAPs) as panacea for all economic ills in developing countries. Structural adjustment programmes administered by international financial institutions (IFIs), such as the International Monetary Fund (IMF), World Bank (WB) and regional development banks require developing countries to reduce barriers to the flow of goods and capital, privatization of domestic economies, inflation control and reduction of governmental bureaucracy in previously protectionist states. These institutions recommend neoliberal stabilization policies based on two main neoliberal principles. First entails deregulation of the market and second is controlling inflation through high interest rates, wage control and public expenditure reduction policies. Structural adjustment loans are provided to countries to overcome their dire fiscal or macroeconomic problems. In return, recipient countries are required to reform their economic policies, according to a neoliberal rubric of economic stabilization, trade and financial liberalization, deregulation, and privatization. Overall combination of these deregulation and deflationary policies at global level led to high unemployment rates and the generation of precarious employment.

Trade liberalization through the reduction of tariff and non-tariff barriers have also led to integration of developing countries in global production system. Many developing countries adopted export-led growth strategy to overcome their economic problems. As many countries in the South have comparative advantage of cheap labour force, therefore they adopted special policy measures in order to attract foreign investment in their countries especially in labour-intensive industries like Textile. As a result, in almost every developing country special export promotion zones were set up to benefit from volatility of global capital, looking for low cost production sites. Different countries have established export-processing zones (EPZs) under different international trade liberalization agreements to promote export. The reduction of tariff and non-tariff barriers has also increased competition for local firms.

Questions about the impact of the neoliberal policies on economic growth, employment and income distribution, from the perspective of developed as well as underdeveloped countries, are yet inconclusive in ongoing debate on globalization. The way this ideological debate for or against globalization is structured has generated many conflicting policy recommendations regarding specific issues like international trade and poverty reduction (Irfan-ul-Haque, 2004). The proponent of neoliberal globalization argues that it has created new opportunities of economic growth and employment generation. However, skeptic of neoliberal globalization often questions this premise of general rise in economic welfare. Despite existing controversies that surround the idea, there is a general consensus that global interdependence has become the fact of life and individuals and societies have no choice to opt out of it. As a historical process, on the one hand globalization has increased choices, access to goods and knowledge, and international communication for humankind. On the other hand, the dominance of neoliberalism as an ideological discourse that is asserted by Bretton Woods Institutions (BWI) has become the main source of controversy and friction. The neoliberal reform agenda is based on ten commandments, which include fiscal discipline, reordering of public expenditure priorities, tax reform, liberalization of the financial sector, exchange rate management, trade liberalization, free flow of foreign direct investment, privatization, deregulation and property rights. This reform agenda pushed developing and underdeveloped countries towards integration with global economy through lowering of trade barriers, deregulation and privatization of state enterprises. This has given birth to a new global production system by integrating developing countries into dominant global structures of trade, finance and production.

Neoliberal Globalization and Transformation of Labour Market

The dominance of neoliberal economic discourse and firms' quest of low-road strategies and practices to shift risk away from the firm are some of the broader trends which have promoted changes in production organization and employment relations. These changes in production organization are mainly related to a reorganization of the division of labour facilitated by developments in the field of communication technologies that caused the *death of distance* in words of Cairncross (1997). This so-called death of distance has provided opportunities to organize more dispersed and functionally integrated global production structures. In global production organization, the production process is broken down into constituent tasks and distributed across the globe depending on the comparative advantages of a particular region. These changes have created possibilities to integrate developing countries in global production processes through extended global supply chains.

The transformations in production organization have differentiating impact on existential conditions of different segments of the population in industrial as well as developing countries. Existing data reveals a general widening in the disparity in income earnings of skilled and unskilled workers. Under auspices of neoliberal policy prescription, developing countries often face conflicting pressures. On the one hand, new liberal policies prescribe liberalization of labour markets in developing countries, which translates into income-earning opportunities for many impoverished workers and their families in developing countries. On the other hand, the organized labour in the industrial countries is demanding for rise in labour standards in developing countries. The liberalization of labour markets and its impact on labour in developed and developing countries is an important issue in the ongoing debate on globalization. Mainstream analysts consider low-skilled, low-wage industrialization as a milestone for the industrial development of exporting countries that is providing employment to millions of people. On the other side, the same processes are worsening labour conditions, and are termed "race to bottom" and "exploitation of labour rights", in both advanced and developing countries through downward harmonization (Hurley & Miller, 2005).

The existing literature support the claim that drive for international competitiveness has contributed to weakening workers' economic position (Barrientos, 2019). It is argued that multinational enterprises (MNEs) have become loosely connected sites and many of them in the core Western locations are employing unprotected and precarious workers through outsourcing their production and services (Lund-Thomsen & Coe, 2015). The restructuring programmes like hyperflexible or flexi-corporatist in the advanced industrialized countries connect MNEs with unprotected workers in the less-developed countries (LDCs) of the South through intricate threads of power. In order to remain competitive in the world market, developing countries are relying on policy measures such as a tight macroeconomic policy, plant-level layoffs and corporate restructuring. These important changes in the production organization and the involvement of unprotected and unrepresented workers within it have entailed economic distress.

Mobile capital of the late twentieth century has acquired freedom from responsibility. Liquid capital always has a possibility to hunt for more peaceful places rather than engaging in tough resistance or lengthy negotiations. Thus, in this view, labour market trade union activity or any kind of government labour support programmes are considered as interferences with the free functioning of labour market. The economy is gradually exempted from political control due to free trade rules and free-floating capital and finances, deregulation, liberalization, flexibility and ever-increasing fluidity. The rapid pace of change due to economic globalization without placing proper safety nets and ensuring due provision of time for cultural adaptation in many developing countries has often backfired, even in the case of well-intentioned efforts (Stiglitz, 2003). Thus, political fragmentation and economic globalization go hand in hand, resulting in worldwide restratification of work and employment. There is intense pressure on developing countries to liberalize their labour markets. Liberalization of labour markets has some adverse outcomes for labour force. Due to trade liberalization, unemployment has increased on account of economic restructuring. Unemployment has also increased with a fall in domestic demand. Although mainstream economic theory does not take into account the gender differences in economic behaviour and outcomes, gender is an important dividing line with multitude of implications for economic, political and social domains. Globalization has reshaped many dynamics of social life including gender relations among many others. When analysing global processes and policies about labour market outcomes, it is important to highlight the gender power relation*s* at both the global and local levels.

Liberalization of labour market policies has detrimental impact on women and has reshaped the conceptual terrain of work and employment conditions. Therefore, ignoring the gender dimension in any theoretical or empirical analysis could result in distorted outcome. However, changes associated with the process of globalization are not entirely negative. Individuals make this process more meaningful in rational steps on a micro level. Centrality of geographical context in analysis of impact of globalization on women is acknowledged (Barrientos, 2019; Sherif, 2014). Thus, it is important to analyse the impact of global production organization on women's lives, on their relationship with the labour market and on the evolution of the gender roles especially from the perspective of developing countries. Detailed specific aspects that affect women life in global economy are discussed in next section.

Women Role as Labour Force in Global Economy

Economic globalization that was promoted through a greater openness to foreign direct investment (FDI) has led to massive increase in women labour force participation. The North American Free Trade Agreement (NAFTA) has substantially increased long-term employment prospects for women. Multinational corporations (MNCs) have a greater share of female labour force in developing countries. These MNCs pay more than their local counterparts do (Gray, Kittilson, & Sandholtz, 2006). Existing literature confirms that women's share of industrial employment has increased dramatically during the last two decades, because there was a pressure to create a new industrial division of labour using flexible forms of production (Chen, 2014). Women workers were considered the ideal workforce for these jobs due to commonly held notions about their docility, submissiveness and dexterity when performing monotonous tasks at low wages under flexible arrangements (Chhachhi, 2006). There was an increase in the demand for an unskilled and flexible female labour force. Numerous studies have found a close relationship between trade liberalization in developing countries and female employment (Barrientos, 2019; Kurian, 2003; Staples, 2006). Figure 2.1 details the condition under which female labour force was integrated into labour market in many developing countries of Global South.

On the one hand, economic globalization that was promoted through a greater openness to foreign direct investment has set in motion a new global production system that created income-earning opportunities for

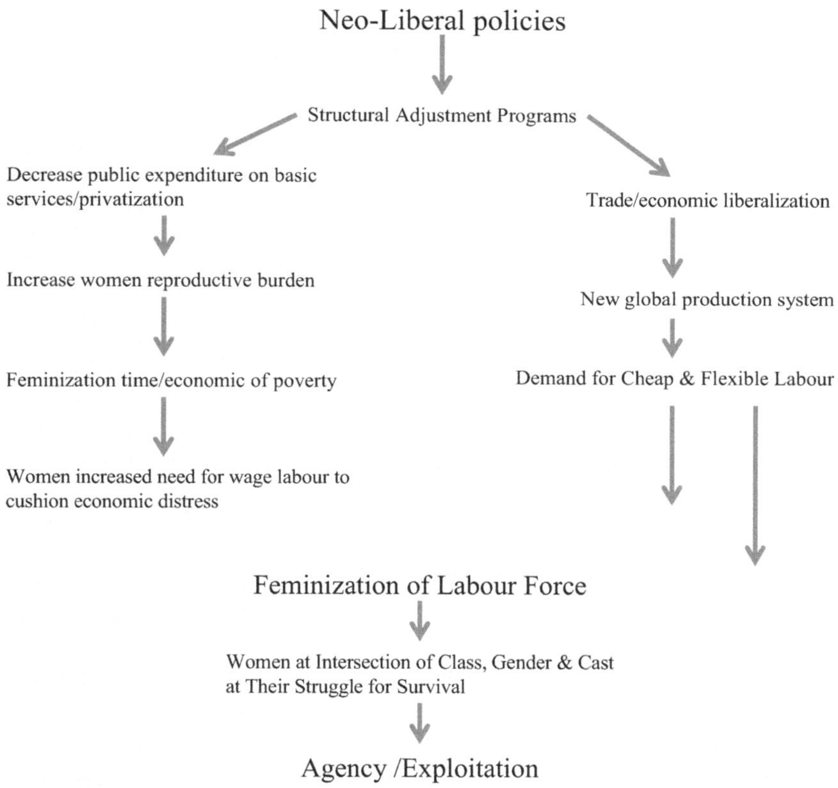

Fig. 2.1 Women in production. (Source: Authors elaboration based on literature review)

women with limited or no marketable skills. On the other hand, the stability and adjustment measure recommended to the developing countries often involves limiting budgetary spending, cutting taxes and privatizing government services. Many studies have reported increased reproductive burden of women due to privatization of basic services. As women share burden of cut in public spending on provision of social services disproportionately, therefore there is increased need for cash income to cushion dwindling household economies of their households. Thus, feminization of labour force has come as no surprise, even in the patriarchal societies.

However, there are conflicting opinions about impact of female labour force participations from perspective of their empowerment and overall well-being. The optimistic school holds that general economic advantage for women will arise in the form of a greater agency for women in the globalization era. Many studies have documented a robust link between neoliberal economic globalization and income growth. This income is also said to spur a sense of self-assurance, encouraging women to be more assertive and escape familial supervision (Acker, 2004; Bhagwati, 2004). In Sen's (1999) own words on the case of paid employment:

> Working outside the home and earning an independent income tend to have a clear impact on enhancing the social standing of a woman in the household and the society. Her contribution to the prosperity of the family is then more visible, and she also has more voice, because of being less dependent on others. Further, outside employment often has useful 'educational' effects, in terms of exposure to the world outside the household, thus making her agency more effective. (p. 192)

According to Marshall (1985), access to paid employment "liberate women from the bondage of the patriarchal extended family, restrictive religious beliefs, and tedious agricultural labour" (Marshall, 1985: 219). It is also argued that due to globalization demand for female technical skills has increased. Consequently, women status has improved due to educational expansion, increased employment opportunities and a reduction in family size. Acknowledged women contribution to family income may help them to liberate from traditional patriarchal bondages and increase the possibilities to live an independent life. Women who were generally excluded from the labour force due to traditional patriarchal structures and limited human capital have newly gained access to paid jobs. This access to cash income allows them not only to meet their own basic needs but also to contribute to the needs of other family members.

A commonly held assumption is that liberalization of markets will generate more income-earning opportunities for women that would ultimately translate into better access to resources both at household level and in public sphere. These changes at labour market and household level are considered to be important mechanisms to break off the traditional barriers that relegate women a secondary status at household level and at societal level. Economic restructuring has created the conditions that are conducive to alter traditional gender roles in different societies. These changes may ultimately lead to reorganization of gender division of labour at household level that is major impediment for women to achieve greater personal autonomy and freedom as public actor. Gender division of work operates at three different levels, namely individual, organizational and societal (Massey, 1984). "Women not only benefit from a greater economic pie, it is also… that their share of the pie increases as the pie becomes bigger" (Apodaca, 1998: 11). In a globalized world, economic and social changes go hand in hand. Thus, changes in economic conditions of women will ultimately pave the way for social change that is required to reaffirm the role of women in society and politics. Better access to employment opportunities and cash income also increases women's quality of life and enhances their general well-being.

However this optimistic view is often challenged on the ground that women's involvement in low-income, low-status and often part-time jobs may reinforce gender inequalities. From a critical perspective, feminization of labour force leads to the concentration of female workers in informal home-based work. These groups, due to their vulnerable position in hierarchy of gender and economic relations, have limited political influence to voice their concerns and to claim and frame their rights (Richards & Gelleny, 2007).

Globalization and Home-Based Work

Competitive environment set by MNCs leads to a permanent search for cheaper and more flexible sources of labour power. Such competitive environment has encouraged a *race to the bottom* and deterioration of work conditions in developing countries (Standing, 1999, 2011). It can be concluded from review of existing literature that though some women had benefited from globalization, the global picture of women as workers is widely discouraging (Sánchez-Apellániz, Núñez, & Charlo-Molina, 2012). Most women work under bad conditions such as low wages, suppression of trade unions and poor opportunities of security or progress (Wright, 1995).

Feminization of labour force in developing countries is often linked to deterioration of working conditions in these countries. There is a general consensus that benefits of globalization are not equally shared. Jobs for women are mostly created in exporting industries, including textiles, electronics, pharmaceutical and computer components, where many women are integrated as informal home-based workers at the lowest ends of global supply chains through extended subcontracting arrangements.

Increased female participation in the informal economy, and particularly within the private sphere of the household, has redefined the boundaries of work and traditional employment. This expansion in the informal sector is linked not only to the capacity of the formal firms to absorb labour, but also to their willingness to do so (Mehrotra & Biggeri, 2007). Transnational hegemonic capitalistic practices co-opt local practices and mould and, even in some cases, deform these for their own benefit. Patriarchy makes the female labour force more exploitable and turns it into a cheap source of profit. Women whose mobility is restricted due to gender norms are increasingly joining the ranks of homeworkers worldwide. Home-based workers are hemmed in by cultural expectations. These women are a captive audience directly or indirectly available for the disposition of multinational or national companies. In sum, the aims of the neo-patriarchy and of multinational and capitalist enterprises reinforce one another: the capitalist subcontracting to homeworkers takes advantage of and thus recreates the gendered order of neo-patriarchy. In other words, neo-patriarchy provides the captive labour force (Wilson, 2003).

A trend towards outsourcing work at the household level has added a layer of invisibility to the economic contribution of female homeworkers. In the case of home-based work, the boundaries of work have been renegotiated between the private sphere of the home and the public sphere of work. As the private realm of the home is increasingly a site of production and consumption for the global economy, traditional forms of industrial relations practice are diminishing at large.

Although the term "home-based work" is very broad, it is difficult to encompass due to lack of consensus on a single definition of the term. However, general definition of the home-based workers includes all kind of remunerative work carried out from inside the home and encompassing the self-employed who are pieceworkers, salaried employees who work for a "middle-man" or a firm; or even unpaid workers in a family enterprise. Home-based workers do wage labour inside or near the house, whereas homeworkers are a subcategory of the home-based workers who work from the home for factories mostly on piece rate. Largely they are involved in industrial outwork. Majority of the women in the developing countries are home workers. They are pushed by the economic deprivation to seek wage labour, but often cannot find regular wage labour and instead work at low piece rates or low daily pay under exploitative conditions without any job security, formal contract or any fringe benefits. They have to cover some production cost themselves, such as the provision of work place, equipment, energy and utility costs and so forth (Mehrotra & Biggeri, 2007).

"Homework" is a broad and confusing term and is sometimes also used interchangeably with home-based work. There are different temporal forms of homework. Traditionally, the term "homeworker" was used for the category of workers involved in manual tasks such as knitting and sewing. In reality, homework is more heterogeneous in nature and it ranges from labour-intensive semi-skilled work to high-tech capital- and information-intensive professional work with huge diversity in the terms of working conditions experienced by different groups of home-based workers. Tietze, Musson and Scurry (2009) argue that the vast breadth and complexity of the phenomenon make it difficult to arrive at a universal consensus on accepted definitions of home-based work. Different groups of individuals are engaged in different types of homework under diverse employment conditions, and a variety of terminologies are used interchangeably in the literature to describe homework, for example industrial outwork, home-based work, homeworking and home production. The variation in defining homeworkers means that constructing an overall picture of homeworking for this disparate population is problematic, because definitional boundaries may effectively exclude certain groups. The diversity of homework activities and the definition of homework also make an international comparison quite difficult, and this has serious outcomes for homeworkers. The ILO (1996) convention on homework defined homework as follows:

> Work carried out by a person in his or her own home or in other premises of his or her own choice, other than the workplace of the employer; for remuneration; which results in a product or service as specified by the employer, irrespective of who provides the equipment, materials or other inputs used, unless this person has the degree of economic independence necessary to be considered an independent worker under national laws, regulations or court decisions. (ILO, 1996)

The ILO convention on homework requires from ratifying states to ensure equality of treatment between employees and homeworkers in their national policies. It follows the union logic and gives home-based workers the status of dependent employees, excluding all those who have a relative degree of sovereignty and economic independence required to be considered an independent worker under national laws, regulations or court decisions. Based on these assumptions, the ILO convention on homework requires that homeworkers must be treated like other workers and demand that states guarantee their right to organize, to equal remuneration, to social security and to a minimum age of employment. The ILO convention on homework also demands the provision of protection against employment discrimination, facilitating access to training and ensuring occupational safety and health, and maternity protection for homeworkers (Freeman, 2004).

Carr, Chen and Tate (2000) have drawn a distinction between homeworkers and home-based workers, later including own-account workers. Home-based workers can be further categorized as own-account workers/employers; persons working on household premises and having a relatively independent status, homeworkers; outworkers who work at home, or in another home other than the employer's/contractor's premises under subcontracting arrangements, having a dependent status, and wage-workers; persons working for wages or salaries in enterprises located in the employer's home (Rani & Unni, 2009). The complexity of home-based work demands for a more comprehensive definition of work in order to make a larger number of homeworkers, a special category of home-based workers, visible in the political economy of production relations and to formulate better informed policies. General and loosely defined constructs can create confusion and marginalize many people in production relations.

Homeworkers are a subset of home-based workers, particularly industrial outworkers who carry out paid work for firms or their subcontractors from their homes, mostly on piece-rate basis. There are two types of homeworkers, namely dependent workers, who produce for subcontractors on a piece-rate basis, and own-account workers, who produce for direct sale. Both groups are markedly different from each other on the basis of the respective positions that they occupy in the production process (Felstead, Jewson, & Walters, 2000). However, employment relationships are more complicated than that, and many homeworkers do not fit into these simple categories since they fall into a grey zone between employees and self-employed. When industrial outwork is not available, many homeworkers have to perform other forms of home-based work to supplement their income. This is often own-account work, for example, preparing food for sale in the local market. Thus, the boundaries between employment and self-employment remain porous for homeworkers. They occupy a distinct niche in the labour market through the distinct organization of their work (Prügl & Tinker, 1997).

Homework is a unique blend of private household and public enterprise production. However, often homework that takes place in family workshops and on kitchen tables is not legally acknowledged and tends to represent an invisible and unprotected workspace. What makes this situation particularly more problematic is that not even the workers themselves perceive them to be "real" workers. From perspective of gender division of labour at household level, women are still responsible for most of unpaid work at household level. In words of Acker (2011), women are encumbered by their obligation to perform day-to-day unpaid work that curtails their possibilities for gainful employment, whereas men are mostly unencumbered in a sense that they are not required to perform unpaid household tasks.

The conditions of their work are not only the outcome of global production processes but are result of the interplay of micro- and macro-level processes. Gender role obligations of unpaid household work and private location of their paid work render their productive activities virtually invisible. Workers are perceived as those who are working outside their homes. In concept of work, unpaid work is generally excluded from the category of work. Such a definition of work has gendered outcome; thus, work needs to be redefined and enlarged to include both paid and unpaid work. Women often face difficulties in combining a labour market career and family obligations. Demands from women are often overshadowed by male-dominated class discourse. Women who work inside their homes in seclusion are both perceived as and perceive themselves as being of higher status than those working in factories or working in the fields as wage labourers. The explanation, Mohanty (1997) notes,

> lies in the redefinition of work as temporary, supplementary, and un-skilled, in the construction of women as mothers and homemakers, and in the positioning of femininity as contradictory to factory work. In addition, the explanation also lies in the specific definition of Third-World, immigrant women as docile, tolerant, and satisfied with substandard wages. (p. 18)

These local beliefs about appropriate gender roles converge and lead to workers' seclusion and are a barrier to women's access to their labour rights and entitlements. This description of lived experiences of women put a great strain on optimism about substantive gains to these women's freedom and agency through involvement in paid work.

The way labour market is organized creates gender inequality in terms of work and employment opportunities. Working and labour market conditions are gendered and have unequal outcome for male and female agents. There are both more proximate mechanisms, such as discrimination, internalization, labour force commitment, cultural devaluation, and distal social macro forces that are generating gender inequalities. The distal forces include economic, organizational, political and cultural forces. Two major forces that are responsible for gender inequality are different types of discrimination on organizational level and the traditional gender division of reproductive work in the household (Gonäs & Tyrkkö, 2015). Women consider themselves as secondary wage earners who are supplementing their family income by using their free time. These women have low human capital and due the ideological construction of women as secondary earner are major factors that push those women who are looking for stable source of income to accept low wages (Fussell, 2000). Their dire economic needs are a hurdle for any kind of organized resistance against exploitative work conditions. Fear of losing income is a major deterrent for these workers.

Home-based workers are widely dispersed in larger areas in and around the cities, and invisible nature of their work make it hard to get accurate statistical data about the number of home-based workers. Mostly men perform all visible activities. In this case, detailed description of local context is important to draw any conclusion about an empowering potential of this kind of work. Power rests in the hands of those actors who have control over the markets, the capital and the returns from the sales. Counting itself cannot remedy oppressive conditions of these workers. Entrenched beliefs about work, gender roles and class shape the women's working life and ultimately affect their conditions of paid work. Paid work inside the confinement of home limits their freedom and agency. The complex interaction between global and local economic and social forces has deeper impact on women agency and freedom. Power exercised by social norms and entrenched belief systems at local level devalue women's economic contributions in private sphere of homes.

Koggel (2003) convincingly argued that having paid work does not automatically translate into agency if work is performed inside the home and invisible and if women have no or limited control on income earned by their paid work. Women paid work in context of economic globalization have gained a new resonance. Does women participation in labour markets enable them to make choices and do things that give them voice, social standing, independence and empowerment in both the public and private spheres? If this is not the case, then we must be cautious about promoting women's labour force participation as a sure way of increasing their freedom and agency.

Women in Global Production: Rethinking About Women Agency and Empowerment

As shown in Fig. 2.1, economic liberalization has led to the feminization of labour force. However, timing of female labour market integration, the forms that it takes, the conditions under which it may enhance women agency and the extent to which paid employment reduces social inequality have been a subject of comprehensive theoretical and empirical investigation in the course of the last 20–30 years. There has been a long-standing debate on whether paid employment created through economic globalization has actually led to a benefit for women. There are two main schools of thought. On the one hand, there is a commonly held assumption that women will lose and will be subjected to higher degree of vulnerability due to the exploitative nature of their jobs. On the other hand, positive impacts of increased income-earning opportunities on women status are registered in many studies. Status of women can be analysed at two distinct levels (Sudarkasa, 1986). First level relates to the condition of women in terms of their rights and obligations. Women status also refers to the relative position of women in gender hierarchy. Richards and Gelleny (2007) argue that first conception of status relates to international legislation about women, which contains specific protection and guarantees. The second conception of "status" is evaluated by using men's status as a reference. Richards and Gelleny (2007) provided a comprehensive list of indicators of women's economic, political and social rights. Economic rights of women include the following: equal pay for equal work; free choice of job; paid employment without needing her husband's permission; equality in hiring and promotion practices; secure jobs; not suffering sexual harassment in the workplace; night work; working in hazardous jobs; and work in the military or the police. Political rights include women's right to vote, run for political office, elected and appointed government positions, political party affiliation and requests to governing parties.

List of social rights refers to the following: same inheritance; getting married on an equal footing with men; travelling abroad; getting a passport; conferring citizenship to children or husband; starting a divorce action; properties acquisition and management and retaining property brought to marriage; participating in social, cultural and community activities; right to education; freedom to choose residence or home; not suffering female genital mutilation in their childhood or adult age; and not suffering forced sterilization. These indicators are used in many studies as important variables to measure the impact of globalization on women quality of life in general terms. When we examine the issue of women's workforce participation in the context of quality of life, the analysis must be responsive to the particularities of context and issues and must be appreciative of diverse human needs and abilities. Many feminist scholars have advanced this argument.

Weaving together analysis of paid work at global and local levels helps to trace interconnections between global forces of power and local systems of oppression. Mohanty (1997) notes that access to paid work is not an adequate measure of economic and social advancement of women. She has suggested a strong connection between capitalism and women exploitation. This assertion was later on tempered by Koggel (2003), who has suggested that women's paid work in a global context has mixed effects. Possibilities for how far one can go on vector of empowerment are largely shaped by the overall context. According to Koggel (2003), jobs that are created by globalization have opened a new window of opportunity that is not otherwise available for women, though conditions under which these women have been employed are far from ideal. Jobs created by MNCs do not automatically increase choices for women that may effectively change their levels of freedom. Instilling appropriate mechanisms can increase the prospect of improvement in working conditions. Paying attention to the women's lives in special socio-economic context in which their working lives are embedded may provide a room for a more complex and sophisticated analysis of equation between access to paid work and women's freedom and agency.

Mohanty (1984) critiques Western feminists notion of agency that glosses over all racial, class or ethnic diversity and ignores historical and cultural specificities. Western feminist ideas of agency often equate agency with voice (resistance), while silence is associated with subordination and abjection. This silence/voice binary has a geopolitical dimension, attributing voice and agency to the Western woman and a suppression of the "historically muted" woman from the Global South (Parpart, 2010; Spivak, 1988). This universally assumed subaltern position of the Southern women has led to a demand to liberate her by nurturing her ability to speak up (Dingli, 2015). Consequently, amplifying women's voice has become the central policy goal of gender and development. Mohanty (2013) argues that such conceptualization of agency completely ignores the complex agency of women of colour as situated subjects and denies the fact that their experience of oppression is incredibly varied and contradictory depending on their individual contexts.

A related dimension of agency is the ability to make and express free choice in the economic domain. Kabeer (2016) argues that the ability to choose is a journey from silence to voice that is important not only for women's agency and empowerment but also for the broader goals of poverty reduction, gender equality and economic development. The instrumentality of this view is clear from the term "smart economics", coined by the World Bank (2012), to refer to how the real purpose of gender equality and women's economic empowerment is to jumpstart economies through faster, more sustainable gross domestic product (GDP) growth. It's no surprise that women's labour market activity and their investments in their children's human capital have become a priority in donor-driven development agendas. Access to income is seen as a clear path to achieve voice and bargaining power. According to the 2014 World Bank Report on *Voice and Agency: Empowering Women for Shared Prosperity*, income and assets "can enhance women's agency by increasing their social status, amplifying their voice, and increasing their bargaining power within the household" (p. 3).

This preoccupation with the voice/agency/empowerment framing in development discourse is a gross simplification of the complex interactions between patriarchy and the neoliberal global economy life. To understand the lives of the women on whose behalf this discourse professes to speak, there is a need to recognize the meaning assigned to agency, which requires a more nuanced and grounded understanding of it. As Spivak (1988) reminds us, speaking on behalf of silenced women recreates the power hierarchies and reinscribes their silence and oppression.

Mahmood (2012) has explored the concept of agency and the alternative means through which women across the world choose to fight the dominant male order and subvert the hegemonic meanings of cultural practices by using them to their own ends. Detailed description of the experiences of women in specific context may help to identify the commonalities of these experiences. Feminist economists generally do not accept ahistorical and universal accounts of experiences shared by all women in the workforce. In order to get a true picture of women empowerment through participation in labour market, we need to examine the broader context as well as localized social practices. Women work is deeply embedded in such customs and practices. Maria Mies's (1982) work on *Lace Makers of Narsapur* provides a vivid example of the local system of oppression that affects labour market outcomes for these women.

Patriarchy and gender subordination are crucial underpinnings to analyse work and employment conditions in Third World countries. However, there are some studies (Lim, 1990) that defend a dynamic historical approach and highlight the need to pay attention to the ways in which women are changing their lives despite facing the negative impact of their work conditions. For instance, Mahmood (2006) claims that by redirecting and recoding the resources offered by religious and cultural traditions, women can make them serve their personal interests and agendas. Women can realize their agency in "small moments of disruption of, and articulation of points of opposition to, male authority" even though women's actions may seemingly be re-establishing *instruments of their own oppression* (Mahmood, 2012: 8).

We must be sensitive to local and global factors while reading accounts of women's work in modern production organization. In order to understand the true outreach of globalization, it must be analysed from the perspective of real experiences of actors in adapting to globalization forces. There is an alternative approach to develop a more constructive debate about the impact of globalization on women. We may take different steps to eliminate negative impacts and to encourage positive ones like cultural change; sustained and mutually agreed action programmes. These positive actions may include different interest groups such as the public sector and business community. Business organizations should make deliberate efforts for removing the glass ceiling in MNCs and including codes of conduct as a part of their corporate social responsibility.

Concluding Thoughts

The paradigmatic shift in industrial organization through liberalization of markets has both winners and losers. From contemporary literature on the organization of work in a global capitalist system of production organization, at least two major patterns in the workforce can be discerned: firstly, a feminization of the labour force characterized by increased female participation in the workforce, and, secondly, the more flexible nature of work signalled by an increasingly large number of people employed as casual, temporary and part-time workers under precarious and unstable conditions (Naz & Bögenhold, 2020). Concentration of women in low-paid and insecure home-based work raises important question: whether jobs created due to feminization of labour force help to improve some aspects of women quality of life or if it rather hurts them further (Richards & Gelleny, 2007). In words of Mills, "Women are neither mere and simple victims, nor free and unchained actors" (Mills, 1999: 11). It is important to acknowledge that feminization of labour force can reinforce gender discrimination but also open up opportunities to challenge patriarchal gender norms through access to cash income. However, this transformation is not automatic and requires instilling appropriate mechanisms. The systematic literature review of homework is conducted in next chapter to glean out how participation in informal industrial homework influences the life conditions of homeworkers. Chapter 3 will examine in detail various issues and controversies that surround informal home-based work created in industrial sector.

References

Acker, J. (2004). Gender, Capitalism and Globalization. *Critical Sociology, 30*(1), 24–46. https://doi.org/10.1163/156916304322981668

Acker, J. (2011). *Why Such Persistent Gender Gaps in Working Life? A Short History of The- orizing Gender Inequality in Work.* Paper Prepared for the Symposium on Conditions for Egalitarian and Sustainable Growth, Karlstad University, September 30, 2011.

Amoore, L. (2002). *Globalisation Contested: An International Political Economy of Work.* Manchester: Manchester University Press.

Apodaca, C. (1998). Measuring Women's Economic and Social Rights Achievement. *Human Rights Quarterly, 20*(1), 139–172. https://doi.org/10.1353/hrq.1998.0001

Barrientos, S. (2008). Contract Labour: The 'Achilles Heel' of Corporate Codes in Commercial Value Chains. *Development and Change, 39*(6), 977–990.

Barrientos, S. (2013). Corporate Purchasing Practices in Global Production Networks: A Socially Contested terrain. *Geoforum, 44*, 44–51.

Barrientos, S. (2019). *Gender and Work in Global Value Chains: Capturing the Gains?* Cambridge: Cambridge University Press.

Barrientos, S., Kabeer, N., & Hossain, N. (2004). *Gender Dimensions of the Globalisation of Production*. Working Paper No. 17. International Labour Office. Retrieved from http://www.oit.org/wcmsp5/groups/public/—dgreports/—integration/documents/publication/wcms_079121.pdf

Benería, L. (2001). Shifting the Risk: New Employment Patterns, Informalization, and Women's Work. *International Journal of Politics, Culture, and Society, 15*(1), 27–53.

Benería, L., & Floro, M. (2005). Distribution, Gender, and Labor Market Informalization: A Conceptual Framework with a Focus on Homeworkers. In K. Neema & L. Benería (Eds.), *Rethinking Informalization: Poverty, Precarious Jobs and Social Protection* (pp. 28–43). New York, NY: Cornell University Open Access Repository.

Beveridge, W. (1944). *Full Employment in a Free Society*. London: Allen & Unwin.

Beveridge, W. (1945). *Why I Am a Liberal*. London: Jenkins.

Bhagwati, J. (2004). *In Defense of Globalization*. Oxford, UK: Oxford University Press.

Bruff, I., & Tansel, C. B. (2019). Authoritarian Neoliberalism: Trajectories of Knowledge Production and Praxis. *Globalizations, 16*(3), 233–244. https://doi.org/10.1080/14747731.2018.1502497

Burchielli, R., Delaney, A., & Coventry, K. (2013). Campaign Strategies to Develop Regulatory Mechanisms: Protecting Australian Garment Homeworkers. *Journal of Industrial Relations, 56*(1), 81–102.

Burchielli, R., Delaney, A., & Goren, N. (2014). Garment Homework in Argentina: Drawing Together the Threads of Informal and Precarious Work. *The Economic and Labour Relations Review, 25*(1), 63–80.

Cairncross, F. (1997). *The Death of Distance: How Communication Revolution is Changing Our Lives*. Knutsford, UK: Texere Publishing.

Carr, M., Chen, M., & Tate, J. (2000). Globalization and Homebased Workers. *Feminist Economics, 6*(3), 123–142.

Carswell, G., & De Neve, G. (2013). Labouring for Global Markets: Conceptualising Labour Agency in Global Production Networks. *Geoforum, 44*, 62–70.

Chen, M. A. (2014). *Informal Economy Monitoring Study Sector Report: Home-based Workers*. Retrieved from http://wiego.org/sites/wiego.org/files/publications/files/IEMS-Home-based-Workers-Full-Report.pdf

Chhachhi, A. (2006). Eroding Citizenship: Gender, Labour and Liberalization in India. In T. Truong, S. Wieringa, & A. Chhachhi (Eds.), *Engendering Human Security: Feminist Perspectives* (pp. 234–276). New Delhi; London: Women Unlimited/Kali for Women; Zed Press.

Chomsky, N. (1999). *Profit Over People – Neoliberalism and Global Order*. New York: Seven Stories Press.

Delaney, A., Burchielli, R., Marshall, S., & Connor, T. (2019). *Homeworking Women: A Gender Justice Perspective*. New York, NY: Routledge.

Dingli, S. (2015). We Need to Talk About Silence: Re-examining Silence in International Relations Theory. *European Journal of International Relations, 21*(4), 721–742.

Felstead, A., Jewson, N., & Walters, S. (2000). *A Statistical Portrait of Working at Home in the UK: Evidence From the Labour Force Survey*. Retrieved from http://www.leeds.ac.uk/esrcfutureofwork/downloads/workingpaperdownloads/fow_paper_04.pdf

Freeman, D. (2004). Homeworkers in Global Supply Chains. *Greener Management International, 43*, 107–119.

Fussell, E. (2000). Making Labor Flexible: The Recomposition of Tijuana's Maquiladora Female Labor Force. *Feminist Economics, 6*(3), 59–79.

Giddens, A. (1998). *The Third Way. The Renewal of Social Democracy*. Cambridge: Polity.

Gonäs, L., & Tyrkkö, A. (2015). Changing Structures and Women's Role as Labor Force. *Nordic Journal of Working Life Studies, 5*(2), 89–108.

Gray, M. M., Kittilson, M. C., & Sandholtz, W. (2006). Women and Globalization: A Study of 180 Countries, 1975–2000. *International Organization, 60*, 293–333. https://doi.org/10.1017/S0020818306060176

Harvey, D. (2005). *A Brief History of Neoliberalism*. Oxford: Oxford University Press.

Hurley, J., & Miller, D. (2005). The Changing Face of the Global Garment Industry. In A. Hales & J. Wills (Eds.), *Threads of Labour: Garment Industry Supply Chains from the Worker's Perspective* (pp. 16–39). Oxford: Blackwell Publishers.

ILO. (1996). *Homework Convention No. 177*. Retrieved from http://www.ilo.org/ilolex/cgi-lex/convde.pl

Irfan-ul-Haque. (2004). *Globalization, Neoliberalism and Labour*. UNCTAD Discussion Paper No 173. Geneva 10, Switzerland.

Islam, M. S. (2008). From Sea to Shrimp Processing Factories in Bangladesh: Gender and Employment at the Bottom of a Global Commodity Chain. *Journal of South Asian Development, 3*(2), 211–236.

Jimenez, M. (2000). Global Change, Economic Restructuring and Labour Market Issues in Mexico City. *International Journal of Manpower, 21*(6), 464–480.

Kabeer, N. (2003). *Gender Mainstreaming in Poverty Eradication and the Millennium Development Goals: A Handbook for Policy Makers*. Ottawa: Canadian International Development Agency.

Kabeer, N. (2016). Gender Equality, Economic Growth and Women's Agency: The 'Endless Variety' and 'Monotonous Similarity' of Patriarchal Constraints. *Feminist Economics, 22*(1), 295–321.

Koggel, C. (2003). Globalization and Women Paid Work: Expending Freedom? *Feminist Economics, 9*(2–3), 163–183.

Kurian, R. (2003). *Vulnerabilities and Opportunities in Gendered Labour Markets: Women Workers in Global Economy and Challenges for Trade Unions.* Working Paper No. 384. The Hague: Institute of Social Studies.

Lim, L. Y. (1990). Women's Work in Export Factories: The Politics of a Cause. In I. Tinker (Ed.), *Persistent Inequalities: Women and World Development* (pp. 101–119). New York: Oxford University Press.

Lund, F., & Srinivas, S. (2000). *Learning from Experience: A Gendered Approach to Social Protection for Workers in the Informal Economy.* Geneva: International Labour Office.

Lund-Thomsen, P., & Coe, N. M. (2015). Corporate Social Responsibility and Labour Agency: The Case of Nike in Pakistan. *Journal of Economic Geography, 15*(16), 1–22.

Lund-Thomsen, P., Lindgreen, A., & Vanhamme, J. (2016). Industrial Clusters and Corporate Social Responsibility in Developing Countries: What We Know, What We Do Not Know, and What We Need to Know. *Journal of Business Ethics, 133*(1), 9–24.

Mahmood, S. (2006). Feminist Theory, Agency, and the Liberatory Subject: Some Reflections on the Islamic Revival in Egypt. *Temenos, 42*(1), 31–71.

Mahmood, S. (2012). *Politics of Piety: The Islamic Revival and the Feminist Subject.* Princeton, NJ: Princeton University Press.

Marshall, S. E. (1985). Development, Dependence and Gender Inequality in the Third World. *International Studies Quarterly, 29*(2), 217–240.

Massey, D. (1984). *Spatial Divisions of Labour. Social Structures and the Geography of Pro-duction.* London: Macmillan Press Ltd.

Mehrotra, K. S., & Biggeri, M. (2010). Children in Homeworker Households in Pakistan and Indonesia. *International Journal of Manpower, 31*(2), 208–231.

Mehrotra, S., & Biggeri, M. (2005). Can Industrial Outwork Enhance Homeworkers' Capabilities? Evidence from Clusters in South Asia. *World Development, 33*(10), 1735–1757.

Mehrotra, S., & Biggeri, M. (Eds.). (2007). *Asian Informal Workers: Global Risk, Local Protection.* New York, NY: Routledge.

Mies, M. (1982). The Dynamics of the Sexual Division of Labor and Integration of Rural Women into the World Market. In L. Benería (Ed.), *Women and Development: The Sexual Division of Labor in Rural Societies* (pp. 1–28). New York: Praeger.

Mills, M. B. (1999). *Thai Women in the Global Labor Force.* New Brunswick, NJ: Rutgers University Press.

Mohanty, C. T. (1984). Under Western Eyes: Feminist Scholarship and Colonial Discourses. *Boundary 2, 12*(3), 333–358.

Mohanty, C. T. (1997). Women Workers and Capitalist Scripts: Ideologies of Domination, Common Interests, and the Politics of Solidarity. In M. Jacqui Alexander & C. T. Mohanty (Eds.), *Feminist Genealogies, Colonial Legacies, Democratic Futures* (pp. 3–29). New York: Routledge.

Mohanty, C. T. (2013). Transnational Feminist Crossings: On Neoliberalism and Radical Critique. *Signs, 38*(4), 967–991.

Munck, R. (2005). Neoliberalism and Politics, and the Politics of Neoliberalism. In A. Saad-Filho & D. Johnston (Eds.), *Neoliberalism – A Critical Reader* (pp. 60–69). London: Pluto Press.

Naz, F., & Bögenhold, D. (2020). Understanding Labour Processes in Global Production Networks: A Case Study of the Football Industry in Pakistan. *Globalization*. https://doi.org/10.1080/14747731.2019.1708658

Parpart, J. (2010). *Choosing Silence: Rethinking Voice, Agency and Women's Empowerment*. Working Paper 297. Gender, Development and globalization Program, Center for Gender in a Global Context. East Lansing, MI: Michigan State University.

Prügl, E., & Tinker, I. (1997). Microentrepreneurs and Homeworkers: Convergent Categories. *World Development, 25*(9), 1471–1482.

Rani, U., & Unni, J. (2009). Do Economic Reforms Influence Home-Based Work? Evidence from India. *Feminist Economics, 15*(3), 191–225.

Rawls, J. (1993). *Political Liberalism*. New York: Columbia University Press.

Richards, D. L., & Gelleny, R. (2007). Women's Status and Economic Globalization. *International Studies Quarterly, 51*, 855–876.

Ryan, A. (1993). Liberalism. In R. E. Goodin & P. Pettit (Eds.), *A Companion to Contemporary Political Philosophy* (pp. 291–311). Oxford: Blackwell.

Sánchez-Apellániz, M., Núñez, M., & Charlo-Molina, J. M. (2012). Women and Globalization. In C. Wankel & S. Malleck (Eds.), *Ethical Models and Applications of Globalization: Cultural, Socio-Political and Economic Perspectives* (pp. 119–140). Hershey, PA: Business Science Reference.

Sen, A. (1999). *Development as Freedom*. New York: Anchor Books.

Sherif, B. (2014). *Women, Work, and Globalization: Challenges and Opportunities*. New York: Routledge.

Spivak, G. (1988). Can the Subaltern Speak. In C. Nelson & L. Gross-berg (Eds.), *Marxism and the Interpretation of Culture* (pp. 271–313). Urbana, IL: University of Illinois Press.

Standing, G. (1999). Global Feminization Through Flexible Labor: A Theme Revisited. *World Development, 27*(3), 583–602.

Standing, G. (2011). *The Precariat: The New Dangerous Class*. New York: Bloomsbury.

Staples, D. E. (2006). *No Place Like Home: Organizing Home-Based Labor in the Era of Structural Adjustment*. New York and London: Routledge.

Stiglitz, J. E. (2003). *Globalization and Its Discontents.* New York and London: Norton and Company.

Sudarkasa, N. (1986). The Status of Women in Indigenous African Societies. *Feminist Studies, 12*(1), 91–103.

Tietze, S., Musson, G., & Scurry, T. (2009). Homebased Work: A Review of Research into Themes, Directions and Implications. *Personnel Review, 38*(6), 585–604.

Wilson, T. D. (2003). Forms of Male Domination and Female Subordination: Homeworkers Versus Maquiladora Workers in Mexico. *Review of Radical Political Economics, 35*(1), 56–72.

World Bank (2012). *World Development Report: Gender Equality and Development.* Washington, DC: World Bank.

World Bank. (2014). *Voice and Agency: Empowering Women and Girls for Shared Prosperity.* Washington, DC: World Bank.

Wright, S. (1995). Women and the Global Economic Order: A feminist Perspective. *The American University Journal of International Law and Policy, 10*(2), 861–887.

CHAPTER 3

Homeworkers in Global Supply Chains: Issues and Controversies

Introduction

The major aim of this chapter is to conduct a systematic review[1] of relevant literature on informal industrial homework to identify major themes and issues in existing research streams. Despite numerous scholarly and empirical efforts on the topic of informal industrial homework, this topic has never been reviewed systematically. Interestingly, most of the recent literature on homework deals with the issues and dilemmas of knowledge homeworkers, and there is less interest in exploring the issues of homeworkers conducting assembling tasks such as seamstresses, packers, and so on. The scope of this review is limited to industrial outworkers, a particular category of home-based workers. Only those studies on homeworkers were included, which were published since 2000 and which deal directly with homework or industrial outwork (see Fig. 3.1 for detail selection process) as an experience of these workers, as opposed to other forms of homework. Although this chapter includes information by many classical studies (Boris & Prügl, 1996; Mies, 1982; Prugal, 1996; Prügl & Tinker, 1997) on homework published prior to 2000, these studies are not included in this chapter due to limitation of selected time frame. This review intends to highlight various approaches adopted by researchers to conduct their

[1] Review that aims to comprehensively identify all relevant studies to answer a particular question, and assesses the validity (or "soundness") of each study taking this into account when reaching conclusions (Petticrew & Roberts, 2006).

F. Naz, D. Bögenhold, *Unheard Voices*,
https://doi.org/10.1007/978-3-030-54363-1_3

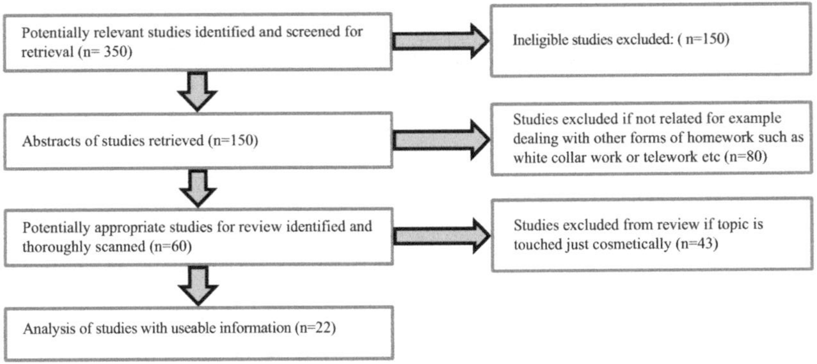

Fig. 3.1 Quorom flowchart of literature review. (Source: Authors elaboration. Petticrew and Roberts (2006))

research and discuss their findings and highlight some of the common problems. These studies are a useful source of information on the issues faced by homeworkers, and many common findings have emerged across the studies (Table 3.1).

Many common characteristics of homeworkers can be gleaned from a review of literature. However, there is also a possibility that such a global picture might disguise some variegated patterns. By reviewing diverse streams of literature on homework, an effort is being made to organize the findings of the review by exploring the diversity of themes and issues in existing literature on homework. However, a neat categorization of different articles in specific sections is not possible, as their content and focus is not easily demarcated and the contribution that they make covers more than one theme (Fig. 3.2).

Contextualizing Homework

Although home-based production is an ancient form of production, various factors have led to the proliferation of home-based work in the global capitalist system of production that characterizes the modern world. It is estimated that there are 250 million home-based workers, including 200 million from the poorest families (WIEGO, 2000). The generalized adoption of neoliberal philosophies and practices especially increased deregulation; and an overreliance on markets to provide regulating functions also facilitated the move (Baylina & Schier, 2002). Deregulation policies further promoted this process as they provide firms with maximum flexibility to switch their production from one place to another in search of cheap labour and lower prices at the expense of vulnerable workers whose limited income and livelihood are constantly renegotiated downwards (Burchielli et al., 2013).

Modern methods of controlling cost and regulating labour have increased all forms of non-standard employment. The new information technologies of the 1980s and 1990s have facilitated retailers to closely monitor and manage their sales and remaining stocks. Due to this new degree of inventory control, retailers are able to minimize the level of stock that they hold at any one time. Thus, in time and lean retailing has become another cost-cutting strategy used by the retailers. Price and flexibility are the most important attributes of modern production organization. Manufacturers responded to these pressures of price and flexibility by subcontracting labour-intensive production to small units and, in some

Table 3.1 Summary of the Literature

Author	*Keywords*	*Themes*	*Methodology*	*Findings*
Felstead, Jewson, and Walters (2000)	Homeworkers, Labour Force Survey, UK	Characteristics of homeworkers	Quantitative	Homeworking confirms many stereotypes associated with home-based work including low pay, feminization and fluidity of space and place.
Baylina and Schier (2002)	Homework, informal economy, Spain, Germany	Characteristics of homework	Qualitative	Homeworking has contradictory outcomes. It is exploitative as well as site of economic opportunity.
O'Hara (2002)	Homeworkers, health and safety	Characteristics of homework	Qualitative (scoping study)	Homeworker's access and information about health and safety issues is limited, and they are marginalized in production relations.
Mehrotra and Biggeri (2002)	Social protection, home-based workers, child labour	Condition of women in home-based economic activities in informal manufacturing and child labour in these activities	Mixed method Survey research Focus groups and case studies	Dual and contradictory nature of home-based work. On the one hand, it could be a source of income, and on the other hand its exploitative nature demand for more public intervention to bring it out from the low equilibrium trap.
Mehrotra and Biggeri (2005)	Informal sector, subcontracting, human development	Human development of homeworking households	Mixed method Survey Research Focus groups and case studies	Education, joint action and social protection are the key answers for human development at the household level.

Mehrotra and Biggeri (2010)	Child labour, subcontracting, Indonesia, Pakistan	Involvement of child labour in homeworking households and its impacts on their capabilities	Mixed method Survey Research Focus groups and case studies	Children from homeworking households have a higher probability of working. There is evidence of the feminization of homework from childhood.
Freeman, D. (2003)	Homeworkers, global capitalism ethical trading initiatives (ETI)	Scope of the problem and the types of issues that surround homeworking	Case study	A step-by-step approach of working to improve homeworking conditions, rather than attempting to exclude homeworkers from global supply chains, is the best way to bring about sustainable improvements in the lives of some of the world's poorest workers.
Williams, P. (2005)	Homeworkers, campaign strategies, UK	Leveraging change in working conditions of homeworkers in UK	Case study	Efforts for raising labour standards for home-based workers will be undermined if other supportive mechanism are not intact.
Burchielli and Delaney (2009)	CSR, homeworkers	Analyses CSR from the perspective of home-based employment	Case study	The case suggests that for CSR to benefit homeworkers, firm behaviour must change, and appropriate regulatory policies must be developed and implemented.
Burchielli, R. et al. (2009)	Homework, informal employment, CSR, ethical networks, supply chains	Explore the concept of ethical network in relation to CSR	Case study	The case suggests that for CSR to benefit homeworkers, firm behaviour must change, and appropriate regulatory policies must be developed and implemented.

(continued)

Table 3.1 (continued)

Author	*Keywords*	*Themes*	*Methodology*	*Findings*
Wilson, T.D. (2003), Staples (2006)	Homeworkers, capitalist system, gender regimes Homeworkers, labour, gender, child care workers	How do gendered power complexes interact with capitalism? How the binary divisions of home-based labor were crisscrossed with other, even more powerful divisions, including sexual, ethno-racial and international divisions of labor	Review Book	Gender regimes thus facilitate capital accumulation based on the exploitation of a cheap, unorganized, flexible labour force. As low-wage homeworkers, domestic laborers and similarly situated workers are made more "visible" through organizing and exposure of all kinds, one can begin to see the intricate governmental relations of social and sexual reproduction on a global scale.
Benería and Floro (2005)	Homeworkers, dynamics of informality, gender relations	A conceptual framework about dynamics of informality with a focus on homeworkers	Qualitative	Nonstandard forms of employment in informal economy have generated inequalities in labour conditions and working life patterns.
Barrientos, S. (2008)	Homeworkers, codes of labour practice, bargaining model	Purchasing practices and global regulations at multiple level of GPN	Qualitative (impact assessment)	There is a positive impact of codes on regular workers but no significant impact on the workers employed through subcontracting arrangements.
Burchielli, Buttigieg, and Delaney (2008)	Homeworkers, mobilization theory	Implications of mapping for organizing theory and practice	Qualitative	Mapping can be used to organize workers who lack a basic worker identity.
Burchielli, Delaney, and Coventry (2013)	Homework initiatives, responsive regulation theory (RRT)	Homeworker protection through regulatory mechanisms	Case study	Both regulatory and social movement strategies are crucial for the protection of homeworkers.

Burchielli, Delaney, and Goren (2014)	Homeworkers, precarious work	Explore the context and characteristics of women garment homeworkers, through the lens of precarious work	Qualitative	The evidence in this paper suggests that the further away from the first-tier factory (or the lower down the supply chain), the more precarious the work is with less likelihood of any union or collective representation.
Delaney, Burchielli, and Connor (2014)	GPN, social upgrading of labour, network regulations	Theories position of female homeworkers through the lens of global production network	Qualitative Review Paper	GPN concept and related theoretical developments such as networked regulation create theoretical space for imagining how homeworkers might establish relationships with other influential actors and work with them to demand a greater share in the value they are helping to produce.
Naz and Bögenhold (2016)	Micro-entrepreneurship Homeworkers Informal Sector Developing Economies	Conceptualizing homework and female micro-entrepreneurship in the context of developing economies	Qualitative	It is argued that female homeworkers who are usually seen as lacking in entrepreneurial spirit are perhaps more enterprising and entrepreneurial than recognized at present.
Delaney, Burchielli, and Tate (2016)	Homework, global production networks, corporate social responsibility, and gender	Applying a feminist analysis to the relationship between production and social reproduction in relation to homework.	Qualitative	Gender-blind CSR responses are inadequate in addressing both homeworkers' poor labour conditions and child labour.
Naz (2017)	Economic responsibility, homework, global supply chains	Working conditions and associated responsibilities in global supply chains	Book	This study shows that women's involvement in homework within the private sphere of the household is shaped by the interplay of gender ideologies and capitalist labor market practices
Delaney, Burchielli, Marshal, and Tate (2018)	Homeworkers, gender, dimensions of justice	The inequities and injustices inherent in homework conditions maintain women's weak bargaining position, preventing them from making any improvements to their lives via their work. The best way to tackle these issues is not to abolish, but to bring equality and justice to homework.		A key finding is that the organizing approach is the only initiative that can achieve positive outcomes in all four dimensions of justice for homeworkers.

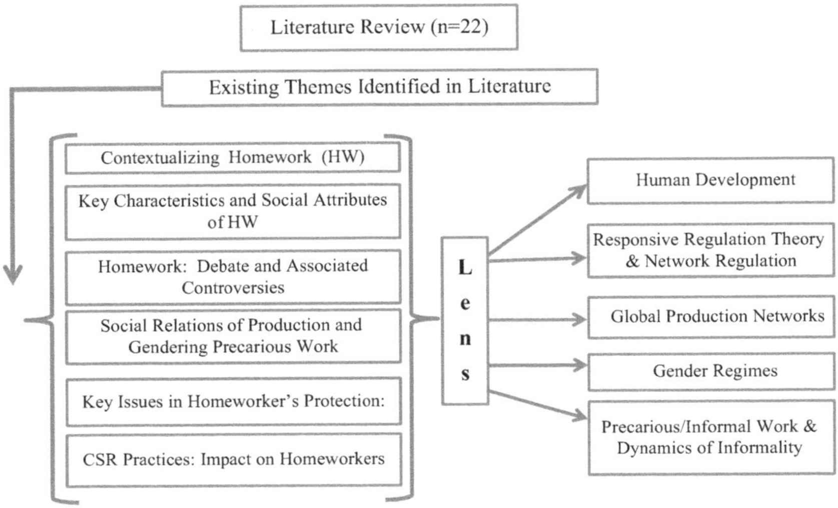

Fig. 3.2 Summary chart of literature review. (Source: Author's elaboration)

cases, at household levels to individual homeworkers. Instead of using a permanent labour force that has to be paid, whether or not there is any work, manufacturers use subcontractors to meet the demands of low price and on-time delivery (Freeman, 2003).

Subcontracting arrangements are beneficial for industry in many different ways. First of all, they do not have to pay social security and other fringe benefits like health insurance and sick leave and so on associated with production in factory using a more formal labour force. In addition, they have been able to shift some overhead costs to homeworkers as well, such as those for light, heat and electricity. Risks associated with the unpredictability of orders during peak and trough production are effectively passed down the subcontracted chains, enabling suppliers to operate competitively. There are many responsible causes for this, but all of them are mainly associated with retailers' need to reduce costs and gain flexibility in a highly competitive environment (Baylina & Schier, 2002; Burchielli et al., 2013; Freeman, 2003; Mehrotra & Biggeri, 2002).

Global economic restructuring has facilitated the retailers to cut their labour costs by outsourcing labour-intensive production to the southern countries, where labour costs are very low and production can be achieved at the lowest cost, so reduction in labour costs is one way of reducing the cost of production. Another strategy to cut the cost is to reduce the volume of held stock at any one time. This reduction helps to decrease not only the storage cost, but it also reduces the amount of capital tied up in form of stored goods that have been purchased but that still is not sold. Improvement in information technology has facilitated such lean retailing. New inventory management systems have made it possible for retailers to keep track of their sale and remaining stock. This new degree of inventory control has resulted in significant cost saving by retailers and has also changed the ordering patterns of retailers, so they can receive the supply when they are ready to sell it.

However, this system has increased pressure on the suppliers to produce high-quality goods at short notice, but at lower cost. Short lead time, low cost, and small and unpredictable orders have become integral attributes of modern production organization. In such a competitive arena where price and flexibility have become an important attribute, manufacturers have found their own ways to remain competitive. One strategy adopted by manufacturers to gain flexibility and reduce cost was to subcontract their work further down the supply chains, all the way to the household level. These changing patterns of employment in the modern economy have contributed to the accelerated growth of homeworking, and homeworking has become a standard part of many supply chains in the process of decentralization of the production process in the twenty-first century (Freeman, 2003).

Homework is part of the informal economy and is not officially calculated. Therefore, statistical information about the extent of homework is patchy and based on or extracted from various empirical study areas, in which homework appears mostly in the broader context of the analysis of the informal economy or of the industrial restructuring of rural areas. Homework is prevalent in both developed and developing economies.[2] The striking reappearance of homework in the west within the informal economy during the 1980s coincides with the appearance of a new production model that changed the geography of European capitalism.

[2] Existing data suggests that approximately 5 percent of labour force in Northern countries is comprised of homeworkers with exception of Australia having 20 percent of homeworkers (Felstead et al., 2000). Data from developing countries is even patchier but estimated figures reveal that there are some 8 million in the Philippines, 20 million in China, and 30 million homeworkers in India (Freeman, 2003).

According to Baylina and Schier (2002), medium-sized and small firms constitute the sporadic network of stable and unstable work in developed economies like Germany. Informal activities have also increased in South Asia, as more and more workers are pushed out of the agricultural sector due to the stagnation in farm income. Surplus labour is involved in both productive and non-productive informal activities as a survival strategy. Informal work is characterized by the lack of social protection and poverty, and it occurs in both developed and developing economies, but outside the formal employment and social protection system (Burchielli et al., 2008).

Global manufacturing is increasingly moving towards buyer-driven manufacturing. Highly competitive global production processes often involve homeworkers at the end of supply chains as a cost-cutting strategy, resulting in a lack of social protection and exploitation of these workers. Exploitation of homeworkers is thus often linked with the international market and predatory practices of multinational companies that end up undermining the labour rights of informal workers integrated in their supply chains (Barrientos, 2013; Mehrotra & Biggeri, 2002; Mezzadri, 2014).

Key Characteristics and Social Attributes of Homeworkers

Historically, homework was carried out by poor women with children, who could thus diversify the source of their family income and support the family. At this point it is of interest to note that homework has also been widely practised in the garment, textile and artificial flower production industries in industrialized countries going back to the Industrial Revolution (Nilsson, 2015). A closer look at the profile of homeworkers reveals that the majority of them are young women with children. A few sectors also have male homeworkers, for example male homeworkers stitch footballs in the football supply chains of Pakistan. In developed countries, most homeworkers are from ethnic minorities. For these people, homeworking is the safest or the only option to work due to racial abuse or attacks (Freeman, 2003). In most of the cases, homeworkers get their work through word of mouth and there is no formal contract. Homeworkers often agree to work on piece rate without having any knowledge of their position in production relations. They may not have any knowledge about the name of the company or companies for whom they are ultimately working. Research reported internationally provides ample evidence that women are overrepresented in homework (Barrientos, 2013, 2019; Burchielli et al., 2014; Felstead et al., 2000; Freeman, 2003)

Although there is some evidence of voluntary entry into informal work, existing research supports that people enter into informal employment relations in the absence of viable alternative options. Clearly, homeworkers are not a homogenous group (Naz & Bögenhold, 2016). However, factors contributing to homework and those contributing to the invisibility of homework converge and exist in combination. The private home-based location of homeworkers contributes to their invisibility, which is a key defining characteristic of their work (Burchielli et al., 2013). Significant characteristics shown by the international studies are that it is a feminine activity that is directly linked with power relations and household divisions of labour. The invisible nature of work is the root cause of many injustices associated with homework. Homeworkers contribute to the global economy but are invisible to the regulators and possibly even to themselves, in the sense that they may not identify themselves as workers. Invisibility is the defining feature of homework (Burchielli et al., 2008; Felstead et al., 2000; Freeman, 2003).

Despite having long-term relations with the employers or subcontractors, homeworkers at best can be categorized as *casual labour*. Homeworkers usually work with the same subcontractors even without a contract due to the cost associated with finding alternatives. There is informal control that governs the stable relationship between homeworkers and the subcontractor community through ties such as a family's debt bondage provision of raw material. This stability of relationship is not balanced with good working conditions. They have none of the benefits that are associated either with regular or casual labour (Mehrotra & Biggeri, 2002).

The demands of homeworking are still high, especially for women. The working day of the homeworkers and the hours spent on homework reveal the error in considering it a flexible form of work. Women's paid productive work cannot be dissociated from their other daily activities. An inherent difficulty and creativity is involved in combining the multiple tasks that female homeworkers are performing. In principle, it is assumed that homeworkers have more opportunities to organize their work independently, but their decisions are not without repercussions for their income and livelihood security. They have limited flexibility in terms of total hours of work, and they cannot decide about the quantity and rhythm of their work without facing serious repercussion on their income and future employment opportunities (Baylina & Schier, 2002).

Therefore, for many homeworkers, this flexibility of homework turns into a self-exploitation involving long hours of work without rest or leisure time in order to secure their livelihood and save their future opportunities for cash income. Homeworkers also assume extra costs in the form of workspace, electricity, heating, telephone and furniture. Unpaid family help is also desired in case of intensive work schedules and demands for the delivery of products. The need for cash income along with social reproduction needs of the family make it hard for women to make their choices independently. Their choices are shaped by the urgency of their needs and the demands of societal gender norms. Homeworkers are not considered as real workers, as their paid work is effectively camouflaged in the popular discourse (Burchielli et al., 2014).

However, despite the precariousness of the work, the need for cash income is the major motivating factor that keeps the homeworkers on the move. Although the need of income might vary on an oscillating scale among female homeworkers, the majority of them are working for their personal and their family's survival. Homeworkers attach contradictory value to their work. The use of space for production purposes, within the private sphere of the household, embodies the possibility of exploitation. Homework performed within the private sphere of the household does not help women to acquire any sort of professional status. However, it may provide room for economic gains by giving them an opportunity to earn some income for their own and their family's needs. However, there is not enough supportive evidence that homework provides opportunities to change gender roles and relations. In relation to opportunities for other forms of gainful employment for women, remuneration of homework can individually be seen as good (Baylina & Schier, 2002; Burchielli et al., 2014; Naz, 2017).

The fear of losing work is the biggest barrier to claiming a better price, especially in the rural areas. Homeworkers are reluctant to benefit from existing protection mechanisms (if any) due to their fear of loss of income. Due to changes in production organization, there is a scarcity of availability of homework, especially in developed countries. Homeworkers in both the northern and southern parts of the world have in common long working days, delays in payments and tight delivery schedules. Dependency is another common feature of homeworking relations. There are some other common denominators related to motivation, which may include factors such as the possibility to combine different tasks, to be their own boss, or few job opportunities (Baylina & Schier, 2002).

Homework: Debate and Associated Controversies

Subcontracting work outside the structure of an ordinary company is part of the neoliberal trend that resulted in massive informalization of the jobs at the end of global supply chains, where many workers are pushed into various types of precarious work arrangements. Multinational companies shift the risk and pressure of deadlines to vulnerable workers at the end of supply chains and reduce their cost and risk in their quest for profit maximization. Changing contractual relationships in the workforce due to subcontracting has outcomes for labour in terms of their health and safety as well as other terms of employment. Homeworking within the formal and informal sector is part of a variety of labour practices, which are faced by the working population at various points in their life cycle. Homework is carried out within the premises of households, either independently or as dependent worker, usually working for subcontractors. Homework has a contradictory charter (O'Hara, 2002).

One stream in research on homework highlights the central role of these earning activities. It is argued that homework provides income-earning opportunities to women for whom there is no choice but to work from home due to their gender-bound roles and responsibilities. Homework provides the opportunity to homeworkers to gain specific skills required for producing these goods at home, increasing the human capital available at the household and local level (Mehrotra & Biggeri, 2002; Mehrotra & Biggeri, 2010). Home-based income-generating activities can lead to human development and can also foster economic development at a local level. The challenge is to find a balance between efficiency and equity. Having the experience of production in a specific sector may also encourage the entrepreneurial capabilities of some workers/subcontractors, and home-based activities and can be a source of emergence of microenterprises. According to Mehrotra and Biggeri (2010), homework within the informal sector has become a functional part of the system with benefits for business and states.

It has gained acceptability at the societal level, too. Homework provides an opportunity to turn the home into a site of economic opportunity, which may also provide an opportunity to women to sidestep personal, social and structural constraints that hinder their access to the labour market or prevent them from earning an income or realizing their professional career. Homeworkers' choices are largely shaped or constrained by gender roles, relations within the families and the regional context (Staples, 2006). Women used to pluriactivity and scant employment alternatives are willing to accept lower wages to supplement their family income. Despite the poor working conditions, women attach a positive value to their work due mainly to the fact that they are able to help their families and are able to influence family decision-making processes within their families. They are more confident about negotiating their family budgets. In a way, it raises their self-esteem and gives them the potential for greater independence and empowerment. Working at home is also reported to have some positive outcomes as well, especially for single mothers or mothers with small children (Barrientos, 2019). Women indicated that homeworking is important for them and something that is *normal* in their life plans. In rural areas where job opportunities are limited for women, homeworking within the informal sector is a socially acceptable form of productive activity for women. For women who assume reproductive work responsibilities due to their assumed gender roles, other forms of work are hard to engage in. Therefore, the broader social context gains relevance in the interpretation of the persistence of homework (Baylina & Schier, 2002).

There are several reasons for the growth of subcontracting activities in many developing countries. It is often beneficial to the local and national economy. It may strengthen inter-industry linkages, enhance entrepreneurial capabilities of subcontractors, bring industry and income-earning opportunities to rural areas. Advantages to employers from subcontracting work to home-based workers are a greater number of recruitment areas for firms, the ability to hire workers according to demand and a minimal risk of unionization. Employers evade safety nets, labour rights and safety in the work place to save costs. However, the employers' advantages turn into sheer disadvantages for homeworkers. The excessive supply of labour pulls down the wages of homeworkers even in the case of highly skilled workers, and working conditions are exploitative due to the lack of alternative income-earning opportunities. Intense global competition in the era of global capitalism has generated a race to the bottom (Benería & Floro, 2005).

During the last three decades, increasing labour market deregulation has reinforced flexibilization. Informalization represents an extreme example of flexibilization, where labour contracts do not even exist. Labour ultimately depends upon the employment generation capacity of capital for survival. This is a reflection of power relations in production processes where flexibilization and informalization tend to increase the relative advantage of capital over labour. New production organization has set the parameters for self-employed labour and home-based work. It is therefore not surprising that inequality is growing not only between labour and capital, but also among the workers themselves.

The individualization of the contract has undermined the bargaining power of the labour force and has decreased the possibility to engage in a collective bargaining process. This situation has enabled the owners and managers to gain a higher share in the production process and shift the risk to individual workers. The way the production process is organized has serious implications for the way cost and risk is distributed among capital and the working population during periods of market instability and cyclical fluctuation. The last few decades have witnessed an increased differentiation in economic well-being among the working population. High-skill labour in high-end jobs is able to get higher returns, whereas most marginalized groups represent unprotected labour with low skills and no job contract (Benería & Floro, 2005; Burchielli et al., 2014; Delaney et al., 2014).

Exploitation by the local supplier is the first step of exploitation of homeworkers in the supply chains. Their problems are further aggravated due to their lack of access to the market. The limitation of contacts with final consumer activities could have a negative impact on homeworkers as well as their families. Negative impacts on economic performance can also result from a low piece rate, as labour of children is also involved to generate additional income. Home-based workers are generally subject to poor environmental conditions, sometimes hazardous occupations or processes, poor lighting and ventilation, non-availability of safety devices, exposure to toxic substances, dangerous gases, postural and spinal disorders, and so on—as many of the studies find (Mehrotra & Biggeri, 2010).

Homework is also characterized by many other forms of exploitation like overwork, insecurity, fear, threat, physical violence, fraud, non-payment, underpayment and withholding of payment. Existence of the exploitative conditions associated with the home-based work keep the homeworking household close to the poverty line. Poor conditions of work and related health issues as well as the low rates of pay hinder home-working households to break out of the poverty trap, especially if home-based work is the main source of income. Homework carried out at the household level has consequences not only for the workers but also for other family members sharing the living space. Two common problems associated with home-based work is that due to the spatial location within the premises of the household, which is considered to be a private sphere, home-based workers are invisible and non-unionized. Despite being clustered in a similar geographical location, homeworkers often work in isolation (Mehrotra & Biggeri, 2005).

Lack of organization and lack of contact with the final consumers are the added disadvantages for home-based workers in terms of having access to their labour rights and other entitlements. Homework has been largely criticized by unions for undermining the interest of the regular labour force by pulling down the wages and working conditions. The lack of organization among home-based workers makes them more vulnerable. Thus, home-based work is characterized by a total lack of social protection. Homeworkers live in cramped conditions. Having limited contact with other workers and no complaint mechanism creates a potential for the exploitation of these workers. A shared sense of homeworking as a labour category does not exist among the homeworking population. The precarious working conditions associated with homeworkers in the informal sector can be attributed to economic, institutional and sociopolitical factors.

It can be safely concluded from the above discussions that market equilibrium generates conditions that undermine human capabilities. There are many institutional factors affecting the earning capabilities and working conditions of the labour force. A lasting impact will not take place without giving due consideration to these sociopolitical and institutional factors. There is rising inequality between labour and capital, which has resulted in a weakening of the bargaining power of labour. Benería & Floro (2005) suggested four interrelated processes that have led to this situation, namely (1) increasing labour market flexibilization, (2) growing inequality in income distribution and diminishing bargaining power of workers, (3) institutional factors such as forms of ownership, production and distribution, and (4) socially ascribed positions in society and within the household.

Social Relations of (Re-)Production and Gendering Precarious Work

The gendered nature of informal work has been extensively documented in the literature (Barrientos, 2013; Burchielli et al., 2014). The stereotypical notion of gender roles contributes to an overrepresentation of women at the informal end of the continuum in home-based production activities. In developing countries, the link between formal and informal enterprises has gradually extended, as increasing numbers of firms, both domestic and international, have become involved with workers outside the traditional work place through subcontracting arrangements. There is a seemingly abundant female labour force in the developing countries that is tapped by the global production networks (GPNs) by creating new forms of putting out systems through which work is provided at the household level. Production is carried out through multilayered networks of firms, subcontractors and home-based workers (Benería & Floro, 2005; Carr, Chen, & Tate, 2000; Freeman, 2003; Prugal, 1996).

There are four main sectors of economic activity, that is, formal economy, public sector, informal economy and the domestic economy. However, there is a multiplicity of work arrangements, and there are definite areas of overlap and labour fluidity within these four sectors of the economy. Informal activities are further subdivided in two groups. The first group involves the bare subsistence activities like street vending, and the second group involves activities that are linked directly or indirectly with the formal production. Market fluctuation shifts the burden of survival on to the individual labourer as firms can effectively hire or lay off labour to adjust to market demands. Under neoliberal regimes, labour flexibility is promoted as a state policy without providing any safety nets during the period of increased employment or underemployment. It is assumed that during this period unpaid household labour of family member will provide a cushion for the subsistence of unemployed or underemployed workers (Benería & Floro, 2005).

Gender is an important axis of differentiation around these processes of labour flexibilization, where women are concentrated in low-end jobs within the informal sector. Although in cultural discourses women's work is constructed as pin money, in most cases homeworking is neither circumstantial nor sporadic. Different reasons for involvement and prevalence of homework are being recognized in the literature, for example low wages paid to male workers in factories, the reserve army of labour available in agriculture and the lack of alternative work for women, which are considered to be the major causes of the survival of homework. People opt for informal work due to a lack of gainful employment opportunities (Benería & Floro, 2005; Burchielli et al., 2014; Delaney et al., 2014).

Strong gender norms and patterns of discrimination are also reflected in economic and social institutions. The ownership of factors of production is linked with the distribution of income/resources, bargaining power and risk. It is a right time to take up this debate again. An institutional analysis of the informal economy reveals the heterogeneity of the working population in terms of earnings and social composition as well as the degree of vulnerability and bargaining power. In terms of organizational forms, the informal economy can be differentiated into at least four major categories: (a) the use of hired wage labour; (b) self-employment and the use of family labour; (c) cooperative forms of production; and (d) hybrid forms combining different institutional and distributional arrangements (Benería & Floro, 2005).

Various institutional factors may include type of work, form of employment, legal/illegal conditions and market destination, which affect wage labour in the informal sector. These institutional arrangements also have implications for income distribution and bargaining power. Labour's access to and control over resources affects their bargaining power in production relations. Workers who have limited resources and are dependent on the employer for the provision of raw material have limited power to negotiate as compared to the workers who have more resources at their disposal. Low-skilled workers who have short work contracts are in a more vulnerable position, and their position in production relations is likely to affect their income and working conditions. There are also certain groups of workers who have less bargaining power by virtue of their ascribed roles within the household and society at large. Female workers are a case in point. They may have limited power and agency to bargain and convert their earnings into a valuable function, including economic security, by virtue of their ascribed gender roles (Benería & Floro, 2005).

The relationship between income and capability is affected by the gender norms and ascribed gender roles that affect income-earning opportunities, workers' choice of work location (whether working at home or with others in a workplace), level of schooling and ownership of assets. Due to their isolation and prevailing gender norms of society, female home-based workers are likely to be at the low end of the income scale on the continuum of labour hierarchy. The structure of the household relations and decision-making processes within the household also affect their income-earning capability. Capabilities are not automatically translated into the functions. As it is claimed by feminists, there is a link between the social reproduction role of the workers at the household level and their role in the labour market. Home-based work enables women who are closely tied to social reproduction work to resolve the contradictions and tensions between paid work and their socially defined reproductive responsibilities (Mehrotra & Biggeri, 2010).

Thus, it is of no surprise that home-based production activities have become an important source of livelihood for women who have no other choice but to combine it with their domestic responsibilities (Carr et al., 2000). The informal environment of home-based work tends to induce vulnerability among homeworkers. Vulnerability is defined as the ability of the household to deal with risk, for example risk associated with a decline in the family income and their attitude towards it. A reduction in the family income can lead to concerns regarding particular functionings including being nourished, sheltered and educated and seeking medical treatment in case of illness. The vulnerability of a household or an individual within a household depends upon the claims or rights over resources in case of risk, shock or economic stress. The less the access to resources, the greater are the chances of vulnerability.

The ability of the individual to function in capability space cannot be simply determined by the existence of employment. Rather, it is the combined outcome of many factors like control over resources—mutual support networks, credit, savings and physical assets. This is especially true during periods of economic shocks. Households with irregular and variable sources of income are more likely to be discriminated against on the basis of a number of social, economic and demographic factors. In the case of economic stress, the burden is not shared equally by the household members. The existence of social networks and trust can be a source of social security during difficult times (Benería & Floro, 2005). The existence of communal mechanisms or institutional arrangements of "generalized reciprocity" within a given community can be a possible source of sharing the risk of homeworking households.

Various local mechanisms of coping with the contingencies have evolved as a part of mutual support systems, like various income maintenance schemes that provide loans. Women play an important role in these informal credit and saving schemes that have evolved to cope with the basic requirements. These informal credit institutions are an important source of security for vulnerable households, because microfinance institutions only target the self-employed or micro entrepreneurs, and participation of poor homeworking households is limited in such schemes. In the face of irregular income streams, poor households design their own strategies to deal with the income shortfalls. Some families use their existing assets or savings as a buffer against income decline. However, when all the household assets and savings have been consumed, the possibility of smoothing falls near to zero. This situation jeopardizes the chances of future income-earning opportunities as well. Homeworkers who need their own resources for production (raw material, equipment etc.) become resource-constrained during income shortfalls, leading to a further decline in their future income. Ethnographic studies do confirm the unequal distribution of income within the household. Therefore, it is important to analyse the effect of labour informality and the way the contribution of each member in the household economy affects the bargaining position and work burden within the household.

Women play a critical role in social reproduction, household maintenance and social asset building or networking. This also has implications for their gender roles and identities as caregivers and income earners. Informal loan arrangements depend upon personal ties and social networks. The intra-household distribution of the work burden resulting from the interplay of gender norms and intra-household negotiation depends upon the relative bargaining power of household members and is subject to change over a period of time. In the case of female homeworkers, it would be of interest to see whether their income is translated to their increased bargaining power at the household level. Does a renegotiation of the division of labour at the household level take place?

However, in cases where gender norms are resilient to changes in income-earning capabilities and income distribution, female homeworkers have to stretch their working time to meet the demands of both productive and reproductive care work. In that case, female homeworkers combine childcare and market work. Looking closely at the different forms of homeworking arrangements may also reveal the mechanisms of the poverty traps and factors contributing to the intergenerational transfer of poverty. Help from other members is also desired to complete the production tasks or to perform household chores, such as cooking and doing errands. Mostly labour of children, especially young girls, is involved, which limits their opportunities and access to education. Girls who are engaged in homeworking activities in turn have limited future opportunities for better jobs and income, thus initiating a circle of intergenerational transfer of poverty in the homeworking families (Mehrotra & Biggeri, 2005).

Future capabilities and entitlements of girls in homeworking households are compromised in order to provide for the survival needs of the family. Thus, these so-called flexible workers do not have the capacity to absorb income variability and are heavily dependent on the subcontractors. Their increased dependence results in a lower mean return on their homeworking activities as compared to less asset-poor households. Case studies from different parts of the world reveal that the inability of homeworkers from poor households to protect their consumption against income risk is likely to have adverse outcomes for their well-being and for productive efficiency (Benería & Floro, 2005). It is clear that the choice for homeworking is highly constrained by gender roles, by relations within the families and by the regional context. Women seem to be suitable for intensive, irregular work, poorly remunerated, informal (in many cases) and home-based, because it is assumed that their productive work is not a high priority in their life. In this sense, female homeworkers are an ideal workforce in the new global economy, cheap, flexible and easy to terminate.

Key Issues in Homeworker's Protection

International supply chains are becoming more and more complicated in our increasingly globalized world. Between the initial manufacturers and the retailers are the complex chains of intermediaries, contractors, subcontractors and agents. Many small-scale producers are involved in these complicated chains, and most of these home-based producers are women. The lack of social protection is one of the outcomes of the companies' predatory practices to hunt for cheap labour in low-cost locations. Factors such as corporate legal identities, structures and capacities pose a serious challenge in the regulation of corporations and supply chains. The magnitude of home-based work and the degree of exploitation demands for a serious intervention to improve home-based work in terms of occupational health and safety, and child labour, as well as household's capabilities, in order to interrupt the intergenerational transfer of poverty.

Factors that keep homeworker families in low equilibrium traps include the involvement of children in home-based work at the cost of schooling, the excessively long hours worked by women, especially young women (the "double burden"), the low piece rates, the unhygienic working conditions and the lack of pension benefits. According to Mehrotra and

Biggeri (2002), without external intervention poor home-based workers may remain at the margin of human capabilities trapped in poverty and will be the source of intergenerational transfer of poverty as well. Under the prevailing scenario, where homework is a rapidly expanding phenomenon, an urgency is felt to push for installing and strengthening protection mechanisms for these workers. However, there are few nations making serious efforts to provide protection to this precarious labour force. Due to the limited recognition of homework, just a few countries have specific legislation for homeworkers. Isolation is a predominant feature of homework. Homeworkers share these characteristics with other homeworkers and remain marginalized at the nexus of gender, race and class.

The specific nature of homeworking makes it difficult to design and implement protection mechanism for homeworkers. A combination of factors like worker invisibility, precariousness of work, predominance of marginalized women, worker isolation and the ambiguity of the employee status of the homeworker contribute to the plight of homeworkers worldwide (Burchielli et al., 2009). Lack of official data on homework contributes to their invisibility in economic and political discourses. Getting data about homeworkers is difficult due mainly to the fact that homeworkers themselves are not sure about their employment status and mostly do not report their activities when data is sought from them. Due to the ambiguous employment status, homeworkers face a difficulty in identifying themselves as workers. Lack of worker status and absence of a shared work context pose serious challenges and difficulties in joining unions to secure legal and social protection. Therefore, attention needs to be paid to the development of the workers identity that is important for workers in the informal economy to establish their social identity (Burchielli et al., 2008).

Many factors hamper the efforts to improve the working conditions of homeworkers and their access to their labour and other human rights and entitlements. Labour laws and legislation are rarely applicable to homeworkers, because mostly they lack any contract or documentary proof of their employment. There is the added difficulty in defining what counts as homework. The nature and boundaries of homework are fluid and shifting. Therefore, it is hard to get accurate data. The informal nature of their work leaves them vulnerable to exploitation by the companies and the subcontractor. There are also some gendered constraints that push women into homework. The ideological construction of work affects the women's ability to perceive themselves as workers.

Their isolation from other homeworkers is also hampering the process of organization of homeworkers. Despite the existence of large numbers of homeworker groups around the world, the vast majority of homeworkers do not know that such groups even exist. In southern countries, approximately 1 percent of homeworkers are in contact with these groups. Although still not ideal, the situation is relatively better in advanced countries. There is an impressive number of homeworker groups around the world, but work done by these associations alone is not sufficient to address the issues of homeworkers on a wider scale (Freeman, 2003).

Traditional labour laws do not provide any protection to homeworkers as their employment status is subsumed under the complex web of the multilayered subcontracting system. They are separated from their employer through many complex, often transnational, subcontracting arrangements with many intermediaries and other forms of informal employment, such as small enterprises and home-based workshops. Employment relations of homeworkers are effectively disguised in supply chains that provide an opportunity to the companies to distance themselves from the responsibilities of the actual terms of the work. Homeworkers are producing for the global market but they are not only invisible to the labour market regulator but to themselves as well, in the sense that the existing normative structure of society hinders their ability to perceive themselves as workers.

Regulatory mechanisms alone are not sufficient to address the issues and problems of homeworkers. As homeworkers are rarely able to gain access to existing protections, there is a need for other social and political mechanisms to provide adequate social protection to homeworkers. Even if protection mechanisms exist, homeworkers are reluctant to claim their legal entitlement mainly due to the fear of losing their work as a backlash from various stakeholders, including firms and political parties, whose interests run counter to those of the homeworkers (Burchielli et al., 2009). The economic imperative to work along with household responsibility makes organization a less attractive option for homework (Burchielli et al., 2008). Broader economic, social and political conditions outline the conditions of homework (Burchielli et al., 2013). Effective regulatory response demands for multi-stakeholder initiatives applied simultaneously for the protection of workers' rights.

Synthesizing the Literature

The main reasons for and advantages of homeworking reported in most of studies were childcare, financial and flexibility, and the main disadvantages were poor pay, isolation and irregularity of work. The main reason identified for employing homeworkers in production chains included flexibility/ dealing with changing workflows, reduced costs, restricted space and solving childcare problems, and the main disadvantage was difficulty with supervision (O'Hara, 2002). Another important factor to understand homework relates to gender, and more specifically to gender exploitation, since homeworkers are mostly women. Economic and social conditions encourage women to opt for the homeworking activities (Burchielli et al., 2013). Extended subcontracting chains effectively disguise employment relations and the responsibility of actual terms and conditions of work is diffused. The neoliberal trend of deregulation has promoted such business practices at the expense of the vulnerable workers whose work is increasingly and dangerously precarious (Benería, 2001).

Under the prevailing scenario where homework is a rapidly expanding phenomenon, urgency is felt to push for installing and strengthening the protection mechanisms for these workers. According to Mehrotra and Biggeri (2010), factors that keep homeworkers' families in low equilibrium traps are the involvement of children in home-based work at the cost of schooling, the excessively long hours worked by women, especially young women (the "double burden"), the low piece rates, the unhygienic working conditions and the lack of pension benefits. Without some external intervention, poor home-based workers may remain at the margin of human capabilities trapped in poverty and will be the source of an intergenerational transfer of poverty as well. The specific nature of homeworking makes it difficult to design and implement protection mechanisms for homeworkers. A combination of factors like worker invisibility, precariousness of work, predominance of marginalized women, worker isolation and the ambiguity of the employee status of the homeworker contribute to the predicament of homeworkers worldwide (Burchielli et al., 2009; Naz, 2017). Lack of worker status and absence of a shared work context pose serious challenges and difficulties in joining unions to secure legal and social protection (Burchielli et al., 2008). Therefore, attention needs to be paid to the development of the workers' identity that is important for workers in the informal economy to establish their social identity.

There is a great similarity in the issues faced by the homeworkers across the world (Delaney et al., 2018) Thus, in late 1980s, many homeworking groups and associations realized that it made sense for local and international organizations to work collectively in order to make the changes that they desired. Workers' use of these broad networks to influence corporate behaviour is an emerging stream in literature, wherein various actors have opportunities to gain and claim legitimacy as regulators in global production networks (GPNs; Delaney et al., 2014). Delaney et al. (2018) strongly advocated homeworkers need to organize to address the imbalances created under capitalism and patriarchy.

Placing homeworkers as actors in the power relation sector within the GPN network framework opens the theoretical space for exploring other ways in which homeworkers might contribute some power in the production network (Coe, Dicken, & Hess, 2008; Delaney et al., 2014). Local, national and transnational nodes of production intersect in GPNs and add to the complexity of the regulatory mechanisms required for this polycentric landscape.

The plurality of actors, variety of mechanisms, relational and the spatial location of actors, with GPN network framework point towards the need for more inclusive and socially responsive mechanisms. Various actors at different nodes of the GPN potentially have the opportunity to claim legitimacy as regulators within this dynamic regulatory field. The GPN concept and related theoretical developments such as networked regulation create the theoretical space for envisaging how homeworkers might establish relationships with other influential actors and work with them to realize their rights (Delaney et al., 2018).

It comes out clearly from the review of literature that homework can be explained not only in economic terms but also in technical, social, territorial and institutional terms. It is not the form of work that can just be placed along marginality and exploitation nor does it just represent the survival of social relations and forms of work doomed for extinction or taken up only in times of crisis. Homework is likely to grow, and, as a model of female employment, will continue to capture the attention of academics as well as practitioners. This literature review confirms that knowledge about homework has grown in depth and breadth over the years. However, the conceptual lens need to be expanded to include the perspective of homeworkers in the theoretical development of the field. There are some other gaps and research areas, which need to be explored further. For instance, it is important to investigate how various forms of regulatory mechanisms such as corporate social responsibility (CSR) may support homeworkers to demand a greater share in the value they are helping to produce (Delaney et al., 2014).

Concluding Thoughts

Existing academic literature on homework paints a complex and variegated picture of homeworking practices. Traditional homework persists in both developed and developing economies, albeit with some differences, indicating the need to consider the geography of work. Various factors that contributed to stimulating the growth of homework under contemporary conditions include the globalization of production through outsourcing and subcontracting arrangements. The generalized adoption of neoliberal policies through increased deregulation and an overreliance on markets to provide regulating functions has facilitated these new production arrangements on a massive scale. Findings from this literature review suggest contradictory evidence about the potential of change through homework. It is manifested from this literature review that, although use of the home space for paid production embodies the possibilities of exploitation, at the same time it must be borne in mind that it also provides opportunities for cash income and boosts their self-confidence and self-esteem. However, the potential of homework to bring strategic changes in gender regimes is not so clear from the existing evidence. Therefore, liberating and empowering potential of homework from the gender justice perspective demands to instil mechanism to realize fuller potential of homework. The next chapter explores these possibilities.

References

Barrientos, S. (2008). Contract Labour: the 'Achilles Heel' of Corporate Codes in Commercial Value Chains. *Development and Change, 39* (6), 977–990.

Barrientos, S. (2013). Corporate Purchasing Practices in Global Production Networks: A Socially Contested Terrain. *Geoforum, 44*, 44–51.

Barrientos, S. (2019). *Gender and Work in Global Value Chains: Capturing the Gains?* Cambridge: Cambridge University Press.

Baylina, M., & Schier, M. (2002). Homework in Germany and Spain: Industrial Restructuring and the Meaning of Homework for Women. *GeoJournal, 56*(4), 295–304.

Benería, L. (2001). Shifting the Risk: New Employment Patterns, Informalization, and Women's Work. *International Journal of Politics, Culture, and Society, 15*(1), 27–53.

Benería, L., & Floro, M. (2005). Distribution, Gender, and Labor Market Informalization: A Conceptual Framework with a Focus on Homeworkers. In K. Neema & L. Benería (Eds.), *Rethinking Informalization: Poverty, Precarious Jobs and Social Protection* (pp. 28–43). New York, NY: Cornell University Open Access Repository.

Boris, E., & Prügl, E. (1996). *Homeworkers in Global Perspective: Invisible No More.* New York and London: Routledge.

Burchielli, R., & Delaney, A. (2009). *Homework and CSR: Can Homeworkers Benefit?* In 15th World Congress of the International Industrial Relations Association (IIRA), 24 August 2009–28 August 2009, Sydney Convention and Exhibition Centre.

Burchielli, R., Buttigieg, D., & Delaney, A. (2008). Organizing Homeworkers: The Use of Mapping as an Organizing Tool. *Work, Employment & Society, 22*(1), 167–180.

Burchielli, R., Delaney, A., Tate, J., & Coventry, K. (2009). The FairWear Campaign: An Ethical Network in the Australian Garment Industry. *Journal of Business Ethics, 90*(4), 575–588.

Burchielli, R., Delaney, A., & Coventry, K. (2013). Campaign Strategies to Develop Regulatory Mechanisms: Protecting Australian Garment Homeworkers. *Journal of Industrial Relations, 56*(1), 81–102. https://doi.org/10.1177/0022185613498662

Burchielli, R., Delaney, A., & Goren, N. (2014). Garment Homework in Argentina: Drawing Together the Threads of Informal and Precarious Work. *The Economic and Labour Relations Review, 25*(1), 63–80. https://doi.org/10.1177/1035304613518476

Carr, M., Chen, M., & Tate, J. (2000). Globalization and Homebased Workers. *Feminist Economics, 6*(3), 123–142.

Coe, N. M., Dicken, P., & Hess, M. (2008). Global Production Networks: Realizing the Potential. *Journal of Economic Geography, 8*(3), 271–295.

Delaney, A., Burchielli, R., & Connor, T. (2014). Positioning Women Homeworkers in a Global Footwear Production Network: Identifying Barriers and Enablers to Claiming Rights, 1–25. https://doi.org/10.2139/ssrn.2497381

Delaney, A., Burchielli, R., Marshal, S. D., & Tate, J. (2018). *Homeworking Women: A Gender Justice Perspective.* New York: Routledge.

Delaney, A., Burchielli, R., & Tate, J. (2016). Corporate CSR Responses to Homework and Child Labour in the Indian and Pakistan Leather Sector. In K. Grosser, L. McCarthy, & M. Kilmore (Eds.), *Can CSR Responses be Inclusive of Informal Women Worker Rights and Priorities?* Leeds: Greenleaf.

Felstead, A., Jewson, N., & Walters, S. (2000). *A Statistical Portrait of Working at Home in the UK: Evidence From the Labour Force Survey*. Retrieved from http://www.leeds.ac.uk/esrcfutureofwork/downloads/workingpaperdownloads/fow_paper_04.pdf

Freeman, D. (2003). Homeworkers in Global Supply Chains. *Greener Management International, 43*: 107–119.

Mehrotra, S., & Biggeri, M. (2002). *Social Protection in the Informal Economy: Home-based Women Worker and Outsourced Manufacturing in Asia*. Innocenti Working Paper No. 97. Florence, Italy: United Nations Children's Fund.

Mehrotra, S., & Biggeri, M. (2005). Can Industrial Outwork Enhance Homeworkers' Capabilities? Evidence from Clusters in South Asia. *World Development, 33*(10), 1735–1757. https://doi.org/10.1016/j.worlddev.2005.04.013

Mehrotra, S., & Biggeri, M. (2010). Children in Home Worker Households in Pakistan and Indonesia. *International Journal of Manpower, 31*(2), 208–231. https://doi.org/10.1108/01437721011042278

Mezzadri, A. (2014). Indian Garment Clusters and CSR Norms: Incompatible Agendas at the Bottom of the Garment Commodity Chain. *Oxford Development Studies, 42*(2), 1–21. https://doi.org/10.1080/13600818.2014.885939

Mies, M. (1982). The Dynamics of the Sexual Division of Labor and Integration of Rural Women into the World Market. In L. Benería (Ed.), *Women and Development: The Sexual Division of Labor in Rural Societies* (pp. 1–28). New York: Praeger.

Naz, F. (2017). The Position of Female Homeworkers in a Global Supply Chain: How do Capitalist Labor Market Practices Interplay with Gender Ideologies? In M. Haase (Ed.), *The Changing Basis of Economic Responsibility. A Look from Perspective of Today*. Springer Publisher.

Naz, F., & Bögenhold, D. (2016). Micro Entrepreneurship and Female Homework in Developing Countries: On the Limited Capacity of Micro Entrepreneurship as Analytical Term. In D. Bögenhold, J. Bonnet, M. Dejardin, & D. Garcia (Eds.), *Contemporary Entrepreneurship: Multidisciplinary Perspectives on Innovation and Growth* (pp. 291–303). Cham, Switzerland: Springer Publishers.

Nilsson, M. (2015). *Taking Work Home: Labour Dynamics of Women Industrial Homeworkers in Sweden During the Second Industrial Revolution*. PhD thesis. Retrieved from https://gupea.ub.gu.se/bitstream/2077/38239/1/gupea_2077_38239_1.pdf

O'Hara, R. (2002). *Scoping Exercise for Research into the Health and Safety of Homeworkers*. HSL Report RAS/02/08. Retrieved from http://www.hse.gov.uk/research/hsl_pdf/2002/hsl02-18.pdf

Petticrew, M., & Roberts, H. (2006). *Systematic Reviews in the Social Sciences: A Practical Guide*. Oxford, UK: Blackwell Publishing Ltd.

Prugal, E. (1996). Home-based Producers in Development Discourses. In E. Boris & E. Prugal (Eds.), *Homeworkers in Global Perspective: Invisible No More* (pp. 39–60). New York and London: Routledge.

Prügl, E., & Tinker, I. (1997). Microentrepreneurs and Homeworkers: Convergent Categories. *World Development, 25*(9), 1471–1482.

Staples, D. E. (2006). *No Place Like Home: Organizing Home-Based Labor in the Era of Structural Adjustment*. New York and London: Routledge.

WIEGO. (2000, October 18–20). *Women Workers in the Informal Sector in South Asia: Creating an Enabling Environment*. Retrieved from http://wiego.org/sites/wiego.org/files/publications/files/Carr-Chen-homebased-women-workers.pdf

Williams, P. (2005). Leveraging Change in the Working Conditions of UK Homeworkers. *Development in Practise, 15*(3-4), 546–558. https://doi.org/10.1080/09614520500075565

Wilson, T. D. (2003). Forms of Male Domination and Female Subordination: Homeworkers Versus Maquiladora Workers in Mexico. *Review of Radical Political Economics, 35*(1), 56–72. http://doi.org/10.1177/0486613402250194

CHAPTER 4

CSR and Home-Based Work: Conceptualizing Social Responsibility in Global Market Economy

Introduction

Economics as we know it today originated from political economy that has clear origin in ethics. There is a persistent philosophical tradition to reflect on the idea of the responsibilities of business. There are two dominant paradigms in history that define the relationship between business and morality of the broader society, namely the theory of moral unity and the amoral theory of business (Shepard, Shepard, James, & Carroll, 1995). The theory of moral unity in pre-industrial *Gemeinschaft* societies rests on the assumption that only one set of moral standards exists within a society and economic entities are not considered as *ethical sanctuaries* (Shepard et al., 1995: 580). The underlying assumption is that social relations and economic activities are socially embedded and governed by the same set of rules, value and norms. In contrast, modern societies are characterized by high levels of social differentiation (Habermas, 1981) as compared to pre-industrial societies and shift from (pre-industrial) *Gemeinschaft* to (industrial) *Gesellschaft* societies, marked by individualism, social fragmentation, weak family ties and competition. Durkheim (1984) provided ample proof in his study of solidarity that social relations change in the market-oriented society from strong ties to a weakening of personal ties. This has resulted in depersonalized relations in organic societies. There is also a shift from integrated social institutions to a high level of functional differentiation.

Modern capitalist societies are increasingly coordinated by means of markets. There are two main perspectives about the role of the market, namely

F. Naz, D. Bögenhold, *Unheard Voices*,
https://doi.org/10.1007/978-3-030-54363-1_4

doux-commerce (gentle business) and self-destruction. The thesis of self-destruction rests on beliefs that capitalism erodes the moral foundation of society. Whereas proponents of doux-commerce assert that capitalism will create a moral environment where society will flourish in respect to economic and social wealth (Aspers, 2011). Supporters of market capitalism regard it as most efficient system with exponential growth and best overall outcome. However, critics are of the view that the development has destroyed other societal values and it has increased inequality at the same time. From the perspective of neoliberal economic theory, market participants are viewed as rational actors whose only desire is to maximize their utility, and economic responsibility does not go beyond what is defined in the laws. According to this perspective, business relationships are not immoral; however, they are not subject to the same moral restraints and practices covering other domains of social relationships (Shepard et al., 1995).

Consequently, in the long-standing tradition of the liberal market economy, responsibilities of commercial agents are narrowly defined and restricted only to negative duties. The core assumption in orthodox economic theory, termed as *Euclidean economics* (Clark, 1921: 132), is that business is a special domain within society with a distinct morality that derives its efficiency from the self-interest of mutually benefiting commercial agents. The market is portrayed as a neutral force linked to economic individualism and personal preferences (Stehr, Henning, & Weiler, 2006). The neoliberal economic theory paradigm has limited space for particularism, sentiment and morality, except for the minimum morality that is defined by law. However, current debates on the moral responsibilities of businesses have begun to question this established principle that the morality of commercial life ought to be a minimum morality (see also Hsieh, 2013), and moral reasoning is gaining ground to explain market behaviour (Dubbink & Liedekerke, 2014). Clark (1916) argued that private enterprises cannot be governed solely by private interest.

> (W)e are coming to see that our everyday business dealings have more far-reaching effects than we have ever realized, and that the system of free contract is by itself quite inadequate to bring home the responsibility for these effects. We have begun to realize the many inappropriate values that are created and the many unpaid damages that are inflicted in the course of business exchanges. (p. 218)

The application of the restrictive economic responsibility model in traditional business economics has striking implications for global society. It leaves the most pressing problems in the domain of supererogatory action and reduces them to issues of mere philanthropy and charity (Clark, 1916). Therefore, a more adequate concept of responsibility is required for the collective age to solve multidimensional large-scale problems (Wettstein, 2012). The normative vacuum created by the dilution of the *Homo economicus* model needs to be filled by altered or new norms and ideas. Major changes in the world scenario are due mainly to the economic globalization, and the declining authority of nation states simultaneously with the rising power of multinational corporations as well as the inclusion of non-state actors in global governance mechanisms demands that we refocus our attention on the normative issues regarding the cross-cultural interface of business and society. However, the transition from one to another mode of thought is fraught with challenges and contradictions. The debate over the appropriate duties of commercial agents has been articulated, particularly in discussions on international business, to demonstrate that the morality of commercial life cannot exclude all positive duties. However, within existing literature, there is a divide on the issue of grounding positive duties either as inescapable moral duties ensuing from the liberal tradition (Dubbink & Liedekerke, 2014; Hsieh, 2013; Young, 2010) or to conceptualize positive duties as an alternative vision of responsibility termed "economics of responsibility" (Clark, 1916), in which business recognizes its responsibility with regard to the public interest (Scherer & Palazzo, 2007; Scherer & Palazzo, 2011). Despite all these contradictory approaches with regard to business responsibility, there is a widely held consensus among scholars that business environment in the twenty-first century is marked by a growing concern about corporate image and responsibility. What follows is an attempt to explore the potential of corporate social responsibility (CSR) to benefit homeworkers located at invisible margins of global supply chains.

Corporate Social Responsibility

A wide range of terminology has been used over the last few decades to explain what is now broadly called corporate responsibility. The earliest conceptualization of social responsibility was outlined in the *Social Responsibilities of the Businessman* (Bowen, 1953) as "obligations to pursue those policies, to make those decisions, or to follow those lines of action which are desirable in terms of the objectives and values of our society" (p. 6). The use of the term "social responsibility" in this context reflects the focus of business during the 1950s and 1960s on doing social good rather than linking it to any benefit. Later, Friedman (1970) forcefully challenged Bowen's idea of social responsibility. According to him, the only social responsibility of a business is to make a profit for its shareholders. An intellectual middle ground was proposed in Carroll's (1979) three-dimensional corporate social performance model, in accordance with which "The social responsibility of business encompasses the economic, legal, ethical and discretionary expectations that a society has of organizations at a given point in time" (p. 500).

Much later, Waddock (2004) defined corporate social responsibility as

> the subset of corporate responsibilities that deals with a company's voluntary/discretionary relationships with its societal and community stakeholders. CSR is typically undertaken with some intent to improve an important aspect of society or relationships with communities or nongovernmental organizations (NGOs) (nonprofits). CSR is frequently operationalized as community relations, philanthropic, multisector collaboration, or volunteer activities. (p. 10)

Blowfield and Frynas (2005) define CSR as

> an umbrella term for a variety of theories and practices all of which recognize: (a) that companies have a responsibility for their impact on society and the natural environment, sometimes beyond legal compliance and the liability of individuals; (b) that companies have a responsibility for the behavior of others with whom they do business (e.g., within supply chains); and (c) that business needs to manage its relationship with wider society, whether for reasons of commercial viability or to add value to society. (p. 503)

A variety of existing CSR definitions acknowledge the social and environmental responsibilities of businesses along with their profit and stakeholder responsibilities. CSR generally falls into what Carroll (2008) termed the "discretionary and ethical responsibilities of business." CSR implies an implicit relation between business and society based on a moral commitment to rights and duties. It is important to acknowledge that the theoretical debate over the concept of CSR has proliferated, with the rise of diverse approaches over the last few decades. Frederiksen and Nielsen (2013) have suggested three plausible approaches. The first one is instrumental approach, which refers to the business side of CSR, namely that *it's good for business*. The second approach is ethical, which is based on the premise that it is the moral obligation of business enterprises to engage in CSR, in that *it's the right thing to do*. The three major ethical theories that occupy a central position in any philosophical debate on the subject are utilitarianism, the ethics of rights and contractualism. Academic discussions on CSR are, by and large, based on these theoretical foundations. The third one is a hybrid approach, which combines features of both instrumental and ethical approaches. The hybrid approach claims that engaging in CSR is both financially and morally good, or that it's good for business and the right thing to do. All these theories differ according to matters of reciprocity and mutual acceptability and also differ according to which specific account of morality they provide.

However, even if consensus can be reached that companies should pay equal attention to avoiding harmful actions and to actively doing good, a new, immediate concern will surface regarding the scope of CSR, namely whose rights companies are morally bound to secure or who should be counted as morally relevant. One way of dealing with this problem, as suggested by Freeman, Harrison, Wicks, Parmar and Colle (2011) is to focus on the stakeholders. Some stakeholder theorists would argue that stakeholder theory has its foundations in libertarian philosophy and has a close affinity with the theory of rights. A stakeholder approach to CSR implies that companies are responsible for their stakeholders, ordinarily understood as the customers, employees, suppliers, shareholders and the local community (Freeman et al., 2011). Stakeholder theory asserts that a business must *recognize* and *manage* relationships with diverse stakeholders in the supply chain (Soundararajan & Brown, 2016).

Despite the current popularity of the notion of CSR, there is empirical evidence which suggests that ethical approaches to CSR in global production networks, although good in theory, are difficult to implement because the role of context in conditioning morality remains largely untheorized in the current literature (Shadnam, 2015). When refracted through the theoretical and ideological lenses of economically advanced countries, entrenched and pronounced issues of labour in developing countries are of little relevance to those located in advance countries, producing instead, in some cases, structurally unjust outcomes. Lund-Thomsen and Nadvi (2010) note, for example, that recent concern about CSR in developing countries is an outcome of the tussle between demands for CSR compliance in developing countries and the search for locally applicable responses to these pressures. This hold true particularly when bringing about sustained improvements in informal workers' conditions in developing countries engaged at the invisible margin of global production network (Lund-Thomsen, Lindgreen, & Vanhamme, 2016). Delaney, Burchielli, and Tate (2016) have argued that the response of CSR towards informal home workers in GPNs is either rejection or tolerance. In sum, the effects of CSR in developing countries are a controversial and understudied area.

CSR in Developing Countries: Issues and Concerns

The concept of CSR has received heightened global attention in recent years and attained a new resonance in the global economy. However, despite the increased attention that is accorded to CSR, very little is known of CSR practices and processes in developing countries (Amoako, 2016). CSR philosophy and practice has largely remained an alien concept in the context of many developing countries or is viewed as part of a "Western imperialist agenda" (Khan & Lund-Thomsen, 2011). According to Jamali (2010), existing literature covering the CSR involvement of multinational corporations (MNCs) in developing countries has been extremely polarized. The Western-centric nature of academic publications on CSR is acknowledged in many studies (Amoako, 2016; Fayyaz, Lund-Thomsen, & Lindgreen, 2015; Jamali & Mirshak, 2007; Khan, Westwood, & Boje, 2010). CSR approaches mainly developed from the perspective of economically advanced countries have little to say about the issues and the interests of those affected by these discourses in developing countries, where CSR interventions occur on behalf of Western corporations (Jamali & Mirshak, 2007; Khan et al., 2010). This lack of attention to the concerns of those who are the target of CSR interventions (Blowfield, 2007) ultimately renders these practices irrelevant for them. Entrenched and pronounced issues of labour in developing countries when refracted through the theoretical and ideological lenses of economically advanced countries bear little relevance for those located in the periphery and, instead, in some cases, produce structurally unjust outcomes. In order to address these issues, CSR literature needs to redress this imbalance of perspective by articulating the issues through active engagement with the developing countries. Existing literature (Beddewela & Fairbrass, 2015; Jamali & Mirshak, 2007; Khan et al., 2010) supports that understanding the national, local context and institutional framework where CSR is implemented is important to better inform practice. According to Beddewela and Fairbrass (2015), CSR is by nature considered to be a voluntary corporate activity that is used by the state and other institutional actors, to engage in indirect means of steering towards the fulfilment of their own goals. Lund-Thomsen and Nadvi (2010) note, for example, that recent concern about CSR in developing countries is an outcome of the tussle between demands for CSR compliance in developing countries and the search for locally applicable responses to these pressures. Lund-Thomsen and Coe (2015), using the case of Nike's production and CSR model in the Pakistani football manufacturing industry, articulate that national contexts for work and employment may place clear limits on what CSR policies of internationally branded companies can accomplish in developing countries. Khan et al. (2010) also put it concisely when they state that resting on universalistic, paternalistic, decontextualizing and atomistic assumptions, Western-led CSR intervention in Pakistan's soccer ball industry brought negative, unintended consequences. Although some alternatives are proposed under the rubric *CSR and Development*, this work is underdeveloped and has largely remained on the fringes of CSR literature. Nonetheless, linking CSR to international development is an important advancement, though claims about the role CSR can play in social and economic development remain largely unsubstantiated (Blowfield, 2007).

MNCs have a lion's share of international trade transactions, and due to their increased power and visibility, there is escalating pressure of social responsibility. In many developing countries, MNCs are expected to fill the gap of defunct governments along the spectrum of their activities. However, the absence of a global legal framework for MNC business activities creates the risk of malpractice, especially in the context of developing and emerging countries (Jamali, 2010). This void and legal abstraction has become even more pronounced in the case of transnational space. The possibility to avoid the increasing pressure of social responsibility is heightened in the case of weak or virtually non-existent environmental regulations that characterize many developing countries. In the context of this regulatory arbitrage (Jenkins, 2005), the debate over the CSR involvement of MNCs in developing countries has become more relevant. Another important challenge for CSR in the transnational context is the aspect of globalization/localization. Building on knowledge gained from the business society and international business, political behaviour literature, Jamali (2010) convincingly argued that in the context of Lebanon the patterns of global CSR are diffused and diluted along the way in view of specific subsidiary endowments and host market characteristics. What materializes at the level of implementation in Lebanon are philanthropic small-scale idiosyncratic CSR activities as token mimetic responses to global directives.

Although the picture is far from clear in terms of relevance and impact of CSR in developing countries, there is at least some empirical evidence that support such claims poorly designed CSR intervention may fail to match the priorities of local stakeholders (Fayyaz et al., 2015). More CSR research in the context of developing countries may offer valuable insights about CSR practice and challenges in the light of different economic, social and cultural conditions. In order to fully understand the impact of Western-based CSR initiatives, it is important to unpack the complexities of existing relations in global production networks that distract them from attending to local priorities where the emerging and understudied area comprises small clusters in developing countries.

CSR in Global Supply Chains

Global supply chains cut across diverse institutional settings with diverse actors and resources at different points in the chain (Tapia, Ibsen, & Kochan, 2015). This paradigmatic shift in industrial organization has extended the scope of analysis beyond the traditional dynamics of the production process that was mainly focused on the production site. The conventional categories of labour and employment increasingly lose their analytical relevance and explanatory potential. Against this backdrop, a variety of frameworks have emerged in the literature that try to capture "network-led development" through the metaphor of a chain. The global value chain (GVC), or global production network (GPN), is a variant of this framework in which production processes are traced from their conceptualization to the final stage.

The GPN approach was developed by the Manchester School of Economics geographers against the backdrop of two other approaches, namely the global commodity chain (GCC) and the global value chain (GVC). These approaches are widely used in the literature as an analytical tool (Barrientos, 2008; Hurley & Miller, 2005; Kurian, 2006). The concept of the GCC was initially developed by Gereffi, Korzeniewicz and Korzeniewicz (1994). According to Gereffi et al. (1994), "GCC consists of sets of inter-organizational networks clustered around one commodity or product, linking households, enterprises, and states to one another in the world-economy" (p. 2). Gereffi classified GCC chains into two types:

producer-driven and buyer-driven commodity chains. Producer-driven chains are mainly governed by large transnational companies (TNC) and have centralized governance structures, whereas buyer-driven chains are controlled by retailers, brand-name merchandizers and trading companies (Gereffi et al., 1994). Production in buyer-driven chains is mostly labour intensive and located at the periphery due to the availability of cheap labour in these countries, whereas high-value activities like designing and marketing are controlled by the core countries, mainly in consumer goods like garments and footwear, and so on. Thus, the relative position of a country in the world economy, due to its comparative advantage, determines the share of each country in the production process.

However, as global production increasingly moved towards high-tech products and services, the term "commodity" was substituted with the idea of global value chains (GVCs). In a GVC, value added at each stage of the production chain is vital to global economic organization. The major focus of GVCs is on inter-firm relationships and particularly on governance issues. However, the inability of value chain analysis to acknowledge fissures and disconnects in the value chain in developing countries is a serious limitation that restricts the scope of analysis. One major but largely valid criticism in GVC research against Gereffi (2005) influential theory of GVC governance is its exclusive focus on inter-sectoral and firm linkages at the cost of labour (Gibbon, Bair, & Ponte, 2008). It is argued that the verticality of value chain analysis fails to see how labour processes are horizontally constituted within the value chain. Chains provide few clues as to the question of social labour processes embedded in supply chains (Newsome, Taylor, Bair, & Rainnie, 2015).

The categorical omission of labour in studies of global production organization is no longer legitimate, this limitation having been overcome by the emergence of the Manchester school, which worked on the development of the concept of global production networks. GPN literature acknowledges the importance of labour within the matrix of other factors that explain global geographies of production and exchange (Coe, Hess, Yeung, Dicken, & Henderson, 2004; Henderson, Dicken, Hess, Coe, & Yeung, 2002; Newsome et al., 2015). Rather than having a simple focus on governance issues like inter-firm power dimensions, GPNs pay heed to their embeddedness in particular local socioeconomic and sociocultural environments that create the possibility to structure GPNs from the bottom up (Lund-Thomsen & Coe, 2015).

Despite the relevance of these analytical frameworks as conceptual tools to understand power relations within global supply chains, it is important to acknowledge that the primary focus of this literature has been on economic development. These approaches concentrate on upgrading countries through the introduction of companies to international markets for products, but the impact of these inter-firm relations on labour and employment conditions in the global production network is often absent in these conceptual frameworks (Robinson & Rainbird, 2013).

According to Henderson et al. (2002), GPNs should acknowledge the "conditions under which labour power is converted into actual labour through the labour process" (p. 448). This means that the integration of labour process theory (LPT) and analysis within chain or network theorizing should be at core of GPNs, and labour should not be treated merely as a factor of production affecting firms' locational decisions and resultant production geographies.

LPT uncovered the underlying mechanism through which the capacity to work is transformed into actual work. Core ideas of LPT are based on Marx's *Capital* and were mainly developed by scholars (Thompson & Newsome, 2004; Thompson & Smith, 2009, 2010). In a nutshell, labour process theory is concerned with exploring the various dynamics of control, consent and resistance at the point (site) of production. The distinctiveness and peculiarities of particular workplaces occupy a privileged position in LPT analysis and theorizing (Robinson & Rainbird, 2013). However, this seemingly narrow focus and the reach of labour process analysis of LPT remain contested (Edwards, 2010), and LPT is criticized for its inability to explain developments within points of production, most notably in relation to gender and race, as well as issues lying outside the workplace, such as non-wage labour, familial ideology and informality.

Conversely, the major strengths of GPNs lie in their explicit acknowledgement of the importance of labour and spatial sensitivity, among other territorial factors, that give GPNs their structure and shape their consequences for both global and local actors. The recent interest of LPT to work at multiple levels of analysis and to extend the level of analysis from the point of production to the dynamics of workplace transformation, political economics and the shifting regimes of accumulation make LPT consistent with projects of GPNs (Newsome et al., 2015). Although this is a relatively underdeveloped area, it is still a promising development. The theoretical landscape of labour process analysis has widened due to the tendency of scholars to adopt the diverse frameworks of global value chains (GVCs) and global production networks (GPNs) rather than to fight framework wars.

According to Newsome et al. (2015), despite claims relating to the inclusion of labour processes, most of the burgeoning literature on GPNs tends to reflect and reproduce an orthodox "factor of production" approach with just a few exceptions (Coe, Dicken, & Hess, 2008; Delaney, Burchielli, & Connor, 2014). However, in recent years there has been a proliferation of attempts to respond to this criticism of GPNs by redressing the *labour deficit* from within economic geography and its subfield of labour geography (Coe et al., 2008; Cumbers, Helms, & Swanson, 2010; Rainnie, Herod, & McGrath-Champ, 2011). Integrating the emphasis of the GPN approach towards a broader network of actors with the interest of LPT to extend the level of analysis from the point of production to the dynamics of the transformation of work and the political economy provides space to conceptualize and empirically investigate how and under what conditions workers are situated in global production organization.

The emphasis of the GPN approach towards a broader network of actors including nation states, international organizations, trade unions, non-governmetal organizations (NGOs) and communities provides space to conceptualize and empirically investigate how and under what conditions homeworkers are situated in GPNs. How do CSR practices that are embedded in wider networks impact homeworkers located at the lowest rungs of GPNs? Both formal and informal institutional processes have to be taken into account when analysing the gains or losses accruing to homeworkers from GPN restructuring, including the kind of restructuring that is outcome of the implementation of CSR policies in GPNs. It is also important to give due attention to both horizontal and vertical relations in GPNs.

The intersection of these two dimensions shapes the terrains of workers' lives as noted by Riisgaard and Hammer (2011), "terrain for labour, is always mediated by the specific social relations of local production and labour control regimes as well as the histories and orientations of the respective actors" (p. 183). Figure 4.1 maps out both horizontal and vertical dimension of GPNs and shows how CSR is embedded in these wider networks of relations. These wider networks of relationships play an important role to determine what is produced, where, when, in which quantity and at what price in GPNs (Lund-Thomsen & Coe, 2015). The vertical dimension of GPN analysis reflects on how internationally branded firms play a role in determining the terms of GPN participation for local

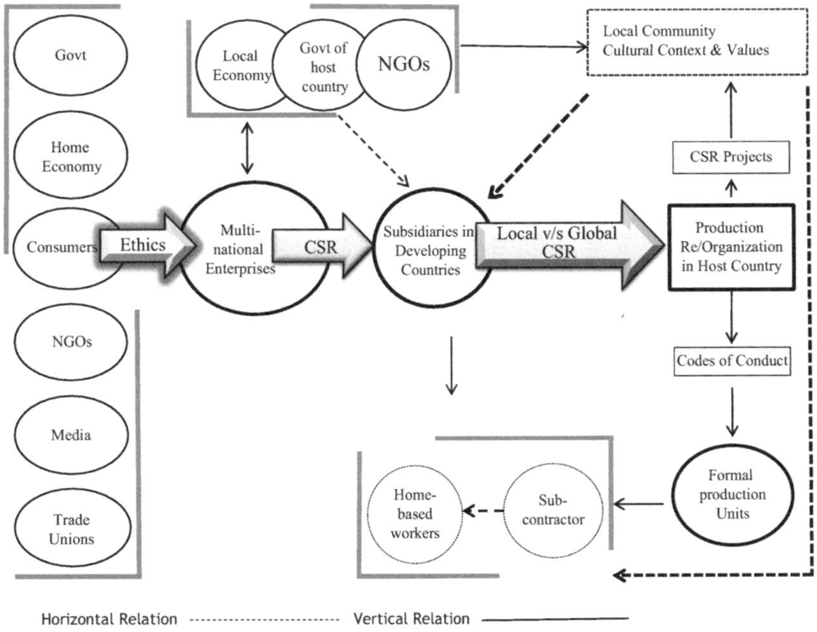

Fig. 4.1 CSR and network of actors in GPNs. (Source: Authors elaboration)

firms, contractors and workers. This relationship is largely shaped by the overall *drivenness* of the network. In buyer-driven networks, international buyers are in a position to exert greater influence on local firms, contractors and workers. This holds true for CSR policies and practices in GPNs. CSR practices are translated and interpreted into national contexts where they are embedded in social networks, business associations and political structures.

CSR Response Towards Homeworkers in Global Production Networks

Rapidly changing dynamics of global production are characterized by the increased outsourcing through complex supply chain arrangements. Production is outsourced to a large number of suppliers around the globe. There is systematic employment of vulnerable casual and contract workers in global production networks (Barrientos, 2008, 2019). Millions of people are employed in the south through subcontracting arrangements and the majority of them are women (estimated 40 million workers employed in garments and 43 million workers employed in special enterprise zones alone (Hales & Wills, 2005). The employment of workers under poor working conditions is driving down the labour standards[1] and labour conditions (Barrientos, 2008). This new production arrangement has fuelled the debate about corporate social responsibility (CSR) on a much broader scale.

According to Williams (2005), tackling the issue of homeworking through CSR suffers from some major flaws. Firstly, in most of the cases, corporate codes are not extended to the homeworkers. Secondly, in some cases, the hasty implementation of codes could also have an adverse impact on homeworkers. According to Delaney et al. (2016), there are two distinct CSR responses to homework in the global production network, rejection or tolerance. When companies *reject* homework, they simply ban it to maintain their pristine corporate image. In the case of *tolerance*, although the corporation accepts homeworkers' presence in their supply chains, it does so without making any improvements in their working conditions.

Xue and Chan (2013) raised question about the motivation of multinational corporations in creating the regulatory rules in chain governance in

[1] International labour standard are laid down through core labour conventions.

response to global campaigns against poor working conditions in global production networks. They argued that CSR initiatives often designed from the vantage point of lead firms either choose to ignore or fail to challenge the existing commercial practices or embedded relations that are fountainhead of poor labour conditions in global production systems. This claim is supported by the fact that despite the widespread implementation of CSR by international brands over the year's corporations' profits increased while there is no significant improvement in labour conditions (Xue & Chan, 2013).

The fluidity of product sourcing in global supply chains demands to reinforce the significance of the internationalist perspective. Raising labour standards for home-based workers is and will always be a challenging task, especially in the case of global supply chains, where poor working conditions are built into the product price (Williams, 2005). Market forces will undermine such efforts, if other supportive mechanisms are not intact, because extending labour standards to the informal sector will increase the cost that retailers are not able to or willing to absorb. Code implementation is expected to be cost-free by many. Only few companies have started to address the issue of homeworkers in their supply chains, and mostly their efforts are concentrated on first-tier suppliers. Not all but some of the MNCs are trying to incorporate these standards in the company codes. Some of these standards include promoting freedom of association and collective bargaining, no discrimination, no child labour and no forced labour (Barrientos, 2008; Barrientos & Smith, 2007).

It is evident from the review of existing literature that codes of conduct have some positive impact on regular workers but have failed to reach more vulnerable casual, migrant and contract workers, many of whom are women (Barrientos, 2019; Barrientos & Smith, 2007). Double bookkeeping and audit frauds hide the true conditions of workers from external auditors. There are many inherent weaknesses in private systems of labour inspection (Blowfield & Dolan, 2008). There is a great similarity in the issues faced by the homeworkers across the world. Thus, in the late 1980s, many homeworking groups and associations did realize that it made sense for local and international organizations to work collectively in order to make the changes that they desire. The workers' use of these broad networks to influence corporate behaviour is an emerging stream in literature, wherein various actors have opportunities to gain and claim legitimacy as regulators in global production networks (GPNs; Delaney et al., 2014; Delaney, Burchielli, Marshal, & Tate, 2018).

GPNs surpass the narrow focus on firms, the way firms use their political, economic and managerial resources to maximize the efficient operation of their production chains, and encompass all relevant actors and relationships. Coe et al.'s (2008) framework of a GPN consists of three mutually dependent and embedded layers. The first layer in a GPN is comprised of formal and informal institutions, such as sociocultural norms and formal institutional mechanisms of the capitalist market system. The second layer refers to power relations between different actors in the GPN, like state, firms, non-government organizations (NGOs), labour and consumers. Homeworkers are part of this second layer. The third layer reflects patterns of inequality and the uneven geographical distribution of benefits (winner and loser) within GPN entities and geographical regions (Coe et al., 2008).

Homeworkers who are commonly referred to as victims of the new production organization model can be conceptualized differently by adopting Coe et al.'s (2008) GPN heuristic framework. In this model, homeworkers can be placed as actors alongside other corporate and non-corporate actors. Placing homeworkers as actors in the power relation sector of the GPN network framework opens the theoretical space for exploring other ways in which homeworkers might contribute with some power in the production network (Coe et al., 2008; Delaney et al., 2014). Local, national and transnational nodes of production intersect in the GPN and add to the complexity of the regulatory mechanism required for this polycentric landscape. The multiplicity of actors, varieties of mechanisms, relational and the spatial location of actors within the GPN network's framework points towards the need for a more inclusive responsive mechanism. Various actors at different nodes of GPN potentially have the opportunity to claim legitimacy as regulators within this dynamic regulatory field (Delaney et al., 2014). Although neoliberal globalization has considerably reduced state protection of labour rights, various forms of other private regulations like multi-stakeholder initiatives, global framework agreements, corporate codes and industry initiatives have to some extent opened up new opportunities and degrees of accountability. Recent theoretical developments related to the concept of GPN such as networked regulation have created the theoretical space for homeworkers to establish relationships with other influential actors to demand a due share in the value they are helping to generate (Delaney et al., 2014, 2018).

In this dynamic regulatory field, various stakeholders play an essential role in regulating corporate activity. However, the effectiveness of multi-stakeholders' initiatives and other non-state forms of networked regulations are contested, but there is also evidence to support the suggestion that workers can also benefit from such private regulations. These developments suggest that regulatory mechanisms have at least some capacity to influence corporate behaviour. There are many such documented cases, where trade unions work in collaboration with NGOs to hold global companies responsible for their corporate responsibility (Barrientos, 2019).

However, there is very limited evidence that such network-regulatory approaches are able to reach homeworkers labouring under precarious and informal work arrangements. Rather there is empirical evidence that clearly suggest that hasty and insensitive implementation of CSR may generate negative externalities for homeworkers. Empirical data presented in next chapter delineate how CSR interventions driven by the exposure of child labour in Sialkot, Pakistan, resulted in the loss of income for many homeworkers due to a shift in production from homes to stitching centres. However, there are also some documented cases, where trade unions work in collaboration with NGOs to hold global companies responsible for their corporate responsibility (Barrientos, 2019). Existing theoretical development in field suggest that regulatory mechanisms have at least opened up opportunities for contestation, which can help leverage change and more gender-equitable improvements for all workers. It can be safely concluded from above discussion that for sustained improvements in conditions of work, especially for homeworkers, require proactive interventions by all actors, including workers, companies, civil society, governments and multilateral organizations.

Concluding Thoughts

Despite all the controversies and contradiction that surround the corporate behaviour there is a widely held consensus among scholars that business environment in the twenty-first century is marked by a growing concern about corporate image and responsibility. However, there is also empirical evidence which suggests that CSR response in global production networks, although good in theory, have led to little change for workers because most brand-name companies, though they earn huge profit, prefer to adopt low price sourcing policy. Existing CSR initiatives are not designed to challenge the existing commercial practices or embedded relations in GPNs. Data presented in the next chapter also support this argument that entrenched and pronounced issues of labour in developing countries are of little relevance to those located in advance countries. This holds true particularly when bringing about sustained improvements in informal workers' conditions in developing countries engaged at the invisible margin of GPNs. Thus, both formal and informal institutional processes have to be taken into account when analysing the gains or losses accruing to homeworkers from GPN restructuring, including the kind of restructuring that is outcome of the implementation of CSR policies in GPNs. It would be a gross simplification of a complex situation to consider home worker as passive recipients of their conditions of work. There are many such documented cases where trade unions work in collaboration with NGOs to hold global companies responsible for their corporate responsibility (Barrientos, 2019). Existing theoretical developments in field suggest that regulatory mechanisms have at least opened up opportunities for contestation, which can help leverage change and more gender-equitable improvements for all workers. However, as convincingly argued by Barrientos (2019), these changes would not take place automatically; rather, they will come through deliberate efforts and social contestations.

References

Amoako, G. K. (2016). CSR Practices of Multinational Companies (MNCs) and Community Needs in Africa: Evidence of Selected MNCs from Ghana. In S. Vertigans, S.O. Idowu & R. Schmidpeter (eds.), *Corporate Social Responsibility in Sub-Saharan Africa*. Cham, Switzerland: Springer International Publishing, pp. 217–240.

Aspers, P. (2011). *Markets*. Cambridge, UK: Polity Press.

Barrientos, S. (2008). Contract Labour: The 'Achilles heel' of Corporate Codes in Commercial Value Chains. *Development and Change, 39*(6), 977–990.

Barrientos, S. (2019). *Gender and Work in Global Value Chains: Capturing the Gains?* Cambridge: Cambridge University Press.

Barrientos, S., & Smith, S. (2007). Do Workers Benefit from Ethical Trade? Assessing Codes of Labour Practice in Global Production Systems. *Third World Quarterly, 28*(4), 713–729.

Beddewela, E., & Fairbrass, J. (2015). Seeking Legitimacy Through CSR: Institutional Pressures and Corporate Responses of Multinationals in Sri Lanka. *Journal of Business Ethics, 136*(3), 503–522.

Blowfield, M. (2007). Reasons to Be Cheerful? What We Know About CSR's Impact. *Third World Quarterly, 28*(4), 683–695.

Blowfield, M., & Frynas, J. G. (2005). Setting New Agendas: Critical Perspectives on Corporate Social Responsibility in the Developing World. *International Affairs, 81*(3), 499–513.

Blowfield, M. E., & Dolan, C. S. (2008). Stewards of Virtue ? The Ethical Dilemma of CSR in African Agriculture. *Development and Change, 39*(1), 1–23. https://doi.org/10.1111/j.1467-7660.2008.00465.x

Bowen, H. R. (1953). *Social Responsibilities of the Businessman*. New York: Harper & Row.

Carroll, A. B. (1979). A Three Dimensional Model of Corporate Social Responsibility. *Academy of management Review, 4*(4), 497–505.

Carroll, A. B. (2008). A History of Corporate Social Responsibility: Concepts and Practice. In A. Crane, A. McWilliams, D. Matten, J. Moon, & D. S. Siegel (Eds.), *The Oxford Handbook of Corporate Social Responsibility* (pp. 19–46). New York: Oxford University Press.

Clark, J. M. (1916). The Changing Basis of Economic Responsibility. *Journal of Political Economy, 24*(3), 209–229.

Clark, J. M. (1921). Soundings in Non-Euclidean Economics. *American Economic Review, 11*(1), 132–143.

Coe, N. M., Dicken, P., & Hess, M. (2008). Global Production Networks: Realizing the Potential. *Journal of Economic Geography, 8*(3), 271–295.

Coe, N. M., Hess, M., Yeung, H. W. C., Dicken, P., & Henderson, J. (2004). Globalizing Regional Development: A Global Production Networks Perspective. *Transactions of the Institute of British Geographers, 29*(4), 468–484.

Cumbers, A., Helms, G., & Swanson, K. (2010). Class, Agency and Resistance in the Old Industrial City. *Antipode, 42*(1), 46–73. https://doi.org/10.1111/j.1467-8330.2009.00731.x

Delaney, A., Burchielli, R., & Connor, T. (2014). Positioning Women Homeworkers in a Global Footwear Production Network: Identifying Barriers and Enablers to Claiming Rights, 1–25. https://doi.org/10.2139/ssrn.2497381

Delaney, A., Burchielli, R., Marshal, S. D., & Tate, J. (2018). *Homeworking Women: A Gender Justice Perspective*. Oxon, UK: Routledge.

Delaney, A., Burchielli, R. and Tate, J. (2016). Corporate CSR Responses to Homework and Child Labour in the Indian and Pakistan Leather Sector. In G. Kate., M, Lauren and K, Maureen. (eds.) *Can CSR Responses be Inclusive of Informal Women Worker Rights and Priorities?* Leeds: Greenleaf.

Dubbink, W., & Liedekerke, L. V. (2014). Grounding Positive Duties in Commercial Life. *Journal of Business Ethics, 120*, 527–539. https://doi.org/10.1007/s10551-013-2003-9

Durkheim, K. (1984). *The division of Labour in Society*. London: Macmillan.

Edwards, P. K. (2010). Developing Labour Process Analysis: Themes from Industrial Sociology and Future Directions. In P. Thompson & C. Smith

(Eds.), *Working Life: Renewing Labour Process Analysis* (pp. 29–46). Basingstoke: Palgrave Macmillan.

Fayyaz, A., Lund-Thomsen, P., & Lindgreen, A. J. (2015). Industrial Clusters and CSR in Developing Countries: The Role of International Donor Funding. *Journal of Business Ethics, 146*, 619–637.

Frederiksen, C. S., & Nielsen, M. E. J. (2013). The Ethical Foundations for CSR. In J. O. Okpara & S. Idowu (Eds.), *Corporate Social Responsibility: Challenges, Opportunities and Strategies for 21st Century Leaders* (pp. 17–33). Berlin: Springer Publishing Company.

Freeman, R. E., Harrison, J. S., Wicks, A. C., Parmar, B. L., & Colle, S. D. (2011). *Stakeholder Theory: The State of the Art.* Cambridge: Cambridge University Press.

Friedman, M. (1970). The Social Responsibility of Business Is to Increase Its Profits. *New York Times Magazine*, pp. 122–126.

Gereffi, G. (2005). The Global Economy: Organization, Governance, and Development. In N. J. Smelser & R. Swedberg (Eds.), *The Handbook of Economic Sociology* (2nd ed., pp. 160–182). Princeton, NJ: Princeton University Press.

Gereffi, G., Korzeniewicz, M., & Korzeniewicz, R. P. (1994). Introduction: Global Commodity Chains. In G. Gereffi & M. Korzeniewicz (Eds.), *Commodity Chains and Global Capitalism* (pp. 1–14). Westport, CT: Praeger Publishers.

Gibbon, P., Bair, J., & Ponte, S. (2008). Governing Global Value Chains: An Introduction. *Economy and Society, 37*(3), 315–338.

Habermas, J. (1981/1987). *The Theory of Communicative Action Life World and System.* Cambridge: Polity Press.

Hales, A., & Wills, J. (Eds.). (2005). *Threads of Labour: Garment Industry Supply Chains from the Worker's Perspective.* Oxford: Blackwell Publishers.

Henderson, J., Dicken, P., Hess, M., Coe, N., & Yeung, H. W. (2002). Global Production Networks and the Analysis of Economic Development. *Review of International Political Economy, 9*(3), 436–464.

Hsieh, N. (2013). Multinational Enterprises and Incomplete Institutions: The Demandingness of Minimum Moral Standards. In M. Boylan (Ed.), *Business Ethics* (2nd ed., pp. 409–422). Hoboken, NJ: John Wiley and Sons.

Hurley, J., & Miller, D. (2005). The Changing Face of the Global Garment Industry. In A. Hales & J. Wills (Eds.), *Threads of Labour: Garment Industry Supply Chains from the Worker's Perspective* (pp. 16–39). Oxford, UK: Blackwell Publishers.

Jamali, D. (2010). The CSR of MNC Subsidiaries in Developing Countries: Global, Local, Substantive Or Diluted? *Journal of Business Ethics, 93*(2), 181–200.

Jamali, D., & Mirshak, R. (2007). Corporate Social Responsibility (CSR): Theory and Practice in a Developing Country Context. *Journal of Business Ethics, 72*(3), 243–262.

Jenkins, R. (2005). Globalization, Corporate Social Responsibility and Poverty. *International Affairs, 81*(3), 525–540.

Khan, F. R., & Lund-Thomsen, P. (2011). CSR as Imperialism: Towards a Phenomenological Approach to CSR in the Developing World. *Journal of Change Management, 11*(1), 73–90.

Khan, F. R., Westwood, R., & Boje, D. M. (2010). I Feel Like a Foreign Agent: NGOs and Corporate Social Responsibility Interventions into Third World Child Labor. *Human Relations, 63*(9), 1417–1438.

Kurian, R. (2006). The Globalization of Domestic Care Services. In T. Truong, S. Wieringa, & A. Chhachhi (Eds.), *Engendering Human Security: Feminist Perspectives* (pp. 147–167). New Delhi/London: Women Unlimited/Kali for Women/Zed Press.

Lund-Thomsen, P., & Coe, N. M. (2015). Corporate Social Responsibility and Labour Agency: The Case of Nike in Pakistan. *Journal of Economic Geography, 15*(16), 1–22.

Lund-Thomsen, P., Lindgreen, A., & Vanhamme, J. (2016). Industrial Clusters and Corporate Social Responsibility in Developing Countries: What We Know, What We Do Not Know, and What We Need to Know. *Journal of Business Ethics, 133*(1), 9–24.

Lund-Thomsen, P., & Nadvi, K. (2010). Clusters, Chains and Compliance: Corporate Social Responsibility and Governance in Football Manufacturing in South Asia. *Journal of Business Ethics, 93*(2), 201–222.

Newsome, K., Taylor, P., Bair, J., & Rainnie, A. (2015). *Putting Labour in Its Place: Labour Process Analysis and Global Value Chains.* London: Palgrave.

Rainnie, A., Herod, A., & McGrath-Champ, S. (2011). Review and Positions: Global Production Networks and Labour. *Competition and Change, 15*(2), 155–169.

Riisgaard, L., & Hammer, N. (2011). Prospects for Labour in Global Value Chains: Labour Standards in the Cut Flower and Banana Industries. *British Journal of Industrial Relations, 49*, 168–190.

Robinson, P. K., & Rainbird, H. (2013). International Supply Chains and the Labour Process. *Competition and Change, 17*(1), 91–107.

Scherer, A. G., & Palazzo, G. (2007). Toward a Political Conception of Corporate Responsibility: Business and Society Seen from a Habermasian Perspective. *Academy of Management Review, 32*(4), 1096–1120.

Scherer, A. G., & Palazzo, G. (2011). The New Political Role of Business in a Globalized World: A Review of a New Perspective on CSR and Its Implications for the Firm, Governance, and Democracy. *Journal of Management Studies, 48*(4), 899–931.

Shadnam, M. (2015). Theorizing Morality in a Context. *International Review of Sociology –Revue Internationale de Sociologie, 25*(3), 456–480.

Shepard, J. M., Shepard, J., James, C. W., & Carroll, U. S. (1995). The Place of Ethics in Business: Shifting Paradigms? *Business Ethics Quarterly, 5*(3), 577–601.

Soundararajan, V., & Brown, J. (2016). Voluntary Governance Mechanisms in Global Supply Chains: Beyond CSR to a Stakeholder Utility Perspective. *Journal of Business Ethics, 134*(1), 83–102.

Stehr, N., Henning, C., & Weiler, B. (2006). Introduction. In N. Stehr, C. Henning, & B. Weiler (Eds.), *Moralization of the Markets* (pp. 1–28). New Brunswick, NJ: Transaction Publishers.

Tapia, M., Ibsen, C. I., & Kochan, T. A. (2015). Mapping the Frontier of Theory in Industrial Relations: The Contested Role of Worker Representation. *Socio-Economic Review, 13*(1), 157–184.

Thompson, P., & Newsome, K. (2004). Labor Process Theory, Work, and the Employment Relation. In B. E. Kaufman (Ed.), *Theoretical Perspectives on Work and the Employment Relationship* (pp. 133–162). Champaign, IL: Industrial Relations Research Association.

Thompson, P., & Smith, C. (2009). Labour Power and Labour Process: Contesting the Marginality of the Sociology of Work. *Sociology, 43*(5), 913–930.

Thompson, P., & Smith, C. (2010). Debating Labour Process Theory and the Sociology of Work. In P. Thompson & C. Smith (Eds.), *Working Life: Renewing Labour Process Analysis* (pp. 11–28). Basingstoke: Palgrave Macmillan.

Waddock, S. (2004). Parallel Universes: Companies, Academics, and the Progress of Corporate Citizenship. *Business & Society Review, 109*(1), 5–42.

Wettstein, F. (2012). Corporate Responsibility in the Collective Age: Toward a Conception of Collaborative Responsibility. *Business and Society Review, 117*(2), 155–184.

Williams, P. (2005). Leveraging Change in the Working Conditions of UK Homeworkers. *Development in Practice, 15*(3–4), 546–558.

Xue, H., & Chan, A. (2013). The Global Value Chain: Value for Whom? The Soccer Ball Industry in China and Pakistan. *Critical Asian Studies, 45*(1), 55–77.

Young, I. M. (2010). *Responsibility for Justice*. Oxford: Oxford University Press.

CHAPTER 5

Dilemmas of Corporate Responsibility in a Globalized World: Empirical Evidences from Global Football Industry

Introduction

During the last few decades, corporate social responsibility (CSR) initiatives have widely proliferated in response to global campaigns against poor working conditions in global production networks. Due to immense pressure from consumers, human rights pressure groups and the presence of fierce competition across the globe, it has become essential for successful and profitable multinational corporations (MNCs) to build a positive corporate image, a corporate image that must be free from any negative connotations. Maintaining this pristine corporate image is especially hard for MNCs operating in the global south, where either the state or local governments are, by and large, lax in implementing existing laws, or existing laws are deficient in meeting international labour standards set by the International Labour Organization (ILO). Consequently, in order to maintain their corporate image and avoid negative publicity, private governance has arisen as a response by global buyers. Plethora of codes of labour standard are introduced by retailers and brand-name firms, which have led to the associated growth of a multibillion social compliance industry involving social auditing and workplace monitoring (Xue & Chan, 2013). In this chapter, we put forward a case of exemplary collaborative venture that was launched in Sialkot, Pakistan, to rid the football industry of child labour, as an illustration of the contestation between the global CSR approaches and local responses. Based on empirical data gathered from football industry of Sialkot, Pakistan, in this chapter we tried to

F. Naz, D. Bögenhold, *Unheard Voices*,
https://doi.org/10.1007/978-3-030-54363-1_5

highlight the limits of gender-blind top-down CSR approaches as a means of improving working conditions at the lowest end of global supply chains. We argue here that effective CSR response requires bottom-up approaches and deeper investigation of broader institutional context that frames the governance of global sourcing from developing countries. Based on analysis of qualitative data, we conclude that currently top-down CSR responses and monitoring mechanisms are facade to avert criticism. We emphasize that in order to make CSR intervention effective and avoid unintended harmful consequences, unheard voices of weaker stakeholders, particularly informal homeworkers in developing countries, should be incorporated in existing frameworks. Admittedly, this is an uphill task in highly dynamic, neoliberal, capitalist global economy, which is marked with unequal power relations between capital and labour. Drawing on literature[1] from global production networks (GPNs) analysis and combining it with insight from feminist political economy, we tried to examine the potential impact of gender-blind CSR strategies on working conditions for homeworkers. This case demonstrates the current failure of instrumental CSR approaches to address labour issues beyond the confines of workplace. However, optimism still prevails that institutional and collective power of wider public, civil society actors and workers may influence companies to design strategies to enhance the scope and effectiveness of CSR policies.

The research, which underpins this chapter, was conducted in Sialkot, Pakistan, between 2013 and 2016. This research led to some other publications as well, which are cited and referenced in various chapters of this book. In this qualitative case study, a triangulation of methods was employed: qualitative interviews and focus group discussions (FGDs) substantiated by secondary sources were used to develop theoretical insight into CSR practices on the margins of GPNs. For the purposes of data triangulation, the interviews were not limited to any one group of informal workers; data were also collected from different groups of football stitchers at various levels in the football supply chain.

An effort was made to include workers from each level of the production organization. One of the authors undertook approximately 40 interviews with factory, centre and home-based workers, investigating the kind of work they preferred. The data used in this chapter were obtained in ten in-depth interviews and four focus group discussions conducted in six different villages in Sialkot, Pakistan. The data collection was not limited

[1] Theoretical background is outlined in previous chapter in detail.

to formal in-depth interviews with football stitchers; many informal and semi-structured qualitative interviews with key informants and other persons living in vicinity were also conducted to supplement the data and map the local football supply chain in Pakistan. The respondents were selected through the snowball sampling technique. Direct participant observations and conversations with local people in selected areas were also used. The formal in-depth interviews were conducted with home-based workers selected by age, gender, marital status and their level of involvement and relevance to the research context. The criterion was set to observe variation in patterns along these dividing lines and to include the perspectives of a broad range of actors. In both stages, the interviews were conducted at the respondents' homes to facilitate the development of rapport and trust between the interviewer and the respondents. Although the qualitative data gathered for this research may not constitute a statistically representative sample of all of the workers in the supply chain, it is illustrative of the types of labour processes and working conditions at the lower end. The interview questions were not fixed and were often revised, based on the spontaneous outcomes, which emerged during the interview; however, a basic skeleton was maintained throughout. The findings that were derived from an analysis of the qualitative data are discussed below.

Contours of the Global Football Industry

Football is regarded as an extremely popular sport, and it is the basis for a major industry across the world that is linked to football (Mahony & Howard, 2001; Manoli, 2018). In terms of its popularity, football has gained a status that is unmatched by any other sport (Pellegrini, Rialti, Marzi, & Caputo, 2020). Football tournaments like the World Championship, the European Championships, and the Union of European Football Associations (UEFA) Champions League are watched across the world. Due to the advent of digital media, viewership has multiplied and has become a truly global sport (Ha, Kang, & Kim, 2017). Its growing viewership and a very large fan base across the globe have not only increased the sales from match and event attendance, but also from associated merchandise and products (Ratten & Jones, 2020). In today's economic climate, the football industry is among the fastest-growing sports industries of the world (Desbordes & Richelieu, 2012). Realizing the potential of this industry, many countries are trying to tap into this emerging market. Global exports of inflatable balls increased from

US$338 million in 2001 to US$817 million in 2005, peaking at US$1.26 billion in 2010 (UN Comtrade, 2011).

The global football industry has some unique features. First, it is dominated by a few brand names like Adidas, Asics, Mitre, Mizuno, Nike and Puma, who organize the global football manufacturing between them. Out of these, Nike and Adidas are the major players of the market and the biggest buyers of footballs. Adidas has a 34 percent market share and achieves sales of $1.57 billion from football-related products, while Nike has $1.7 billion sales in international markets (Nadvi, 2011). The takeover of Reebok by Adidas in 2005 and of Umbro by Nike in 2007 has further concentrated this industry in the hands of just a few international players, thus increasing their profit margins. The second important feature of the football industry is that none of the international brands are producers of footballs, but rather these footballs are sourced from independent suppliers located in distinct production locations and production is concentrated in a particular geographical area, namely South and East Asia. The primary centres for football production are China, Pakistan and Thailand. Together these three countries were responsible for 70.3 percent of total global exports of inflatable balls in 2009 (UN Comtrade, 2011). China has emerged as a leading exporter of footballs in recent years; however, its dominance is limited to machine-stitched and low-end promotional and toy balls. In the area of high-quality hand-stitched balls, Pakistan is the favourite sourcing destination of many leading brands. Traditionally, at the top end, hand-stitched balls are considered to be more reliable and more aerodynamic than machine-stitched balls. Machine-stitched balls do not have the same qualities as premium hand-stitched footballs, but that appears to be changing with improvement in machine stitching technologies. Recent technological advancements and the introduction of the thermo-moulded ball have increased new competitive pressure on Pakistan in the premium quality market as well (Lund-Thomsen & Nadvi, 2010). The emergence of thermo-moulded balls in recent years has shown that high-quality machine-made footballs can compete in quality and performance with the premium hand-stitched balls. China has gradually encroached into Pakistan's niche in the high-end professional match ball market.

On the end market side, the United States and European Union (EU) are major markets for football. As in many other labour-intensive manufacturing sectors, the leading brands coordinate a large and widely dispersed group of global football suppliers who act as original equipment manufacturers (OEM). Global football trade is taking place both through structured and hierarchical global value chains and through dispersed market transactions.

The trend of outsourcing, on the one hand, has created millions of jobs in developing countries and provides livelihood opportunities to workers in these countries and has substantially raised the incomes of many impoverished workers and their families. On the other hand, due to absence or weak enforcement of labour and environment laws in developing countries, there is a widely shared concern that an international social and environmental race-to-the-bottom might be occurring (Lund-Thomsen & Coe, 2015).

The situation has become further exacerbated, because the globalization of the production process has provided flexibility to global firms, allowing them to switch their production process from one country/region/locality to another, to lower their production cost and maximize their profit margins (Gereffi, Korzeniewicz, & Korzeniewicz, 1994). This increased flexibility of global capital along with lean retailing systems has created intense competition among suppliers from low-cost regions in developing countries. Consequently, local producers in developing countries face a challenge in terms of a choice between engaging in the so-called "high road" or "low road" to competitiveness (Lund-Thomsen, Nadvi, Chan, Khara, & Xue, 2012). The high road involves more upgrading strategies through efficiency and moving into higher value added activities. However, the low road to competitiveness is based upon a downgrading strategy that puts additional pressure on local factories in many developing countries to lower their wage costs (Xue & Chan, 2013).

In order to remain competitive in the global arena where price and flexibility have become the most important attributes, suppliers have also designed their own strategies. Many suppliers in developing countries find a solution by subcontracting their labour-intensive activities to smaller units while retaining control of the higher-value activities and the final delivery to the retailer. Work is subcontracted by these small units to producers in the informal sector and further down the chain to home-based workers.

These complex layers of subcontracting in global supply chains have enabled manufacturers to lower their cost of production by reducing their permanent labour force and saving some other overhead costs of production by passing these costs further down the supply chain. Such flexible employment practices hold serious implications for the labour force, with many workers working as home-based workers under precarious conditions at the lowest ends of the supply chains (Mehrotra & Biggeri, 2007). In this process of decentralization, home-based work has become the endpoint of many global and local supply chains. One of the most vulnerable and least visible groups in the global supply chains is that of female industrial homeworkers in developing countries, as they are dealing with intermediary subcontractors rather than their "real" employers at the top of the global manufacturing chain (Lund-Thomsen et al., 2012).

Home-Based Work and Challenges of Social Compliance in Football Industry

Although women's informal paid work is not accounted for in official statistics, even the scarce data that does exist confirms that homework has become an important source of employment for women in many developing countries. Locating and monitoring these homeworkers in supply chains has become a serious challenge for the brand-sensitive consumer goods industries, where compliance with the international standards is a prerequisite for entry into global production networks due to immense pressure from various consumer and activist groups. This has also posed a serious challenge for many suppliers from developing countries to meet the product and process standards to retain their position in global production networks (GPNs), because non-compliance can result in exclusion. The international football industry is a particular case in point, which is facing compliance challenges in its extended global production networks (Nadvi, Lund-Thomsen, Xue, & Khara, 2011). Compliance with international standards and codes of conduct has become a critical challenge faced by football suppliers in developing countries to engage in GPNs. Brand-name companies are increasingly concerned with negative media reports about unethical behaviour in their supply chains that may dent their brand image. Furthermore, suppliers in developing countries are fretting about the increased social and environmental compliance cost.

Recent literature (Lund-Thomsen & Nadvi, 2010) highlights tensions that exist between sourcing policies of brands and their corporate social responsibility (CSR) compliance requirements. On the one hand, due to increased international and local competition, local suppliers are facing intense pressure to reduce lead times and increase their flexibility in production, leading them to assume greater risks and costs. On the other hand, costs that are associated with CSR compliance are rarely, if ever, shared by the brands (Barrientos & Smith, 2007). Due to challenges associated with price and flexibility, home-based production is the best way for suppliers to increase their competitiveness by reducing costs, which could be made possible by counting on the female stitching labour force. Home-based enterprises are cheaper for suppliers to manage. However, fear of being exposed to negative media attention due to the risk of being associated with unethical practices in their supply chains, international brands brush aside opinions and interests of local stakeholders and demand for strict compliance of their codes of conduct (Khan & Lund-Thomsen, 2011).

Often, claims are made about the benefits that codes of conduct supposedly bring to workers and the environment in the developing world. However, evidence of the benefit of these codes for workers in the context of developing countries remains limited and patchy. According to Lund-Thomsen (2008), most of the academic and policy-oriented rhetoric about code of conduct is largely divorced from existing realities of many developing country suppliers, workers and communities. More fruitful engagement with CSR requires bringing in the perspective of those who are often excluded from the debates, namely the intended beneficiaries of these CSR programmes and policies. It is important to distinguish between the compliance with the codes and its ultimate outcome for workers in the developing countries. Divorcing debates about the codes from the existing realities of suppliers, workers and communities may do more harm than good. CSR debates tend to be dominated by the voices of the corporate world, non-governmental organizations (NGOs), trade unions, business school representatives and other delegates and concerns of other groups often fail to find a space. Little or no regard is paid to articulate the world view of workers and their local experiences (Khan, 2007).

Drawing on field data from the football industry of Sialkot, Pakistan, this chapter seeks to contribute to these discussions by looking deeper into the living realities of female home-based workers at the lowest end of football supply chains. Though an emerging stream of literature (Beddewela & Fairbrass, 2015; Jamali, 2010; Jamali & Mirshak, 2007; Khan, Westwood, & Boje, 2010; Kolk & Lenfant, 2010; Lund-Thomsen, 2008; Lund-Thomsen & Coe, 2015) has started to explore CSR dynamics in developing countries, none has explicitly analysed the perceptions of home-based workers located at the lowest nodes of global production networks.

By highlighting the case of football industry in Sialkot, Pakistan, which was brought to the limelight after allegations of child labour in football supply chains by international media and human right groups, we tried to shed light on the challenges associated with transporting Western-based CSR intervention to developing countries. CSR response from the industry, which is to prioritize child labour while ignoring the plight of the local stitchers especially female homeworkers, is detailed in next section to make this point.

Child Labour Controversy and Response from Football Industry

In the sphere of football production, Sialkot, Pakistan, is a famous city in which footballs are produced for major brands like Adidas, Nike, Puma, Select, Litto, Umbro, Mitre, Micassa, Diadora and Decathion. Sialkot caters to 85 percent of the total world demand for hand-stitched inflatable balls, which means 60 million balls annually. However, the reputation of Sialkot was tarnished by the allegations of practices of child labour in the football industry that became a global issue following the broadcast, on 6 April 1995, of a CBS news documentary on the football industry in Sialkot (Khan, Munir, & Willmott, 2007). This news was quickly picked up by media worldwide and intense consumer pressure mounted for remedial action. This story brought many brand-name multinational sports companies including Nike, Reebok and Adidas into the international spotlight. They were accused of hypocrisy and human rights violations in their supply chains. As these brand-name companies depend heavily on their image and brand association, the response was harsh; and to avoid these accusations, some of them immediately terminated their operations in Sialkot (Khan, 2010).

Given this international pressure, the response from global football industry was also very swift and announced the launch of a project in February 1997 to eliminate child labour from football manufacturing. The threat to business also led the Sialkot industrialists to sign the *Atlanta Agreement* in 1997, facilitated by the other three signatories—the ILO, UNICEF and the state body. Consequently, an exemplary collaborative venture was launched in Sialkot to rid the industry of child labour. In order to remove the scandalous taint of child labour from the football industry in Sialkot, a new production regime was introduced, where production was moved from homes to factories and stitching centres. To ensure the elimination of child labour and the monitoring of labour practices in the production facilities, home-based production was banned in the football industry.

However, the exclusive focus on the issue of child labour and the way it was framed in a seemingly benign manner created a *velvet curtain* (Khan et al., 2007: 1056) that obscured other crucial conditions and consequences, especially for stitchers in the industry, who are important but weak stakeholders in the hierarchy of power relations in the production organization of the football industry. The impact of the ban on child labour and associated changes in the production organization gradually unfolded over the years. The exclusion of the voices of the stitching community from debates about child labour in the football industry and production reorganization has social and moral implications. The case of the football industry of Pakistan raises serious questions concerning who has the right to define the illegitimacy of a certain business practice. This chapter argues that divorcing CSR practices from the social and cultural context produces outcomes that might not mirror the interests of intended beneficiaries. What follows is an attempt to explore some unintended consequences of the ethical and seemingly very smooth process of eradication of child labour from the football industry.[2]

Framing the Issue and Solution of Child Labour in Global Football Supply Chain: An Easy Fix for a Complex Problem

In 1995, when international brands and local manufacturers were confronted with the allegations of child labour in the football industry of Pakistan, the issue roused the entire Western media, human rights organizations and the US legislators. Sialkot moved into the focus of heightened global and national concern about child labour and became the site of the investigation against violations of child labour laws by global stakeholders (Khan et al., 2010; Khan & Lund-Thomsen, 2011). The campaign led to

[2] Reasoning on unintended consequences goes back to Adam Smith, whose metaphor of the invisible hand is linked to working principles of unintended consequences. Later, Karl Marx and Max Weber also referred to those ideas but Robert Merton (1936) was an author who explicitly addressed the "unanticipated consequences of purposive social action" (Merton, 1936) by introducing a systematic discussion.

the signing of the Atlanta Agreement by the Sialkot Chamber of Commerce and Industry, the ILO, UNICEF and Save the Children Fund UK in February 1997. Consequently, football stitching was shifted from home-based enterprises to stitching centres[3] to put in place monitoring of child labour in these production facilities.

Prior to the Atlanta Agreement, football stitching was carried out in small home-based enterprises by men, women and children in the villages surrounding Sialkot. Phasing out child labour required the voluntary participation of local manufacturers, who transferred their work from houses to a designated place, which could be monitored by the ILO International Programme on the Elimination of Child Labour (IPEC). The basic criterion for establishing a stitching centre is that there should be at least five stitchers (male, female or both). They should sit together at a designated place and the respective manufacturer must attach a small signboard outside in a specified place, and that should be treated as a stitching centre. In the case of female stitching centres, this limit was reduced to three women. These stitching centres were informal but monitorable work places.

In 2002, the monitoring of these informal work places (stitching centres) was handed over to the Independent Monitoring Association for Child Labor (IMAC).[4] At that time the only issue of monitoring was child labour, though later, in 2003, the monitoring of basic infrastructure like adequate space, sitting arrangement, lighting, ventilation, hygiene, safe drinking water and toilet facilities was also added. However, this condition is waived for the three women's centres. The monitoring process in the football supply chains thus excluded all other core labour rights other than child labour. This exclusion was woven into the monitoring design by choice and not by default. Apparently, this shift means a simple switch from their own homes to other similar places in the same village or some

[3] The "Monitorable Stitching Centres"—declared as such by the ILO-IPEC and later by IMAC—are thus mostly modest abodes of the villagers, dingy shops or private sheds located in rural areas. Outside the shops or sheds, one can see a small sign indicating simply: Stitching Centre. Common village houses turned into centres generally do not have a signboard. Inside these "centres", the IMAC certificate in English and the manufacturer notices in Urdu are found glued to the walls.

[4] In 2007, the IMAC 12-member field team was monitoring more than 2500 football stitching centres for 87 manufacturers. The ILO-IPEC monitoring entailed random physical visits of the centre to ascertain child labour, if any, and filling out a form with basic facts about the centre (i.e. number of workers, amount of work done, wages paid) (PILER, 2009: 23).

other nearby villages. However existing literature (Beddewela & Fairbrass, 2015; Jamali & Mirshak, 2007; Khan et al., 2010) provides ample empirical evidence to support that understanding national, local context and institutional framework, where CSR is implemented, is important to better inform practice. The rest of the chapter echoes the unheard voices of most vulnerable group of workers in football supply chains. It deals with the question how homeworkers perceive the impact of these seemingly non-threatening changes on their lives and livelihood.

Counter-framing the Issue: The Homeworkers Perspective

Economic globalization along with the opening of space also has a space-fixing dimensions. Capital globalization means a new freedom and mobility, whereas labour globalization means localization, a new means of control and uninvited fate. Problem of localized labour in global world is compounded by the fact that localities are losing their meaning-generating and meaning-negotiating capacities because progressive spatial segregation has also caused a breakdown of communication between global and extraterritorial elites, centre of meaning and value production, and the localized rest. Bauman (1998) argued that such demotion of local public space has resulted in ethical dilemmas as there is no room left for local negotiation of meaning. Consequently, extraterritorial messages that are divorced from local experiences rebound more suffering despite all good intentions. The activities of powerful institutional actors to rid the football industry of child labour in order to gain or maintain social legitimacy have produced outcomes for homeworkers' households that failed to surface on the moral radar screens of the international players. In the given socio-economic context of Pakistan, the perceived benefits for children were not beyond the shadow of reasonable doubt (Khan, 2010). One of the outcomes of this shift in production organization was the loss of family income in stitchers household, as many female home-based stitchers had to drop out of the workforce, tumbling their families into deeper poverty (Dubbink & Liedekerke, 2014; PILER, 2009). These darker and harmful unintended consequences (see Fig. 5.1) are also acknowledged in other studies (Khan et al., 2007; Lund-Thomsen & Coe, 2015).

It was evident from the discussions that, in order to remove the stigma of child labour from the football industry, measures that had been

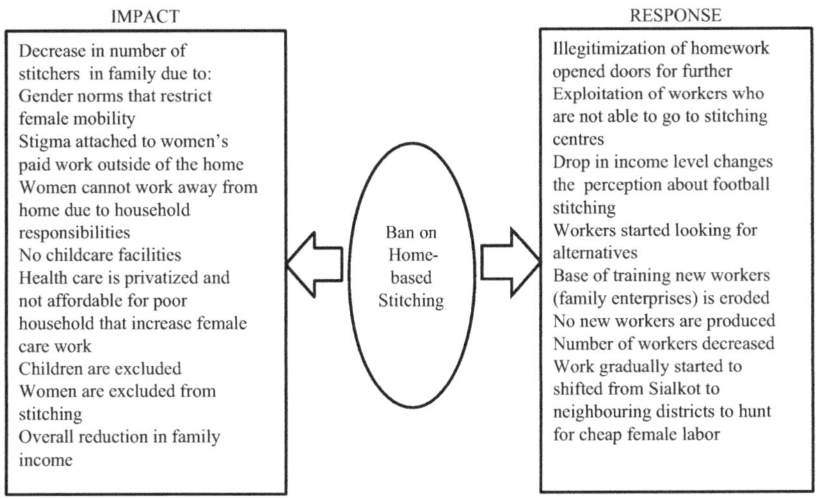

Fig. 5.1 Impact of and responses to ban on home-based stitching in Sialkot, Pakistan. (Source: Authors elaboration)

introduced two decades earlier had gradually unfolded in the form of the stigmatization of football stitching itself. The status of football stitching, which was considered a valuable productive activity and a skill, has declined over the years. A survey commissioned by Punjab Skill Development Fund in 2016 also reports:

> The implementation of Child Labour elimination program during 2007 to 2010 took away a whole slice of potential skilled generation and now the industry is facing acute shortage of new intake and has to rely on older skilled workers. The problem would become worst when the existing older workers will be retired and they would not be replaced by their sons. (p. 26)

Male stitchers who learned this skill as part of their family tradition feel themselves trapped in the profession. It was reported by many respondents that although football stitching is a skill that requires training, nevertheless the income gained from this skilled work is even lower than the wages of unskilled daily wage work in the area.[5] Due to low wages in football stitching, stitchers prefer to opt football stitching as a part time or ad-hoc work, mostly done by women, farmers and general people during their spare time.

The finding that the number of football stitchers has decreased and no new workers are being trained is worth further exploration. It is a red flag for the industry. During a focus group discussion held at a male stitching centre, it was reported that once the village had more than 100 football stitchers; however, just 10 workers were left at the time of the fieldwork. Similar findings also come out of a focus group discussion conducted with the workers of a female stitching centre, where the number of workers has dropped from 36 to 5. Subcontractors reported facing difficulties in finding workers for their stitching centres. The shift from homes to stitching centres not only involves travel time, but also makes it difficult to combine football stitching with household activities. Workers find it hard to remain

[5] A hand-stitcher generally sews three to four footballs a day and earns Rs 80–120 per football, that is, Rs 300–450 per day. The income of a worker who manages to work the entire month can be in the range of just Rs 8000 to 13,000 per month. On the contrary, a construction worker can earn Rs 14,000–15,000 and a mason Rs. 25,000–30,000 per month. Football hand-stitchers are among the country's lowest-paid workers. In 2009, Sialkot's full-time home stitchers were paid by piece rate at around PKR20–30 per ball. They work on average (when orders are sufficient) six to eight hours a day and only make about PKR100–125 (< US$1.50).

attached to football stitching at existing wages and conditions of work. The shift to stitching centres has not been translated into better wages or working conditions for the stitching labour force. These findings are reported in other studies too; for instance, Xue and Chan (2013) argue:

> the most effective solution to the scandal in the mid 1990s, when child labor was discovered in brand-name soccer-ball production, and for which the Atlanta Agreement was signed in 1997, was for the brand-name corporations to raise the piece rate of adult home stitchers. This could be done by giving the subcontractors a higher price and establishing a monitoring system to ensure decent piece rates were being paid. (p. 69)

Data, even from a small sample of stitching centres, show that there are no baseline standards of work or wages in stitching centres. Stitchers in centres have no job contract or other social security benefits. They do not hold the status of employees. Companies hire them through subcontractors, and they do not have any direct contact with the companies for whom they produce their work. Though at one male centre visited during fieldwork, workers were found to have ID cards that entitled them to child education benefit and medical facilities, this is not a standard practice. However, it was an interesting observation that the overall number of stitchers at this centre was lower than at a centre that offered no such benefit, but paid comparatively high wages. This controversial finding was explicitly investigated in two focus group discussions, to gain some insight and assess the stance of the stitchers regarding the contradictory nature of this phenomenon.

According to stitchers working at a stitching centre in Sialkot, an ID card is issued only to those workers who work for the company without a break for one year. In the case of a break from work, the ID card is cancelled. Workers holding cards are bound to work for a company as employees, but without having the status of a regular employee or any other benefit associated with the employment status. The workers' presence is ensured through private monitoring mechanisms and a system of attendance, which ensures their presence at the centre. Workers are not allowed to take work to their homes. They also get a lower piece rate compared to the piece rate provided by other companies. Consequently, it is hard for centre-based stitchers to combine their work with other agricultural activities. According to a subcontractor, it is true that the export companies gives some benefits to workers, but it is hard to work with them, as their terms and conditions are stricter than local firms. They do not allow the establishment of family centres, and work is provided only at main centres. Workers have to complete their work at the centre and are not allowed to take balls to their homes for stitching. However, there are many subcontractors who provide balls to homeworkers, but do so secretly due to imposition of ban on home-based work.

As subcontractors are facing difficulties to hire workers for their stitching centres due to low piece rates, they work with many companies simultaneously, including some companies producing for local markets. This helps them to diversify their source of work and income. Makers get a commission per ball; therefore, it is in their best interest to outsource more balls per day. They also distribute their work to homeworkers to increase their productivity. They prefer to work with companies who have relaxed policies about home-based production.

Female Homeworkers at Crossroads of Production and Social Reproduction

As discussed earlier in Chap. 2, global production system generate paid work for hundreds of millions of workers in emerging and low-income countries, providing income-earning opportunities to significant proportion of women with limited previous labour market access (Kabeer, 2000). Jobs for women are mostly created in exporting industries, for instance sports, textiles, electronics, pharmaceutical and computer components, where many women are integrated as informal home-based workers at the lowest ends of global supply chains through extended subcontracting arrangements (Barrientos, 2019; Xue & Chan, 2013). Increased female labour force participation, particularly within the private sphere of the household, has redefined the boundaries of work and traditional employment. Gender boundaries between paid work and unpaid household work, required for social reproduction, have become blurred in case of homework. The outcome of these labour processes varies across various geographical locations, due to cultural differences in gender norms that shape the division of labour and women's participation in productive and reproductive activities (Barrientos, 2019). Feminist political economy[6] provides important insight on the relationship between production for market and social reproduction in context of global production system. Mainstream

[6] For detailed discussion, see Chap. 3.

economic theory recognizes productive labour for market as a legitimate form of work. However, social reproduction, which involves unpaid labour of women within households and which sustain and reproduce workers (Bhattacharya, 2017), failed to gain due recognition in conventional economic discourse. Social reproduction theory is critical of this universal worker model. Women involvement in paid work using their traditionally acquired skills within the private sphere of household has far-reaching implications for them.

However, despite the strenuous efforts by feminist scholars to highlight systematic gender discriminations in existing economic model, raising labour standards for home-based workers has been a challenging task, especially in the case of global supply chains, where poor working conditions are built into the product price (Williams, 2005). Against the backdrop of the child labour controversy, most of the buyers[7] in football supply chains responded to the issue of child labour in the industry but ignored the plight of homeworkers, located at the crossroads of commercial production and social reproduction.

Female stitchers face a double disadvantage due to their gender role obligations and the existing normative structure of society. The situation is especially hard if there are just one or two female stitchers in a family. Subcontractors confirmed that establishing a female centre is comparatively more difficult. Normally, there are just a few workers in any one village who are willing to work in a centre, and establishing a centre for a very small number is practically not feasible for the makers. A second option for female stitchers is to work in family centres. To establish a family stitching centre also means to provide a workplace in one's own home for the family centre. There is also a condition about the minimum number required to establish a family centre (minimum of four stitchers), which is also hard to meet for many female stitchers. Most of the homeworkers belong to low-social-income strata and their houses are small, even for the needs of their own families. Consequently, a large proportion of the female stitching labour force is effectively deprived of

[7] Nike, a leading brand in football production, cancelled its order of hand-stitched balls to its contracting manufacturer, Saga Sports Private Limited, on the grounds that it violated labour standards and employed child labour. This alone resulted in loss of jobs and income for 7637 people employed by Saga, including 5257 piece rate workers, residing in more than 400 rural settlements in surrounding areas of Sialkot (PILER, 2009).

work and provides room for their own exploitation by subcontractors, as is evident from following extract from a focus group discussion at a family centre:

> The vast majority of female stitchers is receiving no more than 30–35 PKR (approximately 20 cents). In their case, makers (local term for subcontractors) are exploiting these female workers and giving them half of the piece rate compared to what they get from their companies. Different companies have their own piece rate. (FGD 4)

Wages reported at a female stitching centre were almost half, compared to the wages reported at a male centre. A female subcentre visited during fieldwork was reported to be monitored by monitoring teams. In response to the question whether these wages were ever reported by female stitchers to inspectors, respondents categorically stated that they complain about low wages and other working conditions to every monitoring team. However, they never receive any feedback about their complaints. Data reveals that under the new production and existing gender regime, female stitchers with young children and other household responsibilities are left with no other choice but to accept homework at further reduced wages. As the number of male stitchers has also decreased over the years, work has shifted to neighbouring districts to female homeworkers. The development of illegitimization of home-based production has further curtailed the agency of female stitchers to claim their worker identity that may provide the basis of their other labour rights and entitlements in an open manner.

Such a discriminatory wage practice demands some justification and itself puts into question the legitimacy and credibility of monitoring mechanisms, even if it does just have the tunnel vision of children's rights. Data generated in this qualitative study points that income level of the family is directly related to children's right to health, right to education and right to play, to name a few among many other fundamental rights. With the low income earned from football stitching, the welfare of the families of female stitchers depends on whether they are the sole or the main earner in the family; whether they have secondary sources of income; and whether there are other earning members of the family. The poverty risk is higher for families where stitching is the sole source of income, and combining stitching with other forms of work has become difficult, due to the shifting of work from homes to stitching centres and factories. The next section will shed light on the aftermath of this successful collaborative venture, which was signed approximately 20 years ago, with regard to children and their families.

Protection of Child Labour in the Football Industry: An Ethical Dilemma

The term "child labour" refers to "work and economic activities carried out by persons under the age of 18 years, that harms their safety, health and wellbeing and/or hinders their education, development and future livelihoods" (ILO, 2011: 5). Though not included in the list of 39 hazardous occupations for children, child labour in the football industry of Sialkot has been the focus of heightened international concern and academic debate. It is hard to gain accurate estimates[8] of the number of children involved in football stitching, because a vast majority of children help their parents at home. The Atlanta Agreement, and the subsequent project that was launched to eliminate child labour from the football industry, ended with accolades, and the industry successfully positioned itself, especially in the eyes of the Western media and consumers, as responsible actors (Khan et al., 2007). However, the aftermath of this successful collaborative venture with regard to children and their families failed to gain the legitimate attention of the global media, in words of Bauman (1998), a problem of localized existence in a globalized world. The limited focus on child labour created by divorcing it from the larger context, as if child labour exists in a vacuum, casts serious doubts about the benefits for children achieved through this project (Xue & Chan, 2013). The issue of child labour in the football industry was not just linked to children who stitched footballs, but also involved adult workers and socio-economic conditions under which parents made a conscious choice to put their children to wage labour.

Poverty is documented (ILO, 2011) as a major reason for child involvement in wage work worldwide, and Pakistan is not an exception to this norm. Homeworkers' households in Pakistan are below the poverty line and work to stave off poverty (Mehrotra & Biggeri, 2010). Under the existing economic scenario of Pakistan, more earning hands are desired to meet the financial needs of the families. Pakistan has a population of

[8] An ILO estimate placing the number of children at approximately 15,000 (Khan et al., 2007).

180.8 million, of whom 43.6 percent are children aged less than 18 years and 28.6 percent are children aged 5–14 years. Child labour has shown an increasing trend in Pakistan, and the labour force participation rate between the ages of 10 to 14 is reported to be 13.65 per cent (PILER, 2009). There are many factors responsible for this trend in Pakistan. Dire economic needs, falling income level of families, along with a lack of compulsory, adequate schooling facilities are the major push factors for child labour. Low market wages can lead to more child labour and less schooling, when adult income in a household is not sufficient for family needs (Basu & Van, 1998). Responses of participants of focus group discussion vividly illustrate how the issues of children's education, development and future livelihoods are implicated with other social and institutional factors. Some of the barriers and enablers are also identified by respondents, whose verbatim comments speak volumes about the real issues and concerns of stitchers' households.

In the absence of any social security mechanisms, a low piece rate without any guarantee of the continuity of work and high opportunity costs of providing education to children led to the involvement of children in paid work. According to Mehrotra and Biggeri (2010), poverty is a major driving force for women and child labour, and the incidence of child labour is higher in homeworking households. Existing literature on child labour identifies four different categories of children: only working, only studying, working and studying, and neither working nor studying. Although there is no statistical data available to indicate how the decline in family income after the ban on home-based production affected the activity status of these different categories of children, in-depth interviews may point towards some likely scenarios.

> The ban is imposed on home-based production to monitor child labour. But, this has eroded the base of training of a new generation of workers. In the old days, people in their home-based enterprises gradually taught their children this skill and over the years they became KAREEGER (skilled workers). The new generation is not leaning this skill. They are either in schools, if parents can afford this, working in a glove factory, or doing nothing. They just do not want children to stitch footballs, but they don't facilitate to provide them with education by increasing piece rate. Even if you provide a small incentive of 500 PKR to school-going children, enrollment will increase. (Subcontractor)

FGDs show that low piece rate and, consequently, low overall family income are considered as major barrier to a child's education by many respondents. During FGD 3 and FGD 4, it was pointed out that in some cases older children are withdrawn from schools and involved in paid work to support the education of their younger siblings. One of the respondents told researchers that her older son left school in grade five and started to work as a hawker to support the education of his younger sisters. The cost of education is considered high by the majority of respondents. Female FGDs pointed towards the fact that cash income earned from their football stitching is used to support their children's education. In cases where children are withdrawn from schools, the main reason reported was mostly the low family income. Involving children in paid work is not an easy decision for parents who are caught between their dreams of a brighter future for their children and the existing poverty trap. Following transcript from an interview shows how choices of people are shaped and what social and psychological costs are associated with these choices.

> My son and daughter had to leave their school just a few months before their final exams of the 8th and 9th grade. I cannot forgive myself for that. It was not their fault, both of them were very intelligent but I had to involve them in football stitching due to the economic crisis that my family was going through. I cannot sleep at nights when I think about what I have done with my children. I asked God for forgiveness… But I was helpless. I did not have money to afford their schooling. I decided to establish a family centre and teach football stitching to my wife, daughter and son to support my family and provide education to my younger children. (Male stitcher, FGD 4)

Figure 5.2 reveals how conventional top-down approaches about corporate responsibility may lead to such ethical dilemmas.[9] Business ethics is mainly concerned with good and bad or right and wrong behaviour that takes place within an existing context of a business conduct. In a cross-cultural setting, it becomes a major concern to decide as to which sets of norms and standards should be followed. In an increasingly globalized and interconnected world, ethical business practices in cross-cultural

[9]An ethical dilemma is a conflict between at least two ethical principles, both of which could lead to an equally good or an equally bad outcome. In such a situation, obeying one principle leads to transgressing another, whereas both principles seem equally valid.

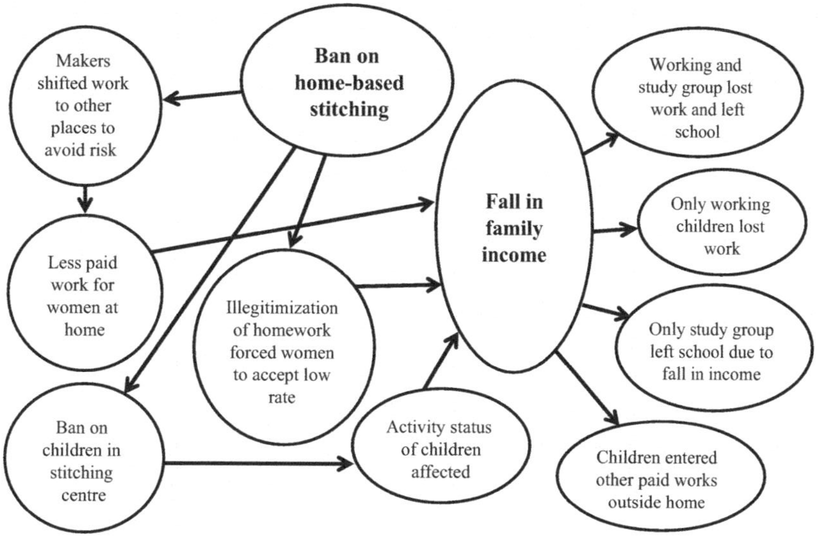

Fig. 5.2 Causal flow of responses to a fall in earnings by homeworking household. (Source: Focus Group Discussions)

settings are desired to include the more difficult and subtle questions of fairness, justice and equity (Clark, 1916; Young, 2010).

These are not easy judgements to make, sometimes leaving communities baffled and ill at ease. Ethical dilemmas such as the one faced by the football industry may result from the conflict between the rightness or wrongness of the actions and the goodness or badness of the consequences of the actions. Apparently, the morally right action of a ban on child labour to protect children's rights resulted in many controversial outcomes for the intended beneficiaries and their families. According to Totaa and Shehua (2012):

> If doing what is right produces something bad, or if doing what is wrong produces something good, the force of moral obligation may seem balanced by the reality of the good end. We can have the satisfaction of being right, regardless of the damage done; or we can aim for what seems to be the best outcome, regardless of what wrongs must be committed. (p. 557)

Situations of this kind demand more serious efforts to resolve such ethical dilemmas, by including all those voices whose interests are at stake. With the rising power of multinational corporations as well as the inclusion of non-state actors in global governance mechanisms, there are demands to refocus our attention on these normative concerns.

Data generated from FGD s confirm that, despite the conditions of work under which stitchers are involved in football production, this income is important for the survival of their families. This holds true especially for female home-based workers, having limited options under the existing opportunity structure of society. Enhanced self-esteem and well-being, reported by female stitchers as compared to their male counterparts, at face value, seem to be a paradoxical finding that demands some further investigation. This might be a reason that despite home-based work being discouraged, it still prevails and is a preferred mode of employment especially for many female football stitchers in Sialkot cluster. In next chapter we have presented a qualitative case study of a football industry in Pakistan to investigate the driving forces and conditions of work associated with the home-based work in GPNs.

Concluding Thoughts

This chapter, by focusing on the industry of Pakistan, argues that, though guided by good intentions, nevertheless the exclusive focus on the elimination of child labour has generated negative externalities especially for female homeworkers in Sialkot, Pakistan. Divorcing the issue of child labour from the social and cultural context produces outcomes that are controversial on ethical and moral grounds as well. This chapter concludes that in an increasingly globalized and interconnected world, CSR practices in cross-cultural settings must be informed by the local context that demands to anticipate the gendered consequences of their CSR strategies. Unintended consequences (Merton, 1936) are so often at work in a way that specific results are intended as a positive vision of development and—vice versa—sometimes exactly the opposite results emerge without the intention of any stakeholder but as an effect, which was not forecasted due to complex situations of decisions and consequences. Public policy at different levels, from social policies up to developmental policies, is full of those examples where decisions are carried out at planning levels with serious and positive intentions but real practice as brought up unintended effects. Despite home-based work being discouraged, it still prevails and is a preferred mode of employment especially for many female football stitchers in Sialkot cluster. Therefore, it is worthwhile to acknowledge that life and work conditions of home-based workers had been transformed in significant ways in the aftermath of the Atlanta Agreement, which was facilitated by the other three signatories—the ILO, UNICEF and the Sialkot Chamber of Commerce and Industry. It come as no surprise that there is no significant change in perceptions of workers about these different work forms (home based, stitching centre based) almost 20 years after the original change took place. This feeds into broader international discussions about how CSR in GPNs can be related to the life and work conditions of home-based workers and can be used as a leverage to bring positive changes in life and work condition of these vulnerable workers by paying attention to their *Unheard Voices*. The case of the football industry of Pakistan also raises serious questions concerning who has the right to define the illegitimacy of a certain business practice and which set of norms and standards should get precedence over others in a cross-cultural setting. "If my activity, though guided by good intentions, generates negative externalities that fall on other subjects, the act which was subjectively just becomes objectively, that is ideopraxically unjust" (Zamagni, 2006: 199).

References

Barrientos, S. (2019). *Gender and Work in Global Value Chains: Capturing the Gains?* Cambridge: Cambridge University Press.

Barrientos, S., & Smith, S. (2007). Do Workers Benefit from Ethical Trade? Assessing Codes of Labour Practice in Global Production Systems. *Third World Quarterly, 28*(4), 713–729.

Basu, K., & Van, P. H. (1998). The Economics of Child Labour. *The American Economic Review, 88*(3), 412–427.

Bauman, Z. (1998). *Globalization: The Human Consequences.* Oxford: Blackwell Publishers Ltd.

Beddewela, E. A. N. D., & Fairbrass, J. (2015). Seeking Legitimacy Through CSR: Institutional Pressures and Corporate Responses of Multinationals in Sri Lanka. *Journal of Business Ethics, 136*(3), 503–522.

Bhattacharya, T. (2017). *Social Reproduction Theory: Remapping Class, Recentering Oppression.* London: Pluto Press.

Clark, J. M. (1916). The Changing Basis of Economic Responsibility. *Journal of Political Economy, 24*(3), 209–229.

Comtrade, U. N. (2011). *United Nations Commodity Trade Statistics Database.* New York: United Nations, Statistic Division.

Desbordes, M., & Richelieu, A. (2012). *Global Sport Marketing: Contemporary Issues and Practice.* New York: Taylor and Francis.

Dubbink, W., & Liedekerke, L. V. (2014). Grounding Positive Duties in Commercial Life. *Journal of Business Ethics, 120*, 527–539.

Gereffi, G., Korzeniewicz, M., & Korzeniewicz, R. P. (1994). Introduction: Global Commodity Chains. In G. Gereffi & M. Korzeniewicz (Eds.), *Commodity Chains and Global Capitalism* (pp. 1–14). Westport, CT: Praeger Publishers.

Ha, J. P., Kang, S. J., & Kim, Y. (2017). Sport Fans in a 'Smart Sport' (SS) Age: Drivers of Smartphone Use for Sport Consumption. *International Journal of Sports Marketing and Sponsorship, 18*(3), 281–297.

ILO. (2011). *Employers and Workers: Handbook on Hazardous Child Labour.* Geneva, Switzerland. Retrieved from http://www.ilo.org/public/english/dialogue/actemp/downloads/projects/cl_handbook.pdf

Jamali, D. (2010). The CSR of MNC Subsidiaries in Developing Countries: Global, Local, Substantive or Diluted? *Journal of Business Ethics, 93*(2), 181–200.

Jamali, D., & Mirshak, R. (2007). Corporate Social Responsibility (CSR): Theory and Practice in a Developing Country Context. *Journal of Business Ethics, 72*(3), 243–262. https://doi.org/10.1007/s10551-006-9168-4

Kabeer, N. (2000). *Discussing Women's Empowerment: Theory and Evidence*. Stockholm: Swedish International Development Cooperation Agency.

Khan, A. (2007). *Power, Policy and the Discourse on Child Labour in the Football Manufacturing Industry of Sialkot*. Karachi: Oxford University Press.

Khan, A. (2010). Discourses on Childhood: Policy-Making with Regard to Child Labour in the Context of Competing Cultural and Economic Preceptions. *History and Anthropology, 21*(2), 110–119.

Khan, F. R., & Lund-Thomsen, P. (2011). CSR as Imperialism: Towards a Phenomenological Approach to CSR in the Developing World. *Journal of Change Management, 11*(1), 73–90.

Khan, F. R., Westwood, R., & Boje, D. M. (2010). I Feel Like a Foreign Agent: NGOs and Corporate Social Responsibility Interventions into Third World Child Labor. *Human Relations, 63*(9), 1417–1438.

Khan, R. K., Munir, K. A., & Willmott, H. (2007). A Dark Side of Institutional Entrepreneurship: Soccer Balls, Child Labour and Postcolonial Impoverishment. *Organization Studies, 28*(7), 1055–1077.

Kolk, A., & Lenfant, F. (2010). MNC Reporting on CSR and Conflict in Central Africa. *Journal of Business Ethics, 93*(2), 241–255.

Lund-Thomsen, P. (2008). The Global Sourcing and Codes of Conduct Debate: Five Myths and Five Recommendations. *Development and Change, 39*(6), 1005–1018.

Lund-Thomsen, P., & Coe, N. M. (2015). Corporate Social Responsibility and Labour Agency: The Case of Nike in Pakistan. *Journal of Economic Geography, 15*(16), 1–22.

Lund-Thomsen, P., & Nadvi, K. (2010). Clusters, Chains and Compliance: Corporate Social Responsibility and Governance in Football Manufacturing in South Asia. *Journal of Business Ethics, 93*(2), 201–222.

Lund-Thomsen, P., Nadvi, K., Chan, A., Khara, N., & Xue, H. (2012). Labour in Global Value Chains: Work Conditions in Football Manufacturing in China, India and Pakistan. *Development and Change, 43*(6), 1211–1237.

Mahony, D. F., & Howard, D. R. (2001). Sport Business in the Next Decade: A General Overview of Expected Trends. *Journal of Sport Management, 15*(4), 275–296.

Manoli, A. E. (2018). Sport Marketing's Past, Present and Future; An Introduction to the Special Issue on Contemporary Issues in Sports Marketing. *Journal of Strategic Marketing, 26*(1), 1–5.

Mehrotra, S., & Biggeri, M. (Eds.). (2007). *Asian Informal Workers: Global Risk, Local Protection*. New York, NY: Routledge.

Mehrotra, S., & Biggeri, M. (2010). Children in Home Worker Households in Pakistan and Indonesia. *International Journal of Manpower, 31*(2), 208–231.

Merton, R. K. (1936). The Unanticipated Consequences of Purposive Social Action. *American Sociological Review, 1*(6), 894–904.

Nadvi, K. (2011). Labour Standards and Technological Upgrading: Competitive Challenges in the Global Football Industry. *International Journal of Technological Learning, Innovation and Development, 4*(1), 235–257.

Nadvi, K., Lund-Thomsen, P., Xue, H., & Khara, N. (2011). Playing Against China: Global Value Chains and Labour Standards in the International Sports Goods Industry. *Global Networks, 11*(3), 334–354.

Pellegrini, M. M., Rialti, R., Marzi, G., & Caputo, A. (2020). Sport Entrepreneurship: A Synthesis of Existing Literature and Future Perspectives. *International Entrepreneurship and Management Journal, 16*, 1–32.

PILER. (2009). *Labour Standards in Football Manufacturing Industry: A Case Study of a Nike Vendor in Sialkot, Pakistan*. Karachi, Pakistan. Retrieved from http://www.piler.org.pk/images/pdf/Labour%20Standards%20in%20Football%20Manufacturing%20Industry%20A%20Case%20Study%20of%20a%20Nike%20Vendor%20in%20Sialkot.pdf

Punjab Skill Development Fund. (2016). *Sports Goods Manufacturing Sector Skills Study*. Retrieved from https://www.psdf.org.pk/wp-content/uploads/2018/11/Final-Report-PSDF-Sports-Goods-Sector-Skills-Study.pdf

Ratten, V., & Jones, P. (2020). New Challenges in Sport Entrepreneurship for Value Creation. *International Entrepreneurship and Management Journal, 16*, 1–20.

Totaa, I., & Shehua, H. (2012). Emerging Markets Queries in Finance and Business: The Dilemma of Business Ethics. *Procedia Economics and Finance, 3*, 555–559.

Williams, P. (2005). Leveraging Change in the Working Conditions of UK Homeworkers. *Development in Practice, 15*(3–4), 546–558.

Xue, H., & Chan, A. (2013). The Global Value Chain: Value for Whom? The Soccer Ball Industry in China and Pakistan. *Critical Asian Studies, 45*(1), 55–77.

Young, I. M. (2010). *Responsibility for Justice*. Oxford: Oxford University Press.

Zamagni, S. (2006). The Ethical Anchoring of Corporate Social Responsibility. In L. Zsolnai (Ed.), *Interdisciplinary Yearbook of Business Ethics* (pp. 31–51). Oxford: Peter Lang, International Academic Publishers.

CHAPTER 6

Home-Based Work and Political Economy of Global Football Production Organization

Introduction

The most decisive factor accelerating, channelling and shaping the information technology paradigm, which has become the guiding organization paradigm of the beginning of twenty-first century, has been the process of capitalist restructuring undertaken since the 1980s. This process led, in a nutshell, to a series of reforms (deregulation, privatization and dismantling of the social contract between labour and capital). According to Castells (2010), four goals were pursued, (1) deepening the capitalist logic of profit seeking in capital–labour relationships, (2) enhancing the productivity of labour and capital, (3) globalizing production, seizing the opportunity of the most advantageous conditions for production and (4) marshalling the state's support for productivity gains and competitiveness of economies. Without the new information technology, the capitalist restructuring would have been much slower, with much less flexibility (Castells, 2010).

When we speak of the *informational societies*, we have to acknowledge that these societies are capitalist societies and that they always experience some degree of cultural and institutional diversity. In a historical time span looking at the last century, if not centuries, we can see a decisive change in the social landscape of human life. Among other historically significant developments, especially those of peculiar interest, are those that are centred on organization of work and the international divisions of labour. These processes have reshaped and still are reshaping our societies and

F. Naz, D. Bögenhold, *Unheard Voices*,
https://doi.org/10.1007/978-3-030-54363-1_6

everything which is interconnected with it (Jin, 2016; Mokyr, 2002). Not only markets and labour markets but also the organization of work and labour are permanently in processes of change, which affect not just the changing contours of work, jobs and opportunities (Sweet & Meiksins, 2017) but also the global–regional diffusion and organization of the capitalist world economy through new and changing markets, the evolution of multiregional economies, globalization and the evolution of knowledge systems in networked clusters with international linkages (Andersson & Andersson, 2017).

Within these worldwide changes the organization of business and of labour in particular multiplies social realities globally, which include social winners with strong labour market positions as well as weak and vulnerable parts which are about disposal of needs and changes in larger organizations and which are parts of globalizing human resource management. The ongoing changes are still part of an ongoing *great transformation* (Polanyi, 2001) which may have no point of end. The emerging literature on the link of sports and entrepreneurial opportunities (Pellegrini, Rialti, Marzi, & Caputo, 2020; Ratten, 2018) is mostly silent regarding the questions that are developed here, namely about how those material items are economically and socially produced in terms of working conditions and working locations. Therefore, this research selected a case of football industry of Pakistan to explore how informal home-based workers are situated at the nexus of global and local production networks. In doing so, we also regard our research as a kind of political economy of sports and its social and economic embeddedness.

This chapter picks up one topical aspect of the global scenario, namely home-based workers in Pakistan being engaged for the production of footballs for an international market in commission of global Western corporations with established brands. Based on extensive primary evidence, the research assesses work conditions of footballs stitchers and seeks to explain the systemic position of home-based workers at the lowest end of global football supply chains. In order to arrive at a more accurate picture of the situation of female home-based workers in the football supply chain, qualitative data obtained through interviews and field observation was subjected to rigorous techniques of qualitative methodology and vetted through triangulation.

Research Context: Organization of Football Production in Sialkot, Pakistan

The football industry of Pakistan is an established name in the world of sports goods and is one of the promising industries of Pakistan providing a livelihood to millions of people directly or indirectly. In Pakistan, there is a long tradition of hand-stitched football production. Football manufacturing in Sialkot dates back to the early 1900s, when Sialkot's leather working caste began to repair and later manufacture footballs for the large British colonial military garrison in Sialkot (Nadvi, Lund-Thomsen, Xue, & Khara, 2011). Sialkot became a supplier of footballs across British India. Approximately 80–85 percent of the high-quality hand-stitched inflatable ball production of the world originates from Sialkot. Sialkot's producers specialize in producing the entire range, including high-quality hand-stitched match balls, medium-quality training balls and lower-quality promotional balls. One major feature of the Pakistani football industry is that it is a labour-intensive and export-oriented industry, which makes extensive use of subcontracting practices. The production process in Pakistan is simple and has a low level of mechanization. The process of cutting and preparing panels takes place in factories and is partially mechanical. However, stitching is a manual process that is outsourced through the process of subcontracting. These balls are stitched at home and are checked for quality assurance in factories. Packing also takes place in factories.

One unique feature of the football industry in Pakistan is that the industry is located in one city called Sialkot, which has a hundred-year-long tradition of stitching footballs. Only 2 percent (approximately 20 firms) of companies in Sialkot are large enterprises that employ more than 250 workers and do business with major brands. About 90 percent are small to medium-sized enterprises (SMEs) in Sialkot (Punjab Skills Development Fund, 2016).

Many famous brands including Nike and Adidas have established their supply chains of premium quality match balls and club balls with the vendors from Sialkot. Most of the larger firms in the Sialkot cluster act as original equipment manufacturer (OEMs) to mega global brands.

Producing for these brands has considerable advantages in terms of production volumes, market access and flows of technical knowledge, but local OEM firms also have to bear the associated cost of being in a captive chain tied to global brands. In the global supply chains of football, the OEM suppliers of Sialkot are vulnerable to the changing sourcing patterns of global brands and face considerable pressure to comply with the buyers' demands. In the current global production system of global supply chains, global lead firms exercise asymmetrical power over their suppliers in various ways—determining what is produced where, under what conditions and for what price (Lund-Thomsen & Nadvi, 2010). In football supply chains, buyers play a significant role in shaping the relations and financial returns that local stakeholders can generate from participating in GPNs. Lead firms are in a position to exert considerable influence over their suppliers in their extended supply chains by deciding what to produce where, under what conditions, and for which prices (Gereffi, 2005). They can also influence the amount of work available to local stitchers by preferring a particular kind of ball over other types of balls; for example, the preference of thermo-moulded or machine-stitched balls over hand-stitched balls has changed the dynamics of the global football industry by moving production from Pakistan to China.

The football industry of Pakistan moved into the international limelight due to its integration into the visible supply chains of many international brands. In 1995, news about the involvement of child labour in the football industry sent shock waves around the world. Under immense international public pressure, a project to eradicate child labour in the industry was started in collaboration with International Labour Organization (ILO) and United Nations Children's Emergency Fund (UNICEF).

Global supply chain governance pressures have altered the traditional forms of production organization in Sialkot. Traditionally, football production in Sialkot was organized on a quasi-cottage-based system. Football panels (the individual hexagonal and pentagonal pieces) were prepared in factories, and, then, through an elaborate chain of subcontractors, these panels were distributed to some 1600 villages surrounding Sialkot, where they were stitched together, mostly in homes. There are no reliable statistics available about the stitching labour force in this industry, and the number varies from estimate to estimate. The stitching workforce estimates vary from a low of just over 30,000 to a high of 65,000 (PILER, 2009). The flexible nature of work makes it hard to get accurate and reliable estimates about the exact number of stitchers associated with the football industry, but the number of registered stitchers was 20,000 in 2014 (Fayyaz, Lund-Thomsen, & Lindgreen, 2015). Besides these formal and informal stitching centres, footballs are also stitched in the homes of individual village-based stitchers. Home-based stitching is a full-time occupation for the majority of female home-based workers who are stitching footballs to cushion their falling income from all other sources. The exact number of these homeworkers is difficult to estimate.

Integration of Female Homeworkers into Football Supply Chains

Until 1970, male workers in small and medium-sized factories and workshops mainly performed football stitching in Sialkot. Due to the introduction of stricter labour laws in 1972, manufacturers shifted more labor-intensive processes like hand stitching from factories to workers' homes, in order to circumvent the labour legislation (Xue & Chan, 2013). This led to the beginning of football stitching as a cottage industry in Sialkot. This trend was further facilitated due to the change of the key raw material in football production from natural to synthetic leather, which was easier to stitch. The decentralization of football stitching resulted in a substantial growth of the industry and facilitated the entry of large numbers of home-based women workers, along with a smaller number of child workers, into ball stitching (Nadvi et al., 2011). For home-based stitchers, football stitching provides a flexible means of work while allowing them to take care of their other household duties and agricultural work. Entire families work as a production unit as together they are able to produce 12 balls per day; this includes the labour of male stitchers, female stitchers and their children. Football stitching involves multiple steps. First, one needs to wax the thread. Sometime stitchers also make holes in the football panels to pass the thread through. And finally, the stitching of footballs that requires more strength is normally done by elders in the family. As children do not have the required strength to stitch entire balls, they are normally involved in waxing the threads.

In order to keep overhead costs down in Pakistan, football stitching is outsourced from factories through extended networks of subcontractors. Outsourcing arrangements initially added flexibility to football production, which was a desired trait in the football industry. Due to the institutionalization of subcontracting arrangements, there is a limited possibility for collective bargaining (Lund-Thomsen, Nadvi, Chan, Khara, & Xue, 2012). In Pakistan, the process of stitching the ball is outsourced through approximately 2450 subcontractors. These subcontractors serve as a link between stitchers and suppliers in football supply chains. Three types of stitchers are identified in the football supply chains of Pakistan, either employed by subcontractors or self-employed or own-account stitchers. They are paid on a piece-rate basis, depending upon the quality of the ball being stitched (Lund-Thomsen, 2012).

Figure 6.1 may help to explain the horizontal and vertical linkages of female home-based workers in the local/global football supply chains. There are 20 large-sized, 50 medium-sized and 400 small or micro firms operating in Sialkot. The industry also houses 2600 registered stitching centres, mostly managed by subcontractors. These registered centres are linked with specific manufacturers and are monitored by the child labour monitoring programmes. There are different types of stitching centres based on their size and location. Large centres in Sialkot accommodate 100 to 500 workers; medium-sized centres have 50 to 100 workers and small centres have 10 to 59 stitchers, whereas home-based stitching centres employ less than 10 stitchers. In addition to these formal enterprises, there are informal home-based stitching centres in Sialkot (UNIDO, 2009).

Empirical Evidences

In terms of the spatial distribution of production organization, there are three major tiers. At the top of the supply chain are a small number of retailers and brand names that govern the chain. They are located in the advanced countries and have greater access to and control over the Western consumer market. They have their own buying houses, and also control research and management, whereas production is carried out in the middle and lower parts of the chain. The middle part represents local vendors and manufacturers in Pakistan. The factories are located in the city, whereas stitching is also organized in stitching centres and home-based workshops surrounding Sialkot city, the hub of football production in Pakistan. Although the football industry is export oriented and linked to the global market, the labour-intensive production model in Sialkot relies heavily on a semi-literate, rural workforce operating in precarious conditions under weak regulatory mechanisms (PILER, 2009). In order to get an overall picture of life and work conditions of the stitchers in the football industry, interviews are carried at various levels in the football supply chain. An effort is being made to include workers from each level of the production organization. Following major themes are extracted from the analysis of the qualitative interviews.

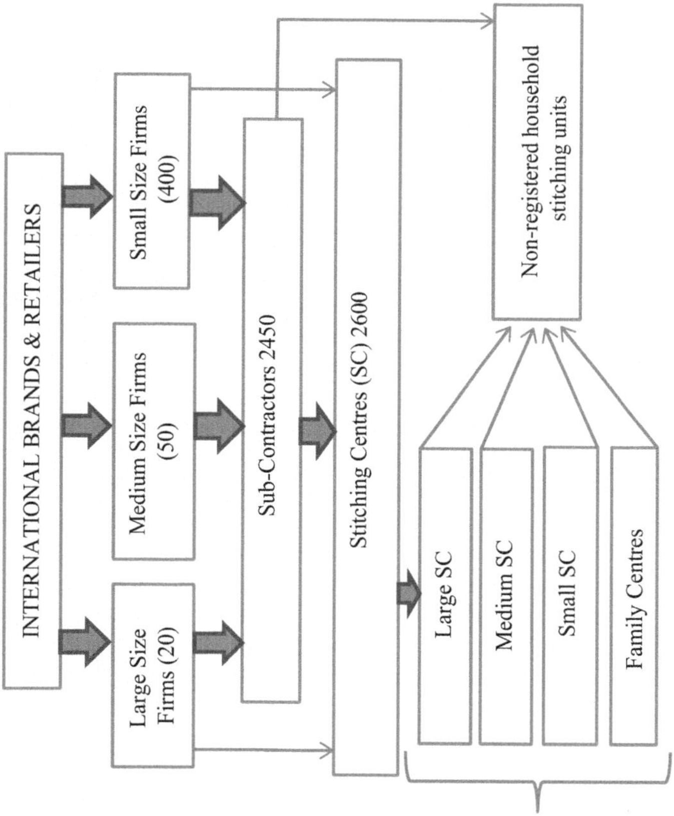

Fig. 6.1 Football production organization Sialkot, Pakistan. (Source: Author's elaboration)

Working Conditions and Wages of Stitching Labour Force at Various Nodes of Football Supply Chain

Although Pakistan looms large on the international football brands suppliers' list, the field data nevertheless reveal that the conditions of football stitchers fall short in terms of most of the principles of decent work and into the category of precarious work in line with Kalleberg (2011) classification. Factories operating in Sialkot hire two types of labour forces: a permanent labour force with job contract and a temporary labour force. The permanent labour force works mainly in management and automatized production units located in Sialkot city. The temporary labour force is hired for labour-intensive stages in football production. Football stitching, which is the most labour-intensive work associated with football manufacturing, mostly involves temporary piece-rate workers hired by firms without any job contracts. The hiring and firing procedure regarding these workers is simple. In order to gain work in a factory, workers have to demonstrate their skill in stitching footballs. They are asked to complete a football, and if they succeed to meet the quality criteria of the firm, they are hired as piece-rate workers without any job contract (Fig. 6.2).

Although there is no gender discrimination in recruitment procedures, inflexible working hours, gender norms about female mobility, along with the structural problems like inadequate transport systems effectively barred women from access to employment in factories. A male factory stitcher confirmed during an interview that there was not even one female stitcher in his factory. Due to the informal nature of their employment, stitchers in the football industry are not issued with a letter of appointment that could entitle them to benefits such as social security or pensions or other form of support from the Employees' Old-Age Benefits Institution (EOBI). Consequently, the majority of the stitching labour force works on a piece-rate basis without any fringe benefits and social securities, and is relatively more mobile. They do not have loyalties or a bond with just one firm. They easily move from one firm to another in search of better conditions, as each firm has its own set of incentives and regulations. Slight variations in the piece rate can provide an incentive for workers to change their workplace.

According to Punjab Skill Development Fund (PSDF, 2016) survey, there are 67 percent contractual workers in Sialkot sports good cluster. Only 8 percent women are working in factories but they too are working on contract basis. The informal nature of employment and the abundance

o f

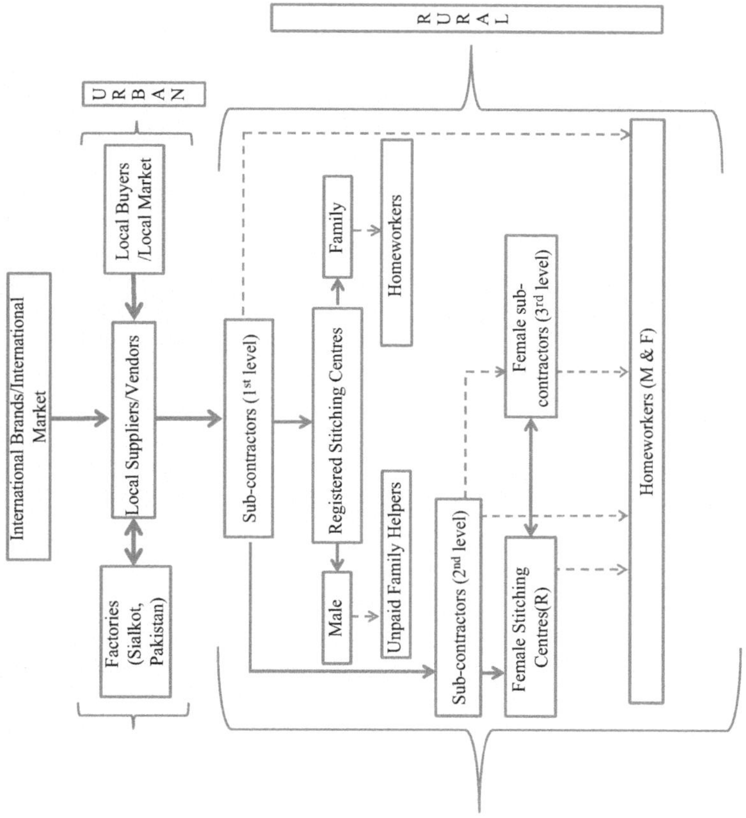

Fig. 6.2 Integration of football stitchers into the global football supply chain. (Source: Naz and Boegenhold (2020))

the labour force willing to work on the basis of these rates due to their dire economic needs create a hurdle, which prevents stitchers from framing and claiming their rights and entitlements through collective bargaining. As most of the stitchers meet their expenditure on the basis of their daily earnings, it is hard to afford any absenteeism from work. It is evident from Table 6.1 that workers who are positioned in factories as stitchers are able to earn relatively better compared to other stitchers in the football supply chain. A piece rate of 100 PKR was reported by a factory stitcher who was interviewed during the field visits. However, while this estimated income shown in Table 6.1 gives us a rough idea about the earnings of a factory stitcher; it is not a true reflection of their earnings.

Their income is dragged down by transportation costs, meals and piece-rate deduction for defective balls, and so on. As football stitchers depend on the daily-income source of football stitching, their daily output plays a crucial role in maintaining their livelihood. Travelling to and from factories also involves a time cost that is exacerbated due to poor road and transport infrastructure in the area. This also affects the overall daily output of the workers, which is reported to be lower in the case of factory-based stitchers compared to the stitchers in stitching centres.

Table 6.1 Earnings in Football Stitching in Pakistan, December 2014

Stitchers	*Sex*	*Daily output*	*Piece rate (PKR)*	*Monthly (26 days) earnings in (PKR)*	*Monthly (26 days) earnings in (EUR)*
Factory-based stitcher	M	6	100	15,600	139.17
Centre-based stitcher	M	7	85 (85–110)	15,470	138.01
Centre-based stitcher	M	7	75 (75–85)	13,650	121.77
Family centre (4 members)	M & F	12	90 (90–95)	28,080	250.51
Female stitching centre	F	3	50	3900	34.79
Homeworker	M	3	60 (60–65)	4680	41.75
Homeworker	F	3	50 (32–55)	3900	34.79
Homeworker	F	3	40	3120	27.83

Source: Field interviews

The daily output reported by the workers at the stitching centre was approximately seven balls per day. Although there is variation in individual outputs, on average a worker in a stitching centre is able to stitch seven balls a day in an estimated time of eight to nine hours. Data shows that the income of centre-based stitchers is slightly less than that of factory workers, but as it involves no travel and meal costs, the gross income of these workers is better. In centre-based stitching, no travel cost is involved, and it is also reported to be relatively flexible in terms of time management. Workers in stitching centres also do not have any job contracts. They connect with the market through subcontractors. Workers at stitching centres reported having no direct link with the factories. They are hired by subcontractors. Work is provided to them at their centre, and the subcontractor is responsible for managing the centre. Two different male centres were visited during the field research, and workers in both centres were operating under different terms and conditions.

For instance, workers at first centre visited during fieldwork reported comparatively lower piece rate compare to second. However, they enjoy certain benefits (health care and child benefit etc.). However, such benefits are provided only to permanent stitchers. They are issued cards by the company after one year of service to the centre. These cards are issued on the basis of the attendance record of workers. Attendance is marked by the mobile inspector of the company once a week. In case a worker is not present on the day of the visit, he is considered absent for a whole week, and any worker who is absent for more than 30 days from work during the course of one year is not entitled to a card. This card entitles workers and their families to medical facilities free of cost and also provides child benefits for children attending school. The amount of child benefit is 1000 PKR (approximately €5.60) after six months. However, it is hard for stitchers to get this entitlement as they juggle multiple economic activities tasks to meet their family needs. At the time of the field visit, there were six permanent stitchers at the centrer holding company cards and others were working part time.

The centre is monitored by ILO teams for child labour and home-based production. Workers are not allowed to take the balls home for stitching. They have to complete their work at the centre. According to the discussion, there is no restriction about home-based production of *desi* (local) balls; these balls are mostly produced by homeworkers. Subcontractors work with many companies at the same time, both local and export firms, to ensure continuity of work at their centres. One interesting finding is that local companies pay even higher rates, but the permanent workers attached with the centre we visited were not allowed to produce ball for any other firm. Subcontractors are responsible for delivering and collecting balls from homeworkers. Rate lists are displayed at each centre so workers at the centre are confident that they cannot be cheated about rates in the centres. However, the same cannot be claimed about the homeworkers with the same degree of certainty. No child under the age of 16 is allowed to work in the centre. Workers at the second stitching centre visited during fieldwork were subjected to the same restriction, but they were not entitled to any benefits like health care and child education benefit. However, due to the high piece rate, there is an estimated income difference of approximately 1800 PKR between the two centres. The centre is monitored by Independent Monitoring Association for Child Labor (IMAC) for child labour and home-based production. Piece rates in this centre range between 85 and 110 PKR. The piece rate varies according to the type of ball, but balls with higher piece rates are hard to stitch and demand more time. The normal reported time for the completion of a ball is approximately 60 minutes, whereas hard balls may take 80 to 90 minutes per ball.

Although workers are not allowed to take the balls home for stitching, they can seek unpaid family help for other tasks like waxing threads at home. Unpaid family help in stitching from female family members was also reported by a stitcher who was interviewed outside a stitching centre. However, this female contribution is not acknowledged as a work in both economic and social discourses.

The illegitimization of home-based stitching, owing to various measures that were adopted after the Atlanta Agreement, by the football manufacturers as *legitimacy-seeking strategies* (Beddewela & Fairbrass, 2015) has opened many backdoor practices in the industry and has undermined the contributions of female stitchers as well as further fragmented the dispersed labour force.

Although the family stitching centre provides an income opportunity for female workers, there are challenges to establishing the centre at home. Firstly, not all companies approve of the stitching cent, and, secondly, it is not possible to establish a family centre for less than four stitchers. Home centres are also monitored by the IMAC to ensure the elimination of child labour in the industry. Family centres are not insured against any risk or health hazards associated with the work. As there is no social security mechanism or assurance of continuity of work, it is reported as a great risk to involve the entire family in football production. In the event of slack periods, the entire family is out of work at the same time, which threatens their livelihood security in the absence of any fallback position (Fayyaz et al., 2015).

The overall productivity reported by the stitchers was three balls per worker per day, which is very low compared to the productivity at the male stitching centres. One of the explanations given by the stitches at the centre was that the average is low due to the low output of female stitchers who have to balance their household responsibilities with their paid work. In their narratives, the contribution of female stitchers in family centres is perceived as a support to male stitchers rather than an independent productive activity. Such construction of women economic contributions reflects how women workers are uniquely situated within political economy of production organization (Amoore, 2002; Barrientos, 2019; Prügl & Tinker, 1997). Another possibility for the stitchers is to work in a female stitching centre. However, there appears to be clear discrimination in terms of wages in male and female centres. Stitchers at the female stitching centre reported a rate of 50 PKR per ball. Overall, the average income from stitching reported by workers at the female centre was approximately 3900 PKR. That is far lower than the income earned by their male counterparts in the industry (see Table 6.2).

Two major reasons for this discrepancy are the differences in wages and the average output of the workers. The major reason for the low productivity of female stitchers reported during the interview is their gender role obligation and associated responsibilities at the household and community levels. At female stitching centres, no other facility is provided except a piece rate. The centre visited during the field visit was organized by a subcontractor through a female supervisor, who was a worker at the centre as well. The supervisor was responsible for checking balls produced at the

Table 6.2 Estimate of Living Wages

Country	*Living wage (EUR)*	*Poverty line (EUR)*	*Statutory minimum wage (EUR)*
Bangladesh	160	132	13
India	170	99	43
Nepal	120	116	70
Pakistan	150	99	80
Sri Lanka	270	200	38

Source: Guzi (2013)

centre and for hiring female stitchers from the community. She was also responsible for providing work to the homeworkers. She was given a commission of 5 PKR per ball for her services. Workplace and other associated expenditure were borne by the subcontractor, a person from the nearby village. All stitchers at the centre were middle-aged married women with children.

The lowest rank in the hierarchy of production organization is occupied by the homeworkers. They receive the lowest rates in the industry. Both male and female homeworkers were interviewed during the data collection process. Male homeworkers combine their work with other forms of paid work. They are hired by subcontractors on a piece-rate basis, and advance payments are made, which creates debt bondage. This is reported as a common practice, and there are no formal mechanisms to organize this. The debt amount varies from worker to worker, and there are no formal conflict resolution mechanisms for settling such debts. This debt burden creates pressure on workers, and they are bound to work under precarious conditions without any formal agreement. There is also a gender difference in terms of piece rate for workers and advance payments. Female homeworkers receive a lower piece rate compared to male homeworkers and claim no or less advance money. Due to debt bondage and a dispersed labour force, there is a limited possibility of collective bargaining. Male homeworkers report that they combine football stitching with other paid work, and female homeworkers combine it with unpaid household work.

Data reveals that in the spatial organization of football production, the further one moves away from the centre, the lower is the piece rate. Gender is a cross-cutting theme in the production organization, and there are clear gender differences in the income level. Male factory-based stitchers and centre-based stitchers earn relatively better. Their income is closer to or relatively higher than the minimum wages in Pakistan. The minimum wage for an unskilled worker in Pakistan was 12,000 PKR (€107.05) in 2014. However, it is disputed whether the minimum wage in Pakistan represents a living wage that covers daily caloric intake, housing, clothing, education, medical and other necessary expenses (see Table 6.2). The situation is even worse for stitchers at the other nodes of the supply chain (see Table 6.2). They are living below the poverty line and their income from stitching is below even the statutory minimum wage of the country.

In the football industry, the stitching labour force is classified as an unskilled or semi-skilled workforce. Seigmann (2008) questioned the classification of the stitchers as unskilled labour on the grounds that ILO classifies assemblers of leather products to the second of four skill levels (ILO, 2012). Football stitchers themselves perceive their work as a form of skilled labour that demands hard work and training.

Driving Forces (Push-and-Pull Factors)

Though the right to decent work under conditions of freedom is granted under the Constitution of Pakistan (Article 3 and Article 37c), an overview of the stitching labour force at various nodes of football supply chain paints both a blue and a gendered picture in terms of minimum standards of decent work and wages. However, despite all the challenges that characterize this sector, a large bulk of the informal labour force residing in more than 400 rural settlements dispersed in three tehsils of the district (Sialkot, Pasrur and Daska)—spread over 3016 kilometres—is associated with the industry. Approximately 41,000–44,000 people were associated with the football industry in 2003–2004 (PILER, 2009). The qualitative data collected during the field research indicate various pull-and-push factors that keep stitchers on move in the football industry of Pakistan. Economic conditions along with geographical distance, local patriarchal values of the stitcher community, modes of recruitment and a diversity of livelihood strategies are a few among many factors that shape the possibilities to engage in football stitching as a mode of earning their livelihood in the villages surrounding Sialkot, Pakistan.

The majority of the respondents interviewed during the course of fieldwork cited dire economic need and lack of alternative earning opportunities as a major push factor to become involved in football stitching. The district of Sialkot has very fertile land that is fed by the Chenab River, Degh Nullah and Aik Nullah (flowing from the Jammu Hills) and the Marala Ravi Link Canal. Almost 50 percent of households in the district of Sialkot, officially described as agricultural households, depending on agriculture and livestock as the source of their livelihood, are compelled to look for alternatives for the reason that the crop production and growth have stagnated over the years due to land fragmentation. High prices of agricultural inputs, low acreage and weather uncertainties have greatly reduced the income of small farmers with small land holdings, and income from agriculture is not sufficient to support family needs. Consequently, agricultural households in the districts had to look for alternatives to support their family. This alternative was provided to the scattered rural population through the informalization of the labour force in the football industry that started during the 1970s due to the decentralization of the production process (PILER, 2009).

The basic automated processes of football manufacturing that include panel cutting, screen-printing and quality control are organized in city-based factories, whereas the labour-intensive process of panel stitching is outsourced in the surrounding villages of the district of Sialkot through a complex chain of subcontractors called *Makers* in the local language. The informalization of the labour force, which has coincided with the technological developments that facilitated the replacement of leather by synthetic material, also makes it easier for women to avail themselves of this income-earning opportunity in order to support the falling income of their families. Synthetic material is much lighter and easier to stitch compared to leather that is hard and demands more strength. Football manufacturers leaned on the untapped female labour force to benefit from the international transformation in the global production organization from the late 1980s onward (Fayyaz, 2011). The biographical histories of respondents confirm that the majority of them are pushed by the dire economic needs of their families and the absence of other income-earning opportunities in the villages. Most of the respondents interviewed during data collection are illiterate or semi-literate. They do not have any other marketable skill. Most of them combine football stitching with other forms of work available in local communities. Due to falling income from agriculture-related activities, one person's income is not sufficient to meet family needs and football stitching has become the main source of income for stitchers to hold over a period of time.

Most of the respondents learned football stitching in the early stages of their lives, either as an income-earning activity or as a part of their family tradition. The majority of them had been associated with the industry for a long time. The other alternative work reported by the male respondents is unskilled daily wage labour as construction worker, which is physically hard work. Therefore, football stitching has become a popular form of work in the Sialkot district since the 1980s. Football stitching was considered a valuable income-earning opportunity, especially in the absence of any education, formal training or better alternatives in rural areas. Stitchers are linked to the production process through their subcontractors, who are responsible for providing work to the stitchers. Although debt servitude is not permissible in Pakistan under the *Bonded Labour Abolition Act* 1992, which declares such advances as illegal, nevertheless in the context of regulatory arbitrage (Jenkins, 2005) weak enforcement mechanisms such as advance payments are reported during the in-depth interviews. Makers give advance payments to the stitchers before engaging them in work. The amount of advance payment varies according to the personal needs of the stitchers and may range between 3000 and 25,000 PKR. Such advance amounts that some workers are not able to settle are reported as a major push factor that barred workers from shifting to other forms of work.

Male stitchers combine football stitching with other forms of paid work, except for the factory worker. Females combined it with household care work and livestock. It is cited as an advantage of football stitching that it is flexible work and can be combined with other types of work to raise the overall family income. Men mostly combined stitching with agricultural work or other paid activities. Stitchers at the centres said that though factories in cities offer a relatively better piece rate, they prefer centre-based stitching. Stitching centres are located in villages, and stitchers either are from the same village or come from nearby villages, which saves travel time, transport costs and even meal costs. A factory-based stitcher interviewed during fieldwork also confirmed that factory-based stitching demands following certain routines, and travel costs and time bring productivity and income down. Factory workers have to produce at their workplace and are rarely allowed to bring work to their homes, whereas stitching centre-based stitchers not only are able to save travel costs, but are also in a position to seek family help to complete their work. Geographical distance matters in the case of poor roads and transport infrastructure that increase travel time and cost for workers. Flexible working hours also help male stitchers to continue their agricultural activities during harvesting and cultivating seasons.

Female stitchers are mostly homeworkers and linked to the market through communal links with subcontractors or male family members. In some cases, subcontractors hire the services of local female subcontractors to gain access to the female stitchers in the area. As in the patriarchal context of Pakistani society male honour is attached to the female bodies, therefore there is a restriction on the free mobility of women, especially young unmarried girls, in the rural context. Patriarchal norms of the society shape gender identities and gender roles (Walby, 1992). A male breadwinner ideology that constructs male hegemonic identity in most of patriarchal societies is hard to maintain in a dire economic situation where male income is not sufficient to provide for the family's needs. Therefore, paid work at home provided an opportunity for women to earn cash income that could be combined with the acceptable parameters of gender role obligations in wider society without challenging hegemonic notions of the male breadwinner ideology (Wilson, 2003). This was evident from the testimony of a female stitcher who was working in a family stitching centre. When she was asked about her contribution to the family income, she was not able to figure out her worker identity, but rather, she perceived her role as a helper to her husband and son in their stitching work.

In the absence of other income-earning opportunities along with gender role obligations, women are even willing to work at a lower price. Subcontractors capitalized on female labour from distant geographical locations further away from the city to increase their profit margin. A variation in the piece rate as reflected in Table 6.1 clearly indicates that female homeworkers are the least-paid workers in the supply chain. There are but few female-only stitching centres in the area. Mostly, young females are not allowed to work in these centres, especially if the centres are located in villages other than the village where they reside. Therefore, they are left with limited choices and opportunity to earn a cash income desired for their family needs. In the absence of other viable options, homework has become an obvious choice for female stitchers from poor families. A female homeworker interviewed during fieldwork reported that her family does not allow her to work outside the home. She herself feels insecure about the outside world. She holds negative perceptions about the female factory workers. She has no education or vocational training. In order to support her husband, she has learned how to stitch footballs from her husband. Her paid work inside the home is acceptable both to her husband and to her extended family. She is obliged to her subcontractor to provide her with work at her home. She reported receiving a low piece rate, but finds it hard to bargain with a male subcontractor.

Stitchers' Perceptions of their Working Conditions

Qualitative data gathered during the field visit shows that the workers' perceptions of their working conditions are mediated through various factors like alternate source of income, landownership, gender and their position in the hierarchy of production organization, albeit not in a linear fashion. The factory worker interviewed during fieldwork, who is positioned higher in terms of piece rate and income, reported many other denominators that play a vital role in influencing his perception about the overall quality of his working life. Overall institutional environment and personal circumstances do play a decisive role in shaping the choices of stitchers in football supply chains. For instance, having no education and no marketable vocational training limits the choices of the workers.

Football stitching is hard work that often causes significant ergonomic problems. All interviewed workers reported different types of muscular such as pain in their shoulders and neck, especially after long working days. A poor health status may reduce the worker's output, which in turn further brings down the income of stitchers that is already lower than the living wages of the country. Low income and the absence of support mechanisms hinder the workers' ability to plan and collectively bargain. In the absence of other viable options and chances of upward mobility, workers are caught in a poverty trap.

Workers in village-based centres visited during fieldwork reported that they receive a lower piece rate compared to the factory-based stitchers, but they cited other advantages that shape their choice to work as a centre-based stitcher. Firstly, centre-based stitching is more flexible compared to the factory-based stitching. Most of the workers at stitching centres combined their stitching work with other forms of work to increase their overall income. Most of them reported that they combine football stitching with agricultural activities. Secondly, working in village-based centres reportedly saved on the time and travelling costs involved in the case of factory-based stitching. Local roads and transport infrastructure make it harder for workers to go to city-based factories.

Thirdly, overall productivity is relatively better in centres due to less travelling time involved in reaching a centre located either in the same or in a nearby village. Lunch costs are also covered in stitching centres. Fourthly, it is also possible to seek family help for stitching. Workers can take some work home, especially from local companies that increase their overall productivity and income. However, in the absence of social security and collective bargaining mechanisms, the overall income of workers is reported to be lower than their family needs. Piece rate is reported to be low when compared to the hard work involved in the stitching of a good quality ball.

Most of the workers perceived their work as low-paid and low-status work. Over the years, football stitching has moved from a valuable income-earning opportunity to a socially devalued form of work. One of the reasons for this shift was reported as being a slow increase in the piece rate. A few years back, it was a popular activity among the young and many boys and girls learned to stitch footballs in home-based workshops through informal training or apprenticeships. At that time, the overall income earned from football stitching was reported to be better in the area, as this was managed as a small family enterprise. However, over a period of time in order to resolve the issue of child labour, the industrial production was shifted from the informal home-based workshops to registered stitching centres. This shift had the unintended consequence of pushing female homeworkers out of work due to prevailing cultural and gender ideologies, and, consequently, family incomes went down. This has gradually changed people's perception about football stitching. It deteriorated from a desirable, productive activity to a socially and economically devalued form of work.

Due to the low social and economic value attached to football stitching, it is gradually dying in the area. Many workers either have left or are planning to leave and no new workers are being trained. "Only those stay in the industry who are not able to do anything else" (excerpt from an interview with a male stitcher). The number of stitchers has reduced in the area. This was also confirmed by a subcontractor interviewed during fieldwork, who explained that he faces difficulty in hiring workers because the income of an unskilled daily-wage worker (*Dehari Mazdoor*) is higher than that of a football stitcher. Therefore, many workers shifted to *Dehari Mazdoor* to meet their family needs. Some of them sold their agricultural lands and went to the Gulf States for work; some started working as street vendors. Workers perceive that there are no chances of mobility; consequently, they do not want their children to learn football stitching. The role and the impact that economic reasoning has on social life and vice versa is also acknowledged in current debates (Douglass, 1991). They want their children to have good jobs. Income from stitching is considered by them as hardly enough for survival. It's a constant struggle. Stitchers in family centres are facing a different set of challenges and insecurities associated with converting the household into a site of production. Though there are no gender differences in wages in family centres, female contributions in family centres are subsumed under the production of the male workers of the family.

Female stitchers working in female-only sub-centres are getting discriminatory wages. They are attached to the production process through complex and multilayer subcontracting chains. A female sub-centre visited during fieldwork is organized by a female subcontractor. She works for a male subcontractor who brings work from another male subcontractor.

Workers at this centre are hired without any job contract. They get the piece rate of 50 PKR per ball, which is much lower than the piece rate given at male stitching centres. This rate further goes down due to deductions made by the subcontractors for defective balls. All female stitchers at the centre are middle-aged married women with children. They believe that their income from football stitching is not enough to meet the entire needs of the family, but still they value it due to a lack of alternative income-earning opportunities for women with household responsibilities.

There are no facilities of childcare, which could free women to look for alternatives in the formal job market. They are driven by the dire economic needs of their families to look for paid work, but cannot distance themselves from their household responsibilities due to the non-existence of any support mechanisms for childcare or care of sick family members. Due to their household responsibilities, women are not able to work in nearby factories in the area. They attach great value to their work. For them, their work is a source of high self-esteem and self-worth. They combine their income with other sources of income and utilize it for managing family budgets. All of them, except one 70 year-old stitcher, have school-going children and they use the cash to support their school-related expenditures.

They have flexible work arrangements at the centre. The average productivity of these workers is three balls per day—which is almost half the productivity of male workers. Consequently, their income is also very low. Major factors that bring down the productivity of workers mentioned during interviews are their household and community responsibilities. Household responsibilities include cooking, cleaning and taking care of children and sick family members. They may also include managing livestock as well in case they own livestock. Due to the existing gender division of labour, men are not expected to contribute to household chores. They help in the management of livestock. Household chores are shared by female family members, and, in the case of female stitchers, they are mostly shared by their daughters. Women also have community obligations that demand time and resources. They are expected to visit friends and family on certain occasions and are also expected to entertain guests at their home.

All these diverse types of responsibilities demand time and leave women time-constrained as well as affect their productive capacity. Respondents mention their community-related responsibilities as a hurdle for them.

The working day of an average female stitcher starts very early. They get up around 4 am. They prepare breakfast, send their children to school, feed their animals and leave for their centre around 10 am. There are six workers in their centre and they enjoy working together. Group work provides them with motivation to work. They reported that they like to work in groups and enjoy talking to each other. They are a closely knitted group. Their work arrangement is flexible and they can also work at home. Their centre is monitored; during the visits by monitoring teams, they are required to be present at the centre. They get advance information about these visits. According to the respondents' views, football stitching is considered as a feminine activity in their area and has community approval, though it is stigmatized for men. Men prefer to work as house painters in a nearby city. Female workers attach positive value to their work, though they are not satisfied with their wage rate, which is very low. They also complain about the lack of facilities in the centres. They complain about working conditions to the monitoring teams, but get no response to their complaints. It is hard to work in the centre, especially during winter, as there are no heating facilities; according to a testimony of a female stitcher, *it feels like working in cold river water.* They also do not have access to credit or advance money or any other fringe benefits. They work as a team and have their informal leader, a female centre supervisor.

They change their subcontractors when they have a better offer from another subcontractor or if they are not satisfied with the behaviour of a subcontractor. As a group, they are better able to bargain and resist at their centre level. They had a larger group in the past. There were 36 stitchers in their group, but over the years many left this work. Most of the women from the village started to work in a nearby glove factory that offers them relatively better wages. Only those are left in football stitching who cannot afford to go out due to their personal life circumstance and household responsibilities.

Next in the hierarchy of production organization are the homeworkers. They work within the premises of their households and are located at the lowest end of the football supply chain. Both male and female homeworkers are associated with football stitching. In the case of female homeworkers, their paid work is completely blended with their household work. A female homeworker interviewed during fieldwork reported to have a good working relationship with her subcontractor, who is also a distant relative. She is obliged to him for providing her with work at home. She has some vague idea about the piece rate paid in some other areas, but she justifies the low piece rate she receives due to the provision of work at her place. Her productivity is three balls per day, and her husband stitches one ball per day. She is happy with her work despite having a low income and some health-related problems due to long hours of football stitching. She reported that she has no debt bondage. She does not take advance money in large amounts. Meanwhile, the male home-based stitcher reported dissatisfaction with his work and income. He is tied to football stitching through debt bondage and is not able to switch to some other form of work. The low income and status attached to football stitching makes him desperate to look for alternatives. The male home-based stitcher also reported exploitation by a middleman who was taking advantage due to debt servitude. Incidences of occasional exchanges of harsh words were also reported.

Theoretical Reflections: Porous Boundaries Between Commercial Production and Social Reproduction

The neoliberal model of capitalism and industrial labor markets limits the definition of work mainly to those activities performed for the labor market outside the home as real work and relegating the rest of the work organization to leisure, crime or housework. This definition of work in terms of employment for wage leads to a reductionist classification of the labor force. According to the International Classification of Status in Employment (ICSE), workers can be either classified as self-employed or wage workers and the employment status of the workers is generally gauged on the basis of two legal criteria, namely subordination and economic dependence. There are two indicators of subordination. The first is the disciplinary power of the work provider and the second is that work is performed under the directions of the work provider (Prügl & Tinker, 1997). Thus, a person is considered to be an employee if he or she is subordinated to the work provider in terms of working hours and a particular way to perform work.

The second important criterion for judging the employment status of a worker is economic dependence. It can be measured through certain indicators, for example worker risk-taking behaviour and his or her opportunity for profit and loss. Risk-taking can be measured in terms of investing capital, providing raw materials, hiring employees, refraining from fixing prices in advance and having only short-term relationships with the provider of work. Nonetheless, opportunity for profit or loss can be gauged by having access to a broad market and possessing marketable skills. However, the diversity of activities and the context in which homeworkers are involved make it difficult to mark the conceptual boundaries of homework based on these criteria. This is especially true in the case of female homeworkers, because they are inserted differently into the labour force, due to their socially constructed gender role obligations and the simplistic interpretation of women's work, which bears the risk of neglecting the heterogeneity of their work and its specific relation to the family and production process. They might not fall neatly into specific legal categories, for example. most of the homeworkers are not under the direct supervision of a work provider; therefore, they do not meet the legal criterion of subordination, and legal criteria to determine employment status of homeworkers often lead to ambiguous results. The employment relationships are more complicated, and many homeworkers do not fit into these simple categories. The boundaries between paid work (production) and unpaid work (social reproduction) remain porous for homeworkers. They occupy a distinct niche in the labour market through the distinct organization of their work, which is largely shaped by existing institutional and normative frameworks.

Social institutions in any society are a reflection of the shared ideologies of their members. Ideologies influence the actors to conceive and enact their roles according to the shared expectations. Consequently, normative structures of society play an important role in determining and shaping the individual choices. Existing literature (Haase, Becker, Nill, Shultz, & Gentry, 2016; Naz, 2017; Wilson, 2003) supports that the interplay of markets, gender ideologies and socio-economic organization is of continuing relevance in understanding the women's productive and reproductive work. In *Capital Accumulation and Women's Labour in Asian Economies* (2012), Peter Custer questioned the interplay between capitalism and patriarchy, which naturalize the contribution of women's reproductive labour towards maintaining workers' productive capacities, in rapidly industrializing Asia. Capital accumulation practices in modern capitalist production organizations, at both the local and the global level, rest on the exploitation of cheap wage labour. Cheap informal wage labour, which is easy to hire and fire, increases the profit by creating more surplus value (Kalleberg, 2011). Women provide a cheap and flexible labour force par excellence in an increasingly informalized and segmented labour market, due to prevailing gender ideologies (Barrientos, 2019). The assignment of low-wage strenuous tasks to women in the informal sector under the pretext of being a secondary earner affects their position in the labour market. Possibilities of collective bargaining also remain muted in the case of women as informal workers due to the construction of their work as an extension of their domestic responsibilities.

Gender ideologies are so deep-rooted that the women cannot fully perceive the disempowering impact of these gendered ideologies (framework of ideas). They may fail to appreciate that their "desirable" behaviour is not natural, but rather tends to be socially constructed. In patriarchal societies, gender norms are embedded in such a way that women are not aware that their habitual choices undermine their own position with regard to their own agency, and their rights in the broadest sense. Women see their dis-empowerment as fitting in with morally virtuous and socially appropriate behaviour. Existing gender norms in Pakistan effectively obscure women's labour in capitalist production processes. A parallel may be drawn between the situation of female and male stitchers at various nodes of a global football supply chain in order to understand how female labour is nested in the gendered social matrix in the global production organization. It may also shed some light on the way capitalist practices intersect with the gender ideology of male domination and female subordination in Pakistan affects, remoulds and articulates local social formations in varied ways.

Among various types of gender/sex system that characterize male domination and female subordination, Pakistani society can be characterized as a patriarchal society. The term "patriarchy" is used with different adjectives to describe various forms of male domination that extend even outside the private sphere (private patriarchy) of the household to the public sphere (public patriarchy) of work (Walby, 1992; Wilson, 2003). Female stitchers in the football industry of Pakistan mostly work as homeworkers. There are various social and structural constraints for female stitchers wanting to join factory-based stitching. Firstly, in the normative structure of Pakistani society, women are primarily defined as homemakers. In the gender division of work, women are responsible for managing the household and care work at home and men are defined as breadwinners at the ideological level. The male breadwinner ideology assumes that the husband should be the primary income provider and the wife should be primarily responsible for the reproductive care work of the family and household (Haase et al., 2016). Consequently, men are mostly exempted from household care responsibilities.

Secondly, in the cultural milieu of rural Sialkot as elsewhere in Punjab, women are expected to adhere to the norms of *Purdah* that restrict women's mobility. Thirdly, in the patriarchal structure of Pakistan, the honour of male family members is attached to the females of their family. This also leads to greater control over female mobility, especially young unmarried girls, to guard their morality, not only by the men, but other women as well. How private patriarchy is supported by public patriarchs is put concisely by a respondent during a field interview, when she narrated:

> It is very difficult to establish a stitching centre for girls. It's a great responsibility and parents are also reluctant to send their daughters to stitching centres. Bad conduct of a girl affects the honour of the family. I provide work to girls at their homes. I have my own daughters and I also take care of all those girls to whom I provide work. I always give their stitching money to their mothers, though sometimes they request some money without involving their parents so they can use this money on their own to top up their mobiles. But I always tell them that it's not good. You should not keep mobile phones. It will affect the honour of your family. You know, if I give them money secretly and they do something wrong, their parents will blame me for that, as I provide them with work. (Female subcontractor)

In words of Cumbers, Helms and Swanson (2010), capital and labour are bound up in a dialectical totality. Capitalist practices intersect with the dominant gender ideology in Pakistan on the micro level, producing an "archipelago (of intersecting and) different powers" (Foucault, 1994: 187). Though women have been stitching footballs since 1980s, they did so within their homes; leaving their home or village for paid work is not a very likely scenario for the majority of women. Therefore, it's not a surprising finding that female stitchers are concentrated in home-based stitching and some also work in stitching centres located in their villages. It was evident from the testimonies of respondents that women's mobility is at best extended up to the boundaries of their own village, thus limiting their choices and opportunities for paid work. Women working in village-based female subcentres earn far less than male centre-based stitchers. The average monthly income of male centre-based stitchers ranges between €121.77 and €138.01, whereas the average monthly income of female stitchers is approximately €34.79. A closer look at the qualitative data shows that this huge difference could be attributed to two major factors. First, there is an immense difference in piece rates. Women working in a village-based female stitching centre visited during the field visit reported a very low piece rate compared to their male counterparts in the main male stitching centres (see Table 6.2). Second, major factor that affects women's income level is the low productivity of women. On average, women produce three footballs per day compared to their male counterparts, who produce an average of seven balls per day. However, no difference in the level of skill was found between male and female stitchers. Workers from both genders reported almost the same stitching time that ranges between 60 and 80 minutes per ball depending upon the material used. However, women are at a relative disadvantage in terms of available time, time poverty is also documented in many other studies (ADB, 2015). As women carry the triple burden that includes their household work, community responsibilities along with their paid work, they are left with no other choice but to juggle multiple responsibilities at the same time. Consequently, they do not have more time for their paid work. The normal day of a female homeworker is characterized by constant oscillation between commercial production and social reproduction.

Social obligations of women consume their productive time, whereas men are relatively free of household and community obligations. The ideological construction of men's role as breadwinners spares them from many other obligations. Female workers, who, despite their paid work, are mainly defined as homemakers, are expected to fulfil their household and community obligations even at the cost of their income loss. Broader economic pressures have opened spaces for women in a previously impermissible area of the labour market, because one person's income is not sufficient to meet an entire family's needs. However, there is a cultural lag, and the normative structure has still not adjusted to new realities. Despite the fact that women are contributing substantial amounts to family budgets, their contributions are undermined by using various gender discourses that relegate their contributions to the realm of extended household obligations of good mothers, wives and daughters, working for the family welfare without challenging the breadwinner ideology or gender division of labour at the household level.

It was evident from the testimonies of female stitchers that their paid work did not relieve them of their other household or community obligations. Their household work is at best shared by other females of the family. In cases where there is no other female at home, the entire burden of household work rests on a female who has to balance her paid and unpaid work. Consequently, the working day of women is relatively much longer than that of the men and does not include a break. Their working day starts earlier and ends later. Following excerpts from an interview show how women are balancing their paid and unpaid work and, in this process, are stretching themselves to their limits.

> I get up early in the morning around 6 am and prepare breakfast for my son and husband. Then I do other household work like cleaning, dish washing, etc. Around 10 am I start stitching footballs and mostly work till 4pm. Then I cook a meal for my family. After that I continue stitching footballs. I usually work till 10 or 11 pm. As I have a backache problem, it is hard for me to sit for a long time, so I have to take a short break after every three or four hours. (Shazia, homeworker)

It was evident from the interviews of female stitchers that married women with grown-up children are in a better position to work in stitching centres compared to young unmarried female stitchers or female stitchers with small children. The testimonies of the respondents clearly show that each woman occupies a unique position at different vectors of class, age, marital status and so on. Consequently, constraints on female mobility are different for women of different age categories. In response to questions about the value of their work, respondents agree on the fact that though it is low paid work, it is better than nothing. At least, cash income from their work helps them to meet *some* of their everyday needs.

Despite the precarious nature of homework, debate remains over the extent to which homeworkers are passive victims of global capital or have agency (Kabeer, 2000). Building on Katz's (2004) work, which breaks down agency into acts of resilience, reworking and resistance, this study supports existing literature (Carswell & De Neve, 2013; Coe & Jordhus-Lier, 2010; Cumbers et al., 2010; Lund-Thomsen & Coe, 2015) that spectrum of agency extends beyond overt and organized protests and counter-hegemonic acts. Agency is also reflected through various creative strategies which help people to live their everyday lives and shape opportunities and possibilities for themselves in the face of oppressive regimes. Access to paid work open up avenues of economic independence, which entails a possibility to provide an avenue for exiting the patriarchal confines (Kabeer, 2000).

In the rural cultural milieu of Pakistani society, restriction on women's work in the public sphere is a symbol of family status. This value is widely shared, and women are not allowed by their male family members to work in centres or in factories due to the visibility of such work. Therefore, they are left with no other choice but to work as homeworkers at lower rates. Homeworkers are the lowest-paid group of football stitchers. A homeworker interviewed during the field visit reported that she is not allowed to work outside the home. Even working as a homeworker is stigmatized in the community, though it is accepted by her husband's family. She is thankful to her husband for allowing her to work despite the fact that he has to face sarcastic remarks from his friends that he cannot provide for his wife. She attaches positive value to her work and considers her paid work as a source of her higher self-esteem and less conflicts within the household.

> My brother is well to do and doesn't want me to stitch football. He asks me why I do this work, if I need money, I should ask him. But you know it is not easy to ask for money, even from brother. If I ask for my needs from my parents it is again disobedience of my husband. They will think that he is not able to provide my needs. It is good that I get work at home otherwise I am sitting idle all the time. Now I have my own money that I can use for my own and my family's needs. (Shazia, homeworker)

It was evident from the responses of the female homeworker that she is working due to the economic situation of her family, but she tries to frame her paid work in a culturally acceptable frame of dutiful and obedient wife (patriarchal bargains). This indicates a clear gap between living realities of individuals and the value they hold and share with the wider society and how they try to bridge this gap by framing their actions in a counter factual manner. Women's paid work reflects on the hegemonic masculine identity of a *breadwinner*; therefore, to gain acceptance, women frame their work as *pin money* (Mies, 1982) earned as a free-time activity.

Such a construction of homework ultimately undermines their contribution at both the household level and at the level of society at large. Female homeworkers are earning even less than male homeworkers, who are relatively more mobile and better able to look for alternatives. They are not tied to their households the way women are due to their gender role obligations. They can combine football stitching with other forms of paid work to increase their overall income.

> I am now 40 years old and I started stitching footballs at the age of 15 as part of my family tradition. However, over the years, the value of this work has decreased due to low income. It is no longer as socially valuable as it used to be in the past when I started this work. People now call us "Footballia". I want to leave this work and want to work as a house painter as that is relatively well paid but I cannot leave this work. I took the advance money at the time of my brother's marriage from my maker, and I am not able to settle yet. I shall pay back this debt and leave this work forever. I want to get married and have a family that is not possible with the income from football stitching. (Rasheed, male homeworker)

However, the way masculinity is constructed and articulated in the social and cultural context of Pakistan, it exerts great pressure on male homeworkers, who find it hard to perform their hegemonic masculine identity of a breadwinner. A male homeworker interviewed during data collection finds it hard to resolve this tension and expresses high levels of dissatisfaction with his work and wages. Male homeworkers are working at the lower end of the supply chain within the private sphere of the household, which is considered as a female domain and is separated from the public domain of work.

Although male homeworkers are not required to do household work, it was an interesting observation that the productivity of the male homeworkers was equal to the average output of female homeworkers. The reported reason for low productivity was the low piece rate that acted as a demotivating factor for male homeworkers, who prefer to do other forms of paid work and stitch footballs as a part-time activity due to debt bondage. Men having a relatively larger horizon of mobility combine football stitching with other forms of paid work. It was evident from the responses of football stitchers that gender ideologies interact with the existing market ideologies in a way that has differential and gendered outcomes for different actors located at various nodes of the football supply chain. The complexity of the homeworkers' situation demands for a definition embedded in the economic, political and social environment of home-based work in order to make a larger number of homeworkers, a special category of home-based workers, visible in the political economy of production relations. In order to understand the effect of homework on the well-being of female homeworkers, we must include their unheard voices into the existing debate about outcome of labour market participation through informal industrial homework, performed at crossroads of production and social reproduction. Chapter 7 will conceptualize and examine in more depth the well-being of homeworkers from their perspective.

Concluding Thoughts

The political and economic spheres are mutually constitutive within the context of social relations. The feminist political economy perspective provides a distinctive ontology and epistemology to view homework from the vantage point of different actors across different social and historical contexts. The fundamental question that needs to be asked in the case of homeworkers is, in what ways are female homeworkers rendered invisible by the economic and political discourses? Amoore (2002) argued that the reorganization of work in a global capitalist system is not unproblematic or inevitable and it becomes manifested in, and contested through, diverse social practices and experiences of workers, particularly unprotected or unrepresented workers like home-based workers, whose voices are unheard in global restructuring discourses. These are the sites where work and political contestation is taking place in the global political economy. In order to understand the positioning of female homeworkers in the global production system and international division of employment, we need to go beyond the existing order and have to consider the historical, political, geographical and social relationships that female homeworkers have with one another, and with the production processes and political geography of work.

References

ADB. (2015). *Balancing the Burden? Desk Review of Women's Time Poverty and Infrastructure in Asia and Pacific*. Retrieved from http://www.adb.org/sites/default/files/publication/177465/sdcc-balancing-burden.pdf

Amoore, L. (2002). *Globalisation Contested: An International Political Economy of Work*. Manchester: Manchester University Press.

Andersson, D. E. & Andersson, Å. E. (2017). *Time, Space, and Capital*. Cheltenham: Edward Elgar.

Barrientos, S. (2019). *Gender and Work in Global Value Chains: Capturing the Gains?* Cambridge: Cambridge University Press.

Beddewela, E., & Fairbrass, J. (2015). Seeking Legitimacy Through CSR: Institutional Pressures and Corporate Responses of Multinationals in Sri Lanka. *Journal of Business Ethics, 136*(3), 503–522.

Castells, M. (2010). The Information Age. Economy, Society, and Culture. *Vol. I: The Rise of the Net-work Society*. Oxford: Wiley-Blackwell.

Carswell, G., & De Neve, G. (2013). Labouring for Global Markets: Conceptualising Labour Agency in Global Production Networks. *Geoforum, 44*, 62–70.

Coe, N., & Jordhus-Lier, D. (2010). Constrained Agency? Re-evaluating the Geographies of Labour. *Progress in Human Geography*: 1–23. https://doi.org/10.1177/0309132510366746

Cumbers, A., Helms, G., & Swanson, K. (2010). Class, Agency and Resistance in the Old Industrial City. *Antipode, 42*(1), 46–73. https://doi.org/10.1111/j.1467-8330.2009.00731.x

Custers, P. (2012). *Capital Accumulation and Women's Labour in Asian Economies*. London: Zed Books.

Douglass, N. (1991). *Institutions, Institutional Change, and Economic Performance*. Cambridge: Cambridge University Press.

Fayyaz, A. (2011). *Collective Success Or Collective Failure? The Sialkot Football Manufacturing Industry's Response to International Labor Standards Pressures in the Early 21st Century*. A Paper Presented at ICSB World Conference Proceedings, Washington, DC.

Fayyaz, A., Lund-Thomsen, P., & Lindgreen, A. J. (2015). Industrial Clusters and CSR in Developing Countries: The Role of International Donor Funding. *Journal of Business Ethics*. https://doi.org/10.1007/s10551-015-2940-6

Foucault, M. (1994). *The Order of Things: An Archaeology of the Human Sciences*. New York: Vintage Books.

Gereffi, G. (2005). The Global Economy: Organization, Governance, and Development. In N. J. Smelser & R. Swedberg (Eds.), *The Handbook of Economic Sociology* (2nd ed., pp. 160–182). Princeton, NJ: Princeton University Press.

Guzi, M. (2013). *Estimating living wage globally - 65 countries*. Retrieved from http://www.wageindicator.org/documents/publicationslist/publications-2013/Estimating%20Living%20Wage%20Globally_201311.pdf

Haase, M., Becker, I., Nill, A., Shultz, C. J., & Gentry, J. W. (2016). Male Breadwinner Ideology and the Inclination to Establish Market Relationships: Model Development Using Data from Germany and a Mixed-Methods Research Strategy. *Journal of Journal of Macromarketing, 36*(2), 149–167. https://doi.org/10.1177/0276146715576202

ILO. (2012). *International Standard Classification of Occupations: Structure, Group Definitions and Correspondence Tables (ISCO-08)*. Geneva, Switzerland. Retrieved from http://www.ilo.org/wcmsp5/groups/public/%2D%2D-dgreports/%2D%2D-dcomm/%2D%2D-publ/documents/publication/wcms_172572.pdf

Jenkins, R. (2005). Globalization, Corporate Social Responsibility and Poverty. *International Affairs, 81*(3), 525–540.

Jin, D. (2016). The Great Knowledge Transcendence. *The Rise of Western Science and Technology Reframed.* New York: Palgrave Macmillan.

Kabeer, N. (2000). *Discussing Women's Empowerment: Theory and Evidence.* Stockholm: Swedish International Development Cooperation Agency.

Kalleberg, A. L. (2011). *Good Jobs, Bad Jobs: The Rise of Polarized and Precarious Employment Systems in the United States, 1970's to 2000's.* New York, NY: American Sociological Association.

Katz, C. (2004). *Growing Up Global: Economic Restructuring and Children's Everyday Lives.* Minneapolis: University of Minnesota Press.

Lund-Thomsen, P. (2012). Labor Agency in the Football Manufacturing Industry of Sialkot, Pakistan. *Geoforum, 44,* 71–81.

Lund-Thomsen, P., & Coe, N. M. (2015). Corporate Social Responsibility and Labour Agency: The Case of Nike in Pakistan. *Journal of Economic Geography, 15*(16), 1–22. https://doi.org/10.1093/jeg/lbt041

Lund-Thomsen, P., & Nadvi, K. (2010). Clusters, Chains and Compliance: Corporate Social Responsibility and Governance in Football Manufacturing in South Asia. *Journal of Business Ethics, 93*(2), 201–222. https://doi.org/10.1007/s10551-010-0561-7

Lund-Thomsen, P., Nadvi, K., Chan, A., Khara, N., & Xue, H. (2012). Labour in Global Value Chains: Work Conditions in Football Manufacturing in China, India and Pakistan. *Development and Change, 43*(6), 1211–1237.

Mies, M. (1982). *The Lace Makers of Narsapur: Indian House Wives Produce for the Global Market.* London: Zed Press.

Mokyr, J. (2002). The Gifts of Athena. *Historical Origins of the Knowledge Economy.* Princeton: Princeton University Press.

Nadvi, K., Lund-Thomsen, P., Xue, H., & Khara, N. (2011). Playing Against China: Global Value Chains and Labour Standards in the International Sports Goods Industry. *Global Networks, 11*(3), 334–354. https://doi.org/10.1111/j.1471-0374.2011.00329.x

Naz, F. (2017). The Position of Female Homeworkers in a Global Supply Chain: How do Capitalist Labor Market Practices Interplay with Gender ideologies? In M. Haase (Ed.), *The Changing Basis of Economic Responsibility: A Look from the Perspective of Today* (pp. 125–147). Berlin: Springer. pp. 125–147.

Naz, F., & Boegenhold, D. (2020). Understanding Labour Processes in Global Production Networks: A Case Study of the Football Industry in Pakistan. *Globalization.* https://doi.org/10.1080/14747731.2019.1708658

Pellegrini, M. M., Rialti, R., Marzi, G., & Caputo, A. (2020). Sport Entrepreneurship: A Synthesis of Existing Literature and Future Perspectives. *International Entrepreneurship and Management Journal, 16,* 1–32.

PILER. (2009). *Labour Standards in Football Manufacturing Industry: A Case Study of a Nike Vendor in Sialkot, Pakistan*. Karachi, Pakistan. Retrieved from http://www.piler.org.pk/images/pdf/Labour%20Standards%20in%20Football%20Manufacturing%20Industry%20A%20Case%20Study%20of%20a%20Nike%20Vendor%20in%20Sialkot.pdf

Polanyi, K. (2001). *The Great Transformation: The Political and Economic Origins of Our Time*. Foreword by Joseph E. Stiglitz. Boston: Beacon Press.

Prügl, E., & Tinker, I. (1997). Microentrepreneurs and Homeworkers: Convergent Categories. *World Development, 25*(9), 1471–1482. https://doi.org/10.1016/S0305-750X(97)00043-0

Punjab Skill Development Fund. (2016). *Sports Goods Manufacturing Sector Skills Study*. Retrieved from https://www.psdf.org.pk/wp-content/uploads/2018/11/Final-Report-PSDF-Sports-Goods-Sector-Skills-Study.pdf

Ratten, V. (2018). *Sport Entrepreneurship: Developing and Sustaining an Entrepreneurial Sports Culture*. Melbourne: Springer.

Seigmann, K. A. (2008). Soccer Ball Production for Nike. *Economic and Political Weekly, 43*(22), 57–64.

Sweet, S., & Meiksins, S. (2017). *Changing Contours of Work: Jobs and Opportunities in the New Economy*. Los Angeles: Sage.

UNIDO. (2009). *Global Value Chains, Local Clusters and Corporate Social Responsibility: A Comparative Assessment of the Sports Goods Clusters in Sialkot, Pakistan and Jalandhar, India*. Technical Paper No. 17. Vienna: United Nations Industrial Development Organization. Retrieved from https://www.unido.org/uploads/tx_templavoila/Global_value_chains_local_clusters_and_CSR.pdf

Walby, S. (1992). *Theorizing Patriarchy*. Oxford, UK: Basil Blackwell Ltd.

Wilson, T. D. (2003). Forms of Male Domination and Female Subordination: Homeworkers versus Maquiladora Workers in Mexico. *Review of Radical Political Economics, 35*(1), 56–72. https://doi.org/10.1177/0486613402250194

Xue, H., & Chan, A. (2013). The Global Value Chain: Value for Whom? The Soccer Ball Industry in China and Pakistan. *Critical Asian Studies, 45*(1), 55–77.

CHAPTER 7

Unheard Voices: Globalization Stories from Invisible Margins

Introduction

It has become a common-sense way of thinking that division of resources within household can be used to enhance the well-being of women in society. Power dynamics within family exert influence on decision-making processes as well as distribution of resources within households. Consequently, in mainstream gender and development discourse,[1] access to paid work is often proposed as a *solution* to tackle the issue of gender inequality (Radcliffe, 2015), but, most of these discussions are embedded in Western liberal philosophical tradition that cherishes enlightened values and lay great emphases on individual actors, rational scientific perspectives and democratic processes. This essentialist perspective may limit our ability to understand the lifeworlds of women whose values have been shaped by non-liberal traditions. Sen (1987) argued that women in traditional societies might not speak up the way liberal economic tradition assumes. They do not think in terms of their individual self-interest; rather, they have an entirely different understanding of the self. He argues that to empower women we need to give women not only resources but also their own sense of individual value. This sense of individual value will help them to find the voice and resist against gender inequality at household level. However, it is important at this point to understand that Western liberal

[1] This discourse is largely built on three important philosophical traditions, namely liberal feminism, colonial development discourse and neoclassical economic theorizing.

F. Naz, D. Bögenhold, *Unheard Voices*,
https://doi.org/10.1007/978-3-030-54363-1_7

tradition were his explanatory framework. Rather than thinking about agency in terms of social context that value interconnectedness and solidarity, he too treated women as autonomous, self-interested subjects.

Here we argued that measuring the well-being of these women through pre-existing analytical categories might produce disembodied voices without context (Cornwall, 2007). Therefore, it is important to investigate as to what extent these pre-existing analytical categories such as agency and well-being, associated with paid work, resonate with the goals and living realities of female homeworkers in global south. To understand their lives, we have to recognize the meaning assigned to homework by homeworkers themselves. This will require a more nuanced and grounded understanding of well-being. Because speaking on their behalf would recreate the same power hierarchies and inequalities that feminist political economy is trying to dismantle. Therefore, in this chapter we have explored the narrative life stories of female homeworkers to understand the meaning and relevance of invisible homework in their lives. Sen's capability approach (CA) has been used as an analytical framework to conceptualize the well-being of homeworkers in global football supply chains.

Mills (1959: 248) states that narratives help to build a connection between *personal troubles* and *public issues*. It is important to acknowledge at this point that these narrative life histories are a collaborative construction of the respondent, the researcher and the reader as well. Though data generated through singular and particular life histories is noisier and may not lead to generalization, it is nonetheless an effective means to bring out the tensions and contradictions of real-life situations (Bathmaker & Harnett, 2010). Context-based individual life histories may help to understand the complex interrelationships. The narrative life history account of female homeworkers in the following section aims at exploring the detail of everyday life homeworkers to gain diversity of insight about the well-being of female home-based workers in the football supply chains. The multidimensionality of well-being is a key red thread that runs through the entire chapter in order to get closer to how female homeworkers experience or construct their own sense of well-being. It is central to the analysis of this inquiry to go a step further and explore how, in the words of Mills (1959), smaller milieux interact with larger structures.

Conceptualizing Human Well-being Through Lens of CA

Disenchantment with traditional income-based measures of well-being in recent years has led to the search for alternative measures of well-being (Binder, 2013). There were many unanswered questions in the basic need approach that led Sen to shift his focus from goods to people. Fundamental questions that posed a serious challenge to the basic need approach were, for example, the following: What are basic needs? Are they the same for everyone at every time? Is consumption at or above some basic level all that we want for people? How do we justify entitlements and what determines these entitlements? (Pressman & Summerfield, 2000) In attempting to address these issues, Sen developed the concept of capabilities, that is, what a person is able to do or be that has intrinsic value in life as compared to the goods that provide instrumental value or utility. Sen tried to expand the basic need approach.

According to Sen, people's ability to do things matters more for their well-being than what people can buy with their income. He argued that development could best be explained as a process of expansion of capabilities of people (Sen, 1983). Thus, freedom and agency to choose have intrinsic value for a good life. The distinction between the notion of functionings (bare achievement) and capabilities (opportunity or freedom) deserves attention. Sen has paid more attention to the notion of capabilities than that of functionings while discussing well-being. Therefore, within Sen's framework, any account of human well-being and development can be seen in the evaluative space of capabilities or functioning (Clark, 2005). Converting capabilities into social functioning is mediated through many social and personal factors.

One major contribution of the capabilities approach is to recognize a different anthropological model, which respects human diversity and is sensitive to pluralism rather than reducing human beings to their utility function. While a utilitarian measure of human welfare would regard a person, for example a divorced woman, to be worse off in terms of economic security, the CA can show that with greater freedom and greater choice, her welfare may have increased (Pressman & Summerfield, 2000). As Sen has stressed continuously, there are many things besides income that create utility or well-being. According to the capabilities approach, deprivation means a lack of certain capabilities, and so the "wealthy but not healthy" may be counted as poor. For Sen, income is not an end in itself, and the end is to increase the functionings and capabilities of people (Pressman & Summerfield, 2000).

Although Sen has not given a definitive list of capabilities, he has mentioned some basic capabilities like basic liberties, freedom of movement, freedom of association and freedom of occupational choice against a background of diverse opportunities; positions of responsibility in political and economic institutions; income and wealth; and the social bases of self-respect. Development could best be explained in terms of these human capabilities (Qizilbash, 2002). Seen from Sen's perspective, well-being is about the expansion of capabilities, that is, to improve human lives by expanding the range of things that a person can be and do, such as to be healthy and well-nourished, to be knowledgeable and to participate in community life. Sen's CA is a perspective that respects human diversity in the assessment of well-being. However, this stance of CA on human diversity poses serious challenges to the application of CA in the assessment of well-being. The existence of empirical diversity renders generalizations less obvious, but the selection of capabilities implies making generalizations and comparisons. However, one of the most difficult tasks in applying the capabilities approach for empirical analysis is deciding which capabilities are most important, as there is a wide range of human capabilities and their relevance or value varies with social context—from one community or country to another, and from one point of time to another. For Sen, each list of capabilities must be context specific, and the context is both the geographical area to which it applies and the sort of evaluation that is performed. What follows is an attempt to evaluate well-being of homeworkers through prism of context-specific capabilities (Naz & Bögenhold, 2020), by analysing the life stories of homeworkers.

Life as Lived: Fahmida's Story

Fahmida had been stitching footballs for 18 years at the time her interview was conducted. Her father Ibrahim worked at the handloom throughout his life, and they were settled in Kammokee, a small town in central Punjab. Her mother, like many women of her generation in Pakistan, was a housewife. She had no formal education and used to work from home to raise additional income for her family by using her traditional skills that she learned as part of her gender role training. She used to do hand embroidery on *dupattas* (a large piece of fabric used by females in Pakistan to cover their head and a symbol of modesty in the cultural milieu). She also spun cotton on a spindle wheel to make threads that were used on handlooms for making traditional fabric for local use. At that time, handlooms were common in rural areas and were considered as traditional family crafts passed down from one generation to the next. So, weaving and spinning were the crafts that women had to be skilled at in these weaver families. Women work as unpaid workers in these home-based enterprises owned and managed by male family members. However, with the advent of power looms, this traditional craft gradually became irrelevant in the context of the rural economy of Pakistan over the years. Fahmida had two brothers and six sisters. She lived in a joint family with her parents and grandparents. Fahmida was the eldest child in the family and had no schooling as she was not allowed by her grandfather to attend the school. In the traditional joint family system of Pakistan, elder male members had more authority and decision-making power. If she had been born in a different era or social class, Fahmida might have gone to school and would have a different life story to tell. Instead, she learnt the traditional crafts of embroidery, and used to do hand embroidery on dresses, attach fancy glass pieces and make bed sheets to raise some income for her family. However, she was able to convince her grandfather to change their family tradition and allow her two youngest sisters to attend school. She considered it as her accomplishment that she was able to send her sisters to school and that one of them had at least primary education and the other one had an education till the eighth grade. She proudly narrated, "I told my grandfather that my time has gone but now it is important for children to get an education. Children should have at least some education." She recalled her childhood with fond memories of her loving parents and grandparents who always took care of her needs. She got married at the age of 20 to her cousin who lived in another small village in Sialkot. This was an arranged marriage decided by her parents. When asked about her feeling about her marriage decision, she simply responded:

I was not asked and my parents themselves decided about my marriage partner. I do not have any objection because one has to marry where one's parents want one. (Source: Excerpt from interview)

She moved to her husband's town after marriage and had been living in the same vicinity for the last 24–25 years. Her in-laws were also weavers, and, like her mother, her mother-in-law also used to spin cotton and her father-in-law worked on handlooms. Her husband was a daily wage labourer, and they lived in a combined family. Her two sisters-in-law worked in a football-stitching centre that was established in the same village. Fahmida was mainly responsible for unpaid household work in her joint family, which was comprised of ten members, and she devoted herself to homemaking and child-rearing. However, in her spare time, she also helped her sisters-in-law to stitch footballs that they used to bring home from their stitching centre and finally mastered the skill over the years. And yet, she worked from home and did not go to the stitching centre because of her household responsibilities and two daughters who needed to be taken care of. Her sisters-in-law brought work for her from the stitching centre. For the initial five years of her marriage, she was mostly doing it as a part-time activity to earn some income and not on a regular basis, because in the joint family system resources were combined and elder family members were responsible to manage household expenditures from resources pooled by all seven brothers and sisters and their parents as well. Therefore, the responsibility and economic burden was shared. Later on, when her sisters-in-law got married and the stitching centre was also closed in their village, she had to look for some other supplier. Fahmida was in her early 30s when she moved into her new home after ten years of marriage. By then her brothers-in-law were also married; hence, their old home was no longer large enough to accommodate them all. Being the eldest in the family, her husband decided to move out with his family. This switch in the family system was an important turn in Fahmida's life, which was now marked with a sense of independence as well as new responsibilities. As she expressed in her own words:

> I was happy in that house too but now I feel even happier because now we manage our own life . . . This is better because now we ourselves are responsible . . . at that time there was no such responsibility. (Source: Excerpt from interview)

Her husband was working as a daily wage labourer, and they had a large family. They were resource-constrained to buy a house according to their family's needs. They had seven children, three daughters and four sons. They were able to afford a small one-room house for the entire family; this was usual for people from same socio-economic stratum in their community. To meet the economic needs of a large family, one person's income was not sufficient. Consequently, Fahmida started football stitching at a regular basis, though her husband was the main provider at that time. It was important for her to raise additional income, because, despite her poor economic situation, she insisted that her children should get education. As her sisters-in-law who provided her work got married and moved to another town, she had to look for some other supplier. Her neighbour introduced her to a subcontractor who provided work to home-based workers and she started to work for him. The situation became further exacerbated for her family, when her husband had an accident that caused serious leg injuries.

He was not able to work, and the responsibility to provide for the family shifted entirely to Fahmida. Her husband was bed-ridden, and she needed money not only to cover her family's expenditure but also for the medical treatment of her husband. In the absence of any social protection or security mechanism and poor state health facilities, it is hard for poor families to afford medical expenditures. Fahmida was not able to earn enough money through her football stitching to meet the economic needs of her family. She got some financial support from her brothers during this critical time, which she recalls with great gratitude and affection. However, she had to make a critical decision to put food on their kitchen table. She taught her elder daughters to stitch footballs. The family was a strong cohesive unit, and the two elder daughters followed their mother's example. At that time they were in grades 8 and 7, respectively, but they had to leave their school and help her mother to stitch footballs full-time to increase their family income.

There were possibilities to work in factories as a stitcher or in stitching centres established in various locations, but Fahmida was not willing to send her daughters to a factory or to the stitching centre. She expressed her sense of insecurity and personal fears related to factory-based work. So, she preferred for herself and her daughters to work from home. Fahmida, along with her two daughters, was able to produce on average 12 balls per day, and with this income they managed their family budget. Though the education of her elder daughters was compromised in the process, which Fahmida regretted very much, with their income she was able to support the education of her five younger children. At the time of the interview, her husband had recovered from his leg injury and was working as day labourer again, but the nature of his work was irregular and there was no guarantee of the continuity of his work. Therefore, for their family, the major regular source of income was football stitching in their constant and ongoing struggle of life.

Life as Lived: Saira's Story

Saira, a 26-year-old young unmarried girl, has been working as football stitcher since the age of 14. She does not remember exactly when she started stitching footballs, but she reports having 15 or 16 years of experience of football stitching. She started to stitch footballs approximately at the age of ten or even earlier. She learned to stitch footballs from her neighbours. She said that at that time her neighbours were using the space on top of their roof to stitch footballs, and she watched them stitching after school and on Sundays. Her mother, who was working as a midwife at the time of the interview, also used to work as a football stitcher in a local football stitching centre and later on started working as a midwife. Saira's father was a chef who worked for people in the community catering for various events like marriage ceremonies or some other events. However, the nature of his work was not regular and was mostly seasonal. They had a large family size, and Saira lived in a one-room house with her parents and six siblings. She said that her father was very devoted and loving and wanted to provide a good education to his children. However, due to his illness he was not able to work properly, and this resulted in a serious financial crisis for their family. Though her mother was also working in a football stitching centre, nevertheless their income was not sufficient for the family's needs in the absence of any other social protection mechanism. Due to the illness of her father, it became difficult for her mother to continue her work at the centre, because she had to come back from the centre to manage household work and attend to guests and look after her husband. Consequently, she switched from centre-based stitching to home-based stitching and at a later stage left this work and started serving as informal midwife in the community. At that time Saira was in the eighth grade. She realized that her education was an additional cost for her family and she must do something to support her family in this time of crisis. By that time she had already acquired the skill of football stitching, and decided to leave her schooling and join her mother in her struggle for the family's survival. She narrated that when she left school, she had a clear idea of what she would do to provide support to her family. She started working in the same stitching centre where her mother used to work. This was a mixed stitching centre, though the number of boys in the centre was just three and there were more than thirty girls working for the centre. Her stitching centre was in the same village and located at walking distance from her home, so for her it was not a problem to go there. In the morning, she was escorted by her mother, and as there were many other women from the village working in the centre, they came back as a group in the evening. It is important to note at this point that in the cultural context of Pakistan, women's mobility is somewhat restricted and often they are escorted by some male family member in a public sphere. In the case of the absence of a male family member, as was the case for Saira, because her father was sick and her brothers were the youngest in the family, mothers or older women in the family escort young girls. There are various ways mobility issues are navigated by women. Saira worked at the centre from 7 am to 4 pm; however, the timing was relatively flexible, as they were paid on a piece-rate basis. It was in their own interest to spend more time to earn better wages; so, there was an inbuilt pressure due to the nature and conditions of work. She worked in that centre for approximately four years, but had to leave her work due to her serious health issues. She developed a cyst in her abdomen that had to be removed. Although she was working with the centre that entitled her to health coverage, she did not have proper information on how to access that. She asked the centre supervisor for help, but she was informed that this was time consuming and that she was required to go to various offices in Sialkot to get approval for the procedure. She did not have any experience of that and neither did her parents; therefore, her father decided to get her treatment done in a private hospital and bear the expenses. Saira said:

> Yes, there were health benefits, but as I told you before that they used to tell me that to get money you have to go to various offices multiple times, so my father decided that it is better to go to a private hospital. (Source: Excerpt from interview)

She was not able to get the medical coverage that she was entitled to due to lack of information and clear guidelines about gaining access. After having a surgery, it was difficult for her to continue football stitching. She left this work for two years, and during this time her sister left her schooling and started football stitching to compensate for the loss of family income. Two years after her surgery, Saira started football stitching again. Though she had an offer, she declined to work with her previous stitching centre, and this time she started working with a new subcontractor under new work arrangements. She started working with a centre, but as a homeworker. This was an interesting arrangement, as she was practically a homeworker; however, in order to get work she was bound to go to a centre once a month or so, when there was an inspection by an ILO team. When asked about this arrangement, she explained that there was no difference in the rate between working at home or at a centre; therefore, she preferred to work from home, and this was the unanimous decision of the workers. So, she was working for a centre that existed on paper, but not on the ground in real terms.

During inspection, some girls are told in advance how to respond to the questions of the inspectors. They are asked about the work conditions, piece rate and other benefits, and they report what they are instructed to say by their supervisor. In response to the question as to why they did not report the actual piece rate and conditions to the inspectors, she gave a very convincing logic"

> We tell them ...? ... we have to work and if they will close the centre then what we will do? So we tell them that we work in the centre and have access to all facilities and we get fair wages as well. (Source: Excerpt from interview)

She is able to earn 2000 to 3000 PKR per week, and some deductions are also made as repair money that brings down her overall income. The approximate deduction from an income around 3000 PKR is about 250 to 300 PKR. She also has some other expenditure like the purchase of wax used on thread and the purchase of some equipment like a wooden frame and punching machine and so on. Her mother is responsible for making the purchases and running the family budget. Saira and her sister hand over their income to their mother, who is responsible for managing it.

As her mother has to go outside the home for her work, Saira and her sister manage all household work, and they juggle between their paid work and their unpaid household tasks for social reproduction.

> We complete our household tasks in the morning and then sit down to do football stitching. I sit from the early morning and my sister first completes household tasks and then joins me in stitching. And when we finish football stitching then we prepare dinner for the family in the evening. (Source: Excerpt from interview)

Her younger siblings attend school; four of them are in public schools, and the youngest sister is in a private school that is more expensive in terms of school fees and related expenditures. Saira was engaged and her fiancé lived in a nearby village at the time of the interview. She was not sure if she would be able to continue her paid work. However, she was concerned about her parents, worrying that after her marriage they would have financial issues, because she was the one who was contributing a major portion to the family budget.

Life as Lived: Shazia's Story

Shazia is a 29-year-old married woman. Her body stature is very lean (weak). She has been married for the last ten years and has no biological offspring. She adopted a son from her sister-in-law. He is 12 years of age and a student of the fifth grade. She wants to provide him with an education at least up to high school or intermediate level. She also aspires to provide him with a religious education so that he can become a Qari (Quran teacher). His age at the time of adoption was 2 years. Shazia lives in a single-room house with her husband and her adopted son. Her house is also her place of work. Her husband owns a donkey cart and works on a daily basis; however, there is no guarantee that he will get work every day. Before switching to daily work (*dehari*) he was also stitching footballs at home. But her husband had to quit football stitching because the overall income from full-time stitching was comparatively low, as he had backache problems and was not able to sit for long stretches of time, which is required in football stitching. Her husband does not have a stable source of income. Therefore, she decided to learn how to stitch balls from her husband to support him. Shazia constructs her personal identity as a good wife. She perceives her contribution to her family budget as part of her gender role obligations to support her husband. Her desire in life is to have her own child and she is undergoing treatment for that too. She perceives her work as a positive activity that not only provides additional income for her family, but is also a source of her high self-esteem. She is happy that she no longer needs to ask her parents or husband for money. She also thinks that her request for money to her parents is a kind of challenge to her husband's masculine identity as a provider. Shazia stitches three balls per day and her husband also stitches one ball, mostly at night, so their productivity per day is four balls. Ball rates fluctuate from Rs 32 to 55, and she is not in a position to negotiate ball rates with her subcontractor for two different reasons, according to her. Firstly, he is male and she cannot bargain with him due to cultural expectations of female docility, and, secondly, she has no other alternative. They also save a portion of their money in a local informal community saving scheme called *commette*.

They use these savings for covering household needs. Shazia is able to get work throughout the year and thinks that football stitching is a stable source of income for her family. Her working day is relatively long. She gets up at 6 am and completes her household chores like cooking, cleaning and so on. by 10 am. From 10 am to 4 pm, she stitches footballs. Then she prepares dinner and again stitches balls at night till her work is finished. Mostly she works till 10 or 11 pm. As she had a back injury in the past, it is hard for her to sit for long hours, but she manages by having short breaks after three or four hours. But, due to constant work, she suffers from back- and hand aches. She has to complete her order within a week and she has to manage her other responsibilities accordingly. Sometimes she has to work longer hours to complete the number of balls that she has to deliver. She is aware that she is getting a low rate, but feels obliged to her subcontractor who provides her work at home. Her justification for accepting low wages is that it is compensation for delivery cost and time, and she also believed that there is no use of protest. She is working due to economic reasons and believes that there are no chances of her upward mobility on the professional ladder due to the low prestige and stigma associated with football stitching. She does not have any contact with other homeworkers except her family members involved in football stitching.

Life as Lived: Shama's Story

Shama is a 50-year-old married women and mother of six children. Her husband is ex-army personnel. He has been paralysed for the last nine years and in bed for the last five years. Her family's economic situation got worse due to the health situation of her husband, who was the sole earner in the family. As there was no other source of income, Shama started to stitch footballs, and, at the same time, she also worked as an agent for a subcontractor to outsource work to homeworkers. Although her husband gets some pension from the state, this income is not sufficient for the family's needs. They also need additional money for her husband's health-related expenditure, though he is entitled to free medical treatment and medicine from military hospitals. However, the combined military hospital (CMH) is in Sialkot city, and they have to bear travel expenses to get his medicine. She also has to provide for her children's education. She has three schoolgoing children. Her elder daughters, who used to help her in stitching and household chores, are married now and live with their in-laws. Therefore, she is responsible for household work, care work of her husband and also her paid work. As part of her responsibility as an agent to a subcontractor, she looks after the centre and counts and checks stitched balls at the centre. She checks balls for defects by inflating each ball. She also delivers balls to homes to women who are not able or willing to work at the centre, though, officially, companies ban home-based work. She receives Rs 5 commission per ball for all these services. In addition to the commission she also stitches footballs. Her productivity is two balls per day. Money that she earns from both these sources is not sufficient for her family needs. She is managing her expenditure thanks to some informal social support mechanisms in the community. For example, the school expenditure of her daughter is met by her daughter's school teachers. She believes that the situation in the football industry is deteriorating over the years and her income level is going down accordingly. There used to be more female football stitchers in her team, and they were able to produce 100 balls per day; so, her commission was Rs 500 per day. With this income, together with money from her stitching work, she was able to manage well. However, the number of her stitchers has reduced from 45 to just 6 and accordingly her income has fallen from 600 PKR per day to 160 PKR per day. Most of the girls who stitched footballs for her have now moved to a nearby glove factory. Those that are left in stitching are not able to go out for work due to their domestic responsibilities or some other reasons. She is also facing competition from another lady in her village who is supplying work to homeworkers. Although her opponent pays a relatively lower piece rate (35 PKR), she provides advance money to her workers to meet their emergency needs. Therefore, most of the female stitchers have a strong loyalty to her and are not willing to work for anyone else.

So far Shama has worked with more than three different subcontractors and left them for various reasons. She suspended her work with a subcontractor due to a boycott by female workers. However, within one week another subcontractor who offered better conditions contacted her, but this relationship also did not last long due to issues of payments. The subcontractor had an accident and spent the workers' payment on his treatment in an emergency and is still not able to make those payments, which amounted to about 12,000 PKR. According to Shama, he normally pays on time, but he was *trapped in bad time* and was not able to repay the money. So she left him and started to work with a new subcontractor. According to her, the new subcontractor is a poor fellow from a nearby village. He is working for another subcontractor and is not able to give advance payments to workers but he pays on time. This indicates towards multiple and complex layers of subcontracting in football industry. He also charges repair cost that on average is about Rs 3 per ball. For every 250 or 200 balls an amount equal to Rs 2200 or 1800 is deducted as repair costs, further bringing down the piece rate. However, as the number of workers in her team has reduced, so has their bargaining power. The life of Shama is a constant struggle, and her working life is complex and does not easily fit into available categories of work. Her agency at work is shaped by her existing opportunity structure in a broader institutional context.

Assessing Well-being of Female Homeworkers

Narrative life histories are not just a way of collecting stories but also involve making sense of those stories by giving a thick description of the lifeworld of people. Table 7.1 provide us a list of context-specific capabilities in the backdrop of which well-being of homeworkers is traced in narrative life stories. In attempting to evaluate the well-being of female homeworkers in the football-stitching industry, we explore the development of basic capabilities along three main but overlapping dimensions—individual, economic and socio-psychological well-being. Economic well-being is evaluated in terms of income and job security. Individual well-being was measured through factors such as job satisfaction, health status, children's education and work–life balance.

However, social well-being is analysed through capabilities such as access to social network support and community engagement. Although these are overlapping spheres, they are separated here for analytical purpose.

Economic Well-Being

To evaluate the economic well-being of female homeworkers, a list of basic capabilities is extracted against which economic well-being is evaluated. Sen defined capabilities as opportunities that individuals have to achieve certain functioning. Thus, capabilities are the individual's ability to do something, whereas functioning refers to achievements. The mutual dependency between functionings and capabilities, as the ability to choose a set of functionings, also depends upon the functionings previously achieved by the individual in his or her life. For example, the directly

Table 7.1 Operationalisation of well-being of female homeworkers

Well-being	*Capabilities*	*Indicators for direct improvement and indirect improvement*
Economic well-being	Income	• *Increase in income* Prospects for increase in income in future
	Labour market participation	• *Direct access to labour market* Possibility for future generations' labour market participation
	Social security	• *Availability of social protection mechanisms (informal)* Improvement for future generations
	Credit	• *Direct access to credit* Indirect access to credit
Individual well-being	Health	• *Improvement in health* Awareness about health issues
	Education	• *Knowledge has increased (literacy)* The possibility of raising this knowledge level for children has increased
	Nutrition	• *Nutrition improved* Increased possibility for better nutrition
	Accommodation	• *Adequate housing for family needs* Increase in income to afford better accommodation
	Domestic and non-market care work	• *Decrease in care work* Prospects of getting access to market care
Social and psychological well-being	Social networks	• *Increased participation in or creation of some types of social networks* Possibility of network creation
	Recreation	• *Involvement in recreational activity* Possibility of future resources for recreation
	Empowerment	• *Control over income, decision-making and mobility* Possibility of increased control in next/future generation (s)

Source: Naz and Bögenhold (2020)

needed functionings for capabilities are good nourishment, health and education (Gandjour, 2008). Sen himself argued that physical health and the absence of poor nourishment are important for people's "liberty to choose to live as they desire" (Sen, 1992: 67). There are other functionings that are indirectly related to the individual ability to do something; mental health is a case in point. In the case of mental health problems, like a mental disorder or negative thoughts, the individual's perception of existing opportunities might become distorted, thus limiting the individual's ability to seize the opportunity (Gandjour, 2008).

Sen's notion of capabilities and functionings provides us with a better and complete understanding of the quality of life of people. The term *functionings* refers to the current or actual life condition of people (Sen, 1993), for example the level of health, happiness, income and nourishment are some of the examples of functionings that a person can achieve. However, the functionings of an individual or family are the result of the choices already made. The standard of living reflects the amount of choices a person can make for different life achievements. People with the highest standards of living have the largest set of possible functionings (Jasek-Rysdahl, 2001). However, functionings are only a partial measure of the standard of living. Sen argued that, in order to have a better understanding of the standard of living, one must include a person's capabilities. However, capabilities are hard to observe directly; therefore, associated functionings are also explored by developing direct and indirect indicators of associated functionings. In-depth conversation with the respective respondent also helped to bring out what capabilities she has *reason to value* and deem relevant for her economic and overall well-being.

From the analysis of life history interviews, it is evident that though homeworkers are playing a very active role in the informal economy, they are nevertheless invisible in the official statistics. None of them have any written job contract. Restrictions on home-based production after the Atlanta Agreement (detailed in Chap. 5) have created a thick curtain that has further marginalized their contribution to the economy. The invisibility of homeworkers and the construction of the illegitimacy of home-based production in the football industry have effectively curtailed the possibility of organization for collective bargaining in the industry as it was very clearly demonstrated from Shama's interview. There are many institutional barriers that impinge on women's capabilities to access the labour market. Without education and formal skills training, choices to gain paid work are limited for female homeworkers. For instance, Fahmida had been doing hand embroidery for local community needs, but flow of that work was irregular and earning was low. She perceived that her capability in football stitching provided her with an opportunity to earn cash income for her families. This gave her a sense of accomplishment and she was glad that she was able to support her family during hard times. Her point of reference was other available options and past experiences.

Thus, there are many institutional factors that affect the capabilities of female homeworkers, for example existing gender norms, age, marital status and existing social and physical infrastructure are but a few. Taking a closer look at narrative life stories reveals that Saira as well as Fahmida's daughters, who were also football stitchers, have limited control and only indirect access over their own income compared to married respondents. Their pattern of work shows that they work like full-time workers but without any benefit associated with regular paid work. Often, home-based work is associated with an increased burden for unmarried homeworkers. In the case of married homeworkers, the responsibilities of care work are shifted to the eldest daughters at the cost of their schooling in some cases.

Though there is no job security and wages are very low, homeworkers reported overall enhanced economic well-being. In relation to opportunities for other forms of gainful employment for women, remuneration of homework can individually be seen as beneficial (Baylina & Schier, 2002; Burchielli, Delaney, & Goren, 2014). Economic well-being of homeworkers is enhanced by their participation in paid work as all of them were pushed by dire economic needs, and for them football stitching was the best possible options to choose from their existing opportunity structure. Major factors that were having negative impact on their working conditions were denial of their work in official discourse. Ban on home-based work has created illegitmization of home-based stitching, which has further pushed down the wages for homeworkers and muted any possibility of organization for their labour rights. The first step towards improvement of working conditions is that companies should admit the existence of these workers in their supply chains. They are adding value to the industry but their work and status are devalued by the industry.

Individual Well-Being

Five capabilities and associated functionings were extracted from the interviews to evaluate the individual well-being of female homeworkers: education, health, accommodation, nutrition and care work (domestic and non-market). An analysis of their= life histories shows that homeworkers attach great value to education. They do believe that education is a vital mean for individual well-being and a better life. They are passionate about providing education to their younger children and siblings to improve their life opportunities. Income earned from football stitching is an important source for them to realize this dream, which also involves sacrifices from elder sisters.

However, there was no evidence to indicate that homework provides opportunities to change gender role obligations at household level. Although women are spending eight to nine hours on football stitching, they are not exempted from their unpaid household work. In the absence of communal or market-based facilities for care work, female homeworkers manage all care work. For instance, although Shama is a full-time stitcher and a subcontractor, she has to manage her household work with help of her daughters and take care of needs of her husband. In terms of health capabilities, respondents reported health issues due to long hours of both paid and unpaid care work. Their working day is long, and most of them complained about problems like obesity, backs pain and stomach aches. However, in struggle of their life they were constantly struggling to improve conditions for their families at cost of their personal health.

In evaluating their life, one point of reference for female homeworkers is their own childhood and family situation. Their involvement in paid work seems to have brought some positive changes in their life: for example, respondents reported that income earned through football stitching had helped them to afford improved accommodation and nutrition. Many studies (Harris, 2003; Naz, 2017; Wapshott & Mallett, 2012) have documented the spatial issues that are caused by the potential overlap of work and non-workspace. However, this gap between academic discourse and homeworkers' perceptions about their living conditions can be explained in terms of individual life circumstances.

On the one hand, home-based work is providing means to the female homeworker to increase respect in the eyes of her family, including self-respect and work satisfaction, by increasing her income as a means to achieve her economic, individual and psychological well-being. On the other hand, homework is often associated with a critical reduction of some basic capabilities, including health, recreation, rest and the capability to take care of her children and other family members (Nussbaum, 2000).

We conclude that homeworking is not a totally negative phenomenon and the local economic system can benefit from the contribution of homeworkers. In turn, homework could also be made beneficial for homeworkers through the evolution of social protection mechanisms. However, this possibility of evolving from low-status survival activity to a valuable professional activity requires strong joint institutional support and some public intervention.

Social and Psychological Well-being

To evaluate the social and psychological well-being of respondents, four major capabilities and associated functionings were identified: empowerment, being respected, recreation and social networks. In terms of social and psychological well-being, both positive and negative perceptions about the empowering potential of paid work and associated well-being were reported. Empowerment was operationalized into two overlapping domains, private and public, and respondents reported association between their income and the enhanced well-being within private sphere of household. Multiple intervening factors affect individual sense of well-being at various stages of a person's life.

In terms of some indicators of empowerment, like control over income, decision-making, sense of self-worth and mobility, respondents reported a relatively improved sense of self-worth as a result of their involvement in paid work. Although the income earned by football stitching was not by itself sufficient for the family's needs, entire families worked together and pooled their resources to manage the family budget. The female homeworkers' control over their terms and conditions of paid work was also very limited. They had no formal job contract; their bargaining power was limited owing to their dependence on subcontractors for the provision of work. Their agency was further restricted by lack of marketable skills and the limited labour market opportunities for women in rural areas.

The working day of the homeworkers and the hours spent on homework reveal the error in considering it a flexible form of work. Women's paid productive work cannot be dissociated from their other daily activities. Women's involvement in paid work does not automatically translate into a revision of the gender contract (Sullivan & Smithson, 2007). Consequently, an inherent difficulty, calling for creativity, was involved in combining paid work with the unpaid reproductive care work that female homeworkers were performing. In principle, it is assumed that homeworkers have more opportunities to organize their work independently, but such decisions are not without repercussions for their income and livelihood security. Homeworkers have limited flexibility in terms of total hours of work, and they cannot decide about the quantity and rhythm of their work without facing serious repercussion on their income and future employment opportunities (Baylina & Schier, 2002).

However, in terms of existing opportunities, female homeworkers perceived working from home as football stitchers to be a much more respected and safe option compared to alternatives.

The life stories of homeworkers clearly reveal marital status as an important denominator for well-being of homeworkers. Unmarried women reported enhanced sense of empowerment associated with their paid work. However, their capabilities for social network participation are low, compared to married women, who have more control over resources and less restrictions on their mobility. Rather than directly confronting mobility constrained posed by patriarchal structure on mobility of young unmarried girls, they prefer to navigate by using various subtle and non-confrontational strategies. It was explained by Saira during her interview that whenever she has to go to the stitching centre, she is accompanied by other women or by younger siblings to avoid social disapproval. As homeworkers are working on a piece-rate basis, they work for nine hours on average to generate more income for their families. That leaves them with almost no time for recreation or participation in communal activities.

Concluding Thoughts

This chapter is based on narrative life histories of limited number of homeworkers; therefore, findings are not representative of industrial homework but at best can be claimed as indicative of working condition in global football supply chains. For homeworkers, access to paid work is more than a source of cash income. Industrial homework has a double role in the lives of female homeworkers, involving frequent trade-offs between various capabilities. It is supported from narrative life histories that homework enhances women's capabilities to earn much needed cash income that in turn is not only a source of their self-worth and satisfaction but is a source of their enhanced well-being. In the context of their lifeworld, income-earning opportunities are reported to command more respect from their family members in general. In the socio-cultural context of Pakistan where interconnectedness and solidarity serve as high values, family support is a capability that is highly appreciated by homeworkers. However, this subjective view of female homeworkers could not be used to mask some clear disadvantages and critical reductions in some basic capabilities faced by them in the system of global production organization. Life stories of homeworkers reflect reductions in capabilities of health, recreation and social protection. It is evident from the statements of respondents that in the complex socially, economically and spatially embedded life stories of female homeworkers, their individual perception of well-being is highly tangled and multidimensional. They are not satisfied with the wages but consider stitching as the most reliable source of income that is helping to enhance the capabilities of future generations. The sense of well-being and the choices made by homeworkers are relational and not necessarily individualistic in the context of industrial home-based work performed by women in rural areas of Pakistan. Although income earned through homework is low, with many deficits of labour and human rights, from the workers' perspective this is still considered an improvement under their existing opportunity structure. As opposed to the commonly held assumption of well-being that focuses on either the material aspect of well-being or subjective experiences of individuals, this study encompasses a broader definition of well-being that is informed by existing academic debates and intersubjective experiences of work and well-being by including unheard voices of female homeworkers. While industrial homework is not negative per se, a lack of collective action and of support through public intervention is the major hurdle to realizing its full potential to contribute to well-being. Considering the industrial organization of the football industry, where homeworkers are mostly clustered in a specific geographical location, the possibilities of fostering human development are comparatively higher with the right institutional support, because this natural clustering reduces the transaction costs for any development initiative.

References

Bathmaker, A. M., & Harnett, P. (2010). *Exploring Learning, Identity, and Power Through Life History and Narrative Research*. New York: Routledge.

Baylina, M., & Schier, M. (2002). Homework in Germany and Spain: Industrial Restructuring and the Meaning of Homework for Women. *GeoJournal, 56*(4), 295–304.

Binder, M. (2013). Subjective Well-Being Capabilities: Bridging the Gap Between the Capability Approach and Subjective Well-Being Research. *Journal of Happiness Studies, 15*(5), 1197–1217.

Burchielli, R., Delaney, A., & Goren, N. (2014). Garment Homework in Argentina: Drawing Together the Threads of Informal and Precarious Work. *The Economic and Labour Relations Review, 25*(1), 63–80.

Clark, D. A. (2005). Sen's Capability Approach and the Many Spaces of Human Well-being. *The Journal of Development Studies, 41*(8), 1339–1368.

Cornwall, A. (2007). Buzzwords and Fuzzwords: Deconstructing Development Discourse. *Development in Practice, 17*(4–5), 471–484.

Gandjour, A. (2008). Mutual Dependency Between Capabilities and Functionings in Amartya Sen's Capability Approach. *Soc Choice Welfare, 31*(2), 345–350.

Harris, L. (2003). Home-based Teleworking and the Employment Relationship: Managerial Challenges and Dilemmas. *Personnel Review, 32*(4), 422–437.

Jasek-Rysdahl, K. (2001). Applying Sen's Capabilities Framework to Neighborhoods: Using Local Asset Maps to Deepen Our Understanding of Well-being. *Review of Social Economy, 59*(3), 313–329.

Mills, C. W. (1959). *The Sociological Imagination*. New York: Oxford University Press.

Naz, F. (2017). The Position of Female Homeworkers in a Global Supply Chain: How Do Capitalist Labor Market Practices Interplay with Gender ideologies? In M. Haase (Ed.), *The Changing Basis of Economic Responsibility: A Look from the Perspective of Today* (pp. 125–147). Berlin: Springer.

Naz, F., & Bögenhold, D. (2020). Understanding Labour Processes in Global Production Networks: A Case Study of the Football Industry in Pakistan. *Globalization*. https://doi.org/10.1080/14747731.2019.1708658

Nussbaum, M. (2000). *Women and Human Development: The Capabilities Approach*. Cambridge: Cambridge University Press.

Pressman, S., & Summerfield, G. (2000). The Economic Contributions of Amartya Sen. *Review of Political Economy, 12*(1), 89–113.

Qizilbash, M. (2002). Development, Common Foes and Shared Values. *Review of Political Economy, 14*(4), 464–480.

Radcliffe, S. (2015). Gender and Postcolonialism. In A. Coles, L. Gray, & J. Momsen (Eds.), *The Handbook of Gender and Development* (pp. 35–46). London: Routledge.

Sen, A. (1983). Development: Which Way Now? *The Economic Journal, 93*, 745–776.

Sen, A. (1987). *Gender and Cooperative Conflicts*. Working Paper 18. Helsinki, Finland: World Institute for Development Economics Research.

Sen, A. (1992). *Inequality Reexamined*. Oxford, UK: Oxford University Press.

Sen, A. (1993). Capability and Wellbeing. In M. Nussbaum & A. K. Sen (Eds.), *The Quality of Life* (pp. 30–53). Oxford: Oxford University Press.

Sullivan, S., & Smithson, J. (2007). Perspectives of Homeworkers and Their Partners on Working Flexibility and Gender Equity. *International Journal of Human Resource Management, 18*(3), 448–461.
Wapshott, R., & Mallett, O. (2012). The Spatial Implications of Homeworking: A Lefebvrian Approach to the Rewards and Challenges of Home-Based Work. *Organization, 19*(1), 63–79.

CHAPTER 8

What Lessons Did We Learn?

Overview

The *Unheard Voices* is a truly interdisciplinary enterprise of investigation combining divergent academic lenses covering economics and political economy, development studies, industrial relations, social inequality studies, economic sociology, ethics and gender studies altogether. The interdisciplinary nature includes key words such as gender, work, and political economy as major topics bridging a diversity of knowledge domains and synthesizing discussions, which must be sought, found and fitted together like, puzzle pieces. The authors hope that those academic adventures have successfully hit their target. The book tries to argue theoretically and empirically and intends to balance both areas of investigation to one harmonized unit. So much academic literature has evolved on gender studies, especially during the last 20–30 years, that we are nevertheless optimistic to add one research lens which may be comparatively less explored, which is women working in the so-called Third World countries as workers of global supply chains.

The book *Unheard Voices: Women, Work and Political Economy of Global Production* is an interplay between two authors working as academics in distant places, split between two continents. In so far, they belong both in persona each to the so-called underdeveloped and developed world. What we found out is that the semantic distinction between those two (or even more) worlds does not make too much sense if we narrow down to concrete empirical questions of industrial relations and global political

F. Naz, D. Bögenhold, *Unheard Voices*,
https://doi.org/10.1007/978-3-030-54363-1_8

economy. Both worlds are so interwoven that they cannot be treated in isolation, as different worlds; the opposite is true. They are highly interdependent and governed by diverse modes of corporate strategies of international management, international labour markets, diverse sets of governmental structures and forms of financial and political power. The twenty-first century gives proof of the fact that we are a "one-world" society with world citizens who have very different life histories, work situations, and aspirations; and, at the end, extremely varying destinies weather in the form of life awards, health situation, or life expectancy.

Theoretical Landscapes

The rhetorics of capitalism have been repeated numerous times (Stiglitz, 2006). Key messages are division of work, decentral planning in corporations rather than in state agencies and competition operationalized by firms based on free property. Competition, communication and the interplay of all those items will foster productivity as driving force of economic development. The raise of economic development will lead automatically to an increase of wealth and prosperity in economy and society, so the sounding of the basic assumptions comes up which we all are hearing so often. All this is not completely right or wrong but it is too empty and too sterile, and therefore it is misguided and just only one part of the full truth. The problem with those statements is that they treat capitalist economies as if they exist in a vacuum but in reality capitalism does not exist in a vacuum. Instead of dealing with *economies in abstracto*, we deal almost with *economies in concreto*, meaning that economies have concrete institutions by which they differ among each other. Especially, different economies are linked to different societies which frame looking and working of each citizen. In other words, economies shape societies while societies shape economies. The reciprocal penetration of economy and society lead to the fact that different economies look always somehow similar and, simultaneously, specifically different. Culture matters (Harrison & Huntington, 2000) was a sound summary of a view which highlights cultural variables as forces which make the difference between *economy in abstracto* and *economy in concreto*.

Of course, institutional economics, in recent times starting with D.C. North (1990), is all about the integration of institutional elements into a concept of economy (Hodgson, 2000). These institutions include not only the system of law and governmental institutions but also all other regulations and how procedures in a society are working as well. Especially, the organization of labour markets, the principles of industrial relations and the system of education and further education in societies but explicitly also the working of the institution family and rules of trust and reciprocity, hence the principal codes of social norms governing a society which are almost interwoven with normative implications brought up by (different) religions, all these factors determine how societies concretely look. *Economics in abstracto* does not ask for those elements since it treats the analysis of capitalism independently, whether it is capitalism in Belgium, Bangladesh, Botswana or Brazil; but these countries differ considerably among each other. These countries do not share the same level of productivity and wealth. They have different labour market data, ratios of mortality and life expectancies, and also they don't share the same paths of historical development. One of the most critical neglects of *economics in abstracto* is that history as important variable of development was increasingly ignored. In the twentieth century, economics has started to forget history (Hodgson, 2001). History of economic theory was abolished or pushed to different other disciplines, almost to philosophy or science theory and economic and social history; as domains of investigation were outsourced to faculties of history, they were of increasingly less interest to economists. The academic adequate understanding of economic development is incomplete if we do not respect history and understand the social embeddedness of economic institutions and social behaviour.

Reasoning about globalization and the international system of economic and social relations is a very complicated academic issue in which we always must ask ourselves which are the specific elements in *concreto* and which *in abstracto*. Comparing international figurations of economic relations includes always the analysis of competitive economic advantages of nations. The understanding of prosperity and poverty refers always to a framework of historical explanations. Acemoglu and Robinson (2012) have dealt with the question why similar-looking nations differ sometimes greatly in their economic and political development. They conclude that history is the key since,

> It is a historical processes that, via institutional drift, create the differences that may become consequential during critical junctures. Critical junctures themselves are historical turning points. And the vicious and virtuous circles imply that we have to study history to understand the nature of institutional

> differences that have been historically structured. (Acemoglu & Robinson, 2012: 432)

The reader learns from Acemoglu and Robinson (2012) not only the need to dig deeply into historical issues to gain an adequate command of analysing to solve contemporary problems (see also Bögenhold, 2020), but also that economic and social developments are not simple highways always leading in the same direction. The global world is a complex puzzle with different subtle own logics, which is also integrated into international regulations of financial institutions. In this respect, Stiglitz used his famous formulation: "The global financial system is not working well for developing countries. Money is flowing uphill, from the poor to the rich" (Stiglitz, 2002: 245). The conclusion by Stiglitz is that "what is needed, if we are to make globalization work, is an international economic regime in which the well-being of the developed and developing countries are better balanced: a new global social contract between developed and less developed countries" (Stiglitz, 2002: 385).

The book *Unheard Voices. Women, Work and Political Economy of Global Production* is almost about processes of international integration and the question of how globalization processes effect lives of female (home) workers in a region of Pakistan who are producing goods for the sports industry as part of global supply chains.

Home-Based Work and Political Economy of Global Capitalist System

In recent times of Covid-19 crisis, home and office have met again to commonly practise new forms of home-offices; while these two spheres were historically separated for many decades in many countries, our field of investigation in the study of this book was always holding and having a kind of *home-office*. Homeworkers do their work activities at home; they are mostly regarded as a relic of premodern forms of working. However, for two reasons it shows that these activities are mostly relevant now when home and offices increasingly merge into home-offices; our explored workers have been working (and living) all the time in *home-offices*, although sometimes in very precarious social and material relations.

The word *economics* was introduced by the philosopher Xenophon in Ancient Greece. Combining *oikos*, meaning household, with nomos, meaning rules or norms, he invented the art of household management (Raworth, 2018: 11). Since then, economics evolved and went a very special way during the twenty-first century (Medema, 2019). On the way, economics forgot not only its own history but also its own links to different other disciplines. Household was no longer a place to analyse production in modern capitalism. What we are seeing now is that (female) homework has a firm location within the international *perfect storm* of rising inequalities (Milanović, 2016), it is part of one and the same game of global inequalities worldwide where legal and ethical constraints may come into clash.

Many contemporaries believe in capitalism as an autonomous machine which affects development including progress and prosperity by its own. Schumpeter is regarded as one of the pioneers of *evolutionary economics.* He viewed capitalism as *a form or method of economic change* (Schumpeter, 2000 [1942]: 82). *Creative destruction* serves as the title of a chapter in the book *Capitalism, Socialism, and Democracy* (Schumpeter, 2000) in which he deals with the modus operandi of competition which exists always as a development with a fragile balance of *coming* and *going* of firms, entrepreneurs, goods, ideas, mentalities and ideologies. Although Schumpeter is often regarded as academic hero of entrepreneurship and innovation, he was highly sceptical about the endogen creativity of capitalism to achieve a balance between creativity and destruction. In one chapter, he posed the question, *Can capitalism survive?* and he did not hesitate to answer, *No, in my opinion not.* He actually felt that socialism would eventually supplant capitalism. So far, Schumpeter can be said to have underestimated the potential innovation sources of capitalism. Schumpeter argues against some predominant economic thought at his time which was characterized as being static. In opposition to that, Schumpeter conceptualized economy being in a constant flux of economic and social change. Schumpeter frequently discussed the parallels and divergences of his thought and Marxism: "The essential point to grasp is that in dealing with capitalism we are dealing with an evolutionary process. It may seem strange that anyone can fail to see so obvious a fact which moreover was long ago emphasized by Karl Marx" (Schumpeter, 2000: 82).

Creative destruction is a contradictory expression which seeks to highlight the fact that competition and economic development are parts of the overall economic game. Creative destruction has to be seen in a wider context of innovation and entrepreneurship for which Schumpeter is well known. Entrepreneurs are treated as agents to introduce new inputs into the economy.

The book locates the empirical place of investigation to a region in Pakistan in order to investigate modes of the working of global capitalism. This procedure is just seemingly paradox but shows that one has to embed the analysis of the social, economic, political and ethical situation into the cultural and historical context of people and their life stories in order to find in the particular situation of people elements of a universal principle of our current world society. The living of poorly paid people have an ultimate link to the fun toys of other people in Western countries, where young generations wear sports clothes very often just as leisure clothing style.

Reconnecting this discussion to *creative destruction* shows that the international dimension of the world economy is increasingly neglected, especially the embeddedness of economies in global strategies of large international corporations and governmental policies which, both, enable partly the game of market forces. The most decisive factor (historically) accelerating, channelling and shaping the information technology paradigm was (and still is) the process of capitalist restructuring undertaken since the 1980s. This process led to a series of reforms (deregulation, privatization and dismantling of the social contract between labour and capital). Four goals were pursued: (1) deepening the capitalist logic of profit seeking in capital–labour relationships, (2) enhancing the productivity of labour and capital, (3) globalizing production, seizing the opportunity of the most advantageous conditions for production and (4) marshalling the state's support for productivity gains and competitiveness of economies. Without the new information technology, the capitalist restructuring would have been much slower, with much less flexibility (Castells, 2010).

Always new and emerging technologies have become more central so that among the wealthiest and most powerful industrial companies there were enterprises spanning a wide range of industries, the chemical or pharmaceutical industry, banking, insurances, energy, or food industries. Looking at the most powerful companies worldwide in terms of stock market capital, the landscape of the wealthiest companies has changed. Today, the top five companies in the world are Apple, Microsoft, Alphabet, Facebook and Amazon. All these companies are US-based firms, which operate globally and which are ultimately linked to the so-called digital age of capitalism. Among them, only Apple is centrally engaged in manufacturing, although this is carried out mostly in China, whereas the other big companies are primarily centred on developing, producing and selling software or running internet applications (Facebook, Google). Amazon is mainly engaged in selling and logistics. All these big ventures are knowledge intensive; they were created just a few decades back as start-ups by regular individual people, and they serve as impressive examples for hundreds or thousands of other young companies, giving the message that creativity combined with knowledge may matter, especially in the digital world. In other words, turning good ideas into opportunities and vice versa seems to have become one of the challenges of recent times. This view of modern capitalism corresponds to the idea that we can observe a paradigm change from managerial capitalism to entrepreneurial capitalism (Audretsch & Thurik, 2000), in which changes in economy and society multiply the dynamics and push forward elements of creative innovation and the need and power to raise permanent newness.

In parallel with those developments towards the so-called entrepreneurial societies, we observe a new division of labour and social contracts worldwide so that the domains of knowledge creation remain in developed countries, whereas labouring processes are almost outsourced to countries in those parts of the world offering cheap labour. In our case of football production, we see that entrepreneurial companies, being almost located in Europe and North America, concentrate their entrepreneurial potential almost at storytelling about corporate social responsibility (CSR) (Boje & Khan, 2009). Storytelling is a primary way by which entrepreneurs maintain the currency of their reputation. While marketing and corporate reputation literatures recognize corporate social responsibility as an eminent component of a company's brand strategy, the role of storytelling is not addressed by them. Entrepreneurs strengthen their brands through telling stories about their CSR initiatives. Such CSR stories improve the image of entrepreneurs with consumers, help them gain legitimacy for their labour practices and assist them in attracting other resources required for their continued success (Boje & Khan, 2009: 9). A careful examination of all entrepreneurship semantics shows that entrepreneurship is very often just a rhetoric which sometimes has poor content (Örtenblad, 2020).

Citizen premium and citizen penalty (Milanović, 2019) are so closely related to our orchestration of a world society since the living of members of one group is visibly related to the living (and working) of the other group. The reader finds himself or herself led on a journey through the study, where we learn about the regional cluster in Pakistan where football production is primarily going on, we learn diverse social and economic situations. This part reads very much as being a trip into unknown terrain, at least for many contemporary Western readers. However, we explicitly understand the research as exemplary research for an understanding of a political economy of globalization and the related international division of work. The study deals with a country in which several millions of working people receive their wages on a daily or weekly basis. The authors refer to links between political economy, business ethics in general and CSR strategies in particular. One of the lessons is that that multiplying the income of female homeworkers might be a solution to care for those actors without creating trouble for companies which employ homeworkers, since the share of wage or salary very often only accounts for a small share of the final budget calculation of a football. Taking this into consideration, the reader sometimes gains the impression that CSR is in danger of being just rhetoric cosmetic of global inequalities.

The interviews carried out with homeworkers and with other experts in companies and in public organizations are one source of empirical investigation. Another one is the discussion on the division of labour and companies and the relevant supply chains in the industrial sector of the football industry. We come with diverse empirical cases of supply chains. We describe the social and economic situation of football stitchers doing the job as female homeworkers and deliver numerous individual cases. Reading those cases provides systematic data to the reader. In so far, the told stories start to *live*, since we get to know concrete circumstances. Based upon qualitative—and in so far selective—interviews, the reader will find figures for different analytical categories like decent work and wages, relevant push-and-pull factors motivating people to do the jobs they do, and, finally, perceptions of living, expressions of well-being and happiness and ideas for further aspects of own living and the living of one's kids. It is shown that stitching can be organized in different forms, namely factory-based stitching, family centres, female subcontractors and, lastly, homeworkers.

The *Unheard Voices* also deals with gender ideologies in which it can be shown that the construction of gender has serious and different implications for men and women. In the end, economic conditions along with geographical distance, local patriarchal values of the stitcher community, modes of recruitment and a diversity of livelihood strategies are a few among many factors that shape the possibilities to engage in football stitching as a mode of earning their livelihood in the surrounding villages of the place of investigation, which was Sialkot, Pakistan. Most of the respondents interviewed during data collection are illiterate or semi-literate. They do not have any other marketable skills. Most of them combine football stitching with other forms of work available in local communities. Male homeworkers reported that they combine football stitching with other paid work and female homeworkers combine it with unpaid household work.

If we want to frame the issue of corporate responsibility in the global football supply chain, the study refers necessarily to companies and to workers and to systems of industrial organization. We learn to look through different lenses and also to see practical difficulties, which are discussed in the case of protection of child labour as well. These are serious *ethical dilemmas*. For instance, mainstream development theory, which has its roots in Western traditions, does not consider children as independent economic actor. According to Boyden and Levison:

> In effect, economics represents children as dependents who thereby personify household and societal costs, there being no workable theory of children as economic agents. Investment in children is assessed in terms of its role in increasing their economic productivity as adults rather than its potential for furthering the interests and welfare of children themselves. This is extremely important because economic policies nevertheless have a major effect on all policies about children, and therefore on children. (Boyden & Levison, 2000: 10)

Such framing of *normal* childhood fails to acknowledge variations of childhood experiences. Notions of childhood not only vary in cross-cultural settings but there are also considerable differences among different classes in the same culture. Different understanding of childhood have resulted in variation on discourse about child labour in various societies (Khan, 2010). Quoting the ILO: "The term child labour refers to ‚work and economic activities carried out by persons under the age of 18 years, that harms their safety, health and well-being and/or hinders their education, development and future livelihoods" (ILO, 2011: 5). However, the implementation of regulations to forbid child labour and to send kids to school has earnest implications for families to compensate lost income which child labour was potentially contributing to the family income. The study shows that different agencies (local governments, factories, workers, families) have sometimes differing perceptions of the phenomenon and that the rightness or wrongness of CSR strategies very often needs a much closer view than opinions from distant Western research desks suggest. The situation is serious as too often family incomes are so poor that even small financial contributions matter to sustain everyday life.

Finally, the book discusses ideas on conceptualizing the well-being of female homeworkers from the perspective of the capability approach (Sen, 1990). Economic interaction takes place within pre-existing institutions, lending it a social dimension that is hard to play down. In the same vein, the individual's well-being in any society cannot be completely divorced from the broader economic context. Sen's major contribution in the field of economics is to resist the desocialization of economics and challenge the philosophical foundation of traditional economic theory. Traditional welfare economics holds that individuals are rational beings, and free exchange will increase the well-being of these rational actors (Pressman & Summerfield, 2000). Sen (1983, 1993) expanded the notion of human well-being beyond consumption and developed better measures of poverty and inequality. He has introduced a different view of human economic agents having some intrinsic worth rather than being just rational utility maximizers. His notion of well-being also encompasses development of human potential by increasing the options available to individuals in any society. Sen asserted that when making normative evaluations about a valuable life, the focus should be on what people are able to be and to do, and not just on the material resources that they are able to consume. In this line of argument, known as the capability approach (CA), Sen (1987, 1992) built more realistic assumptions about economic science based on the notion of entitlements and human capabilities.

Choices can only be made in the context of available options. Thus, it makes sense to evaluate well-being in terms of broadening the available options or, in other words, by an expansion of capabilities. Based on the analysis of data gathered through narrative life history interviews, we intend to highlight the contradictory nature of industrial homework. On the one hand, if left to the devices of the free-market economy, it could be a source of exploitation of workers that not only puts serious constraints on their human development, but could also be a possible source of intergenerational transfer of poverty and depreciation of human capital. On the other hand, the implementation of policies divorced from the local institutional context is equally harmful and can have unintended consequences, which may deprive people of their sources of livelihood.

Industrial homework has a double role in the lives of female homeworkers that involves frequent trade-offs between various capabilities (Naz & Bögenhold, 2020). The response of female homeworkers on three-dimensional scale of well-being supports that homework enhances women's capabilities to earn cash income that in turn is not only a source of their self-worth and satisfaction but is a source of their enhanced well-being. In the context of their lifeworld, income-earning opportunities are reported to command more respect from their family members in general. However, this subjective view of homeworkers should not be used to mask some clear disadvantages and a critical reduction in some basic capabilities faced by female homeworkers in the system of global production organization. Critical reductions in capabilities of health, recreation and social protection are reported by the respondents. In terms of educational capabilities, more resources are reported to be directed towards the education of children that may increase education and the earning capabilities of future generations. However, the full-time involvement in homework to earn more income in some cases also compromises the education of mostly elder daughters, who have to share care work and take care of younger siblings, as there are no institutional facilities for child care in rural areas of Pakistan. It is argued that with right institutional support industrial homework may help to enhance the capabilities of homeworkers and their families, which in turn supports the goals of local development. The empirical data presented in *Unheard Voices* reveals that the lives of female homeworkers are intimately bound up in the dynamics of global production organization and the local institutional context. Female homeworkers are inherently at a disadvantage in the power asymmetry that exists between labour and capital in a global economy. Exploring the individual life histories not only highlights the processes of challenging and negotiating norms, but also sheds light on structural constraints that impose real barriers to the transformative potential of such actions.

Concluding Thoughts

The *Unheard Voices* delves into relatively unchartered territory of the invisible margins of global supply chains and hopefully will stimulate open discussions regarding the alternative economic choices by bridging gaps between economic and social domains. Incorporating ethical considerations into economic thinking and evaluating the limits and potential of such choices is a step towards fairness in the economic system. The idea of incorporating ethical consideration is not entirely new; rather there has been a persistent tradition in the history of economic thought. Economics as we know it today originated from political economy that has its clear origin in ethics. Adam Smith, whose ideas laid the foundation of economics and of the modern capitalist system, despite his panegyric of a free and unfettered market, had proposed a tripartite model of society comprised of three different but interrelated modes of social control: moral rules, law and the market.

It is important to underline at this point that industrial homework is not negative per se. However, a lack of collective action and of support through public intervention is the major hurdle to realizing the full potential of homework. Considering the systemic asymmetries of power between footloose global capital and informal home-based workers, who are relatively weaker stakeholders with limited ability to organize, it's inevitable to provide them institutional support to improve their working condition. We conclude that the possibilities of fostering human development of home-based workers are comparatively higher with the right institutional support. There is a need for more effective legislation and enforcement mechanisms for female homeworkers. The governments should extend the legal rights to the entire working population, including the female homeworkers, who are excluded from the enumeration as informal workers. The services of female homeworkers should be enumerated in the national accounting system, and they should be granted recognition as workers in official statistics. The evaluation of their contribution to the national economy and its recognition can bring some positive change to the existing situation through making them more visible. Another important strategy to improve the conditions of homeworkers is to support their efforts to organize themselves. It is evident from the data that homeworkers have contacts with their fellow workers but that the system of subcontracting works in such a manner that they are severely constrained in their sense of solidarity and common identity. Their contacts with one another are largely fragmentary and there are few, if any, public meetings of homeworkers. The purpose of helping the women to organize themselves, for example in a network, is to enable them to make contacts and frame their demands, but also better to understand just how important their position is in the production process overall. Civil society institutions can play an effective role in supporting organizations of female homeworkers to make claims, to acquire labour rights and improve respect for those rights by other parties. There is also a need to increase awareness among homeworkers about existing support mechanisms in the industry. Finally, efforts should be made to develop coordinated CSR policies at the local level with consultation of all stakeholders including female homeworkers. Providing training facilities needed for women homeworkers in their immediate vicinities in terms of acquiring skills will help them earn a better income. This will not only help the women to increase what they earn through their work, but is also important for the growth of the industry through the development of human capital. We sincerely hope that *Unheard Voices* echoes the voice of informal home-based workers in global supply chains and will hopefully initiate a critical reexamination of corporate strategies and policies in various cross-cultural contexts and especially in the context of developing countries.

References

Acemoglu, D., & Robinson, J. A. (2012). *Why Nations Fail: The Origins of Power, Prosperity and Poverty*. London: Profile.

Audretsch, D. B., & Thurik, R. (2000). Capitalism and Democracy in the 21st Century: From the Managed to the Entrepreneurial Economy. *Journal of Evolutionary Economics, 10*, 17–34.

Bögenhold, D. (2020). History of Economic Thought as an Analytic Tool: Why Past Intellectual Ideas Must Be Acknowledged as Lighthouses for the Future. *International Advances in Economic Research, 26*(1), 73–87.

Boje, D. M., & Khan, F. R. (2009). Story-Branding by Empire Entrepreneurs: Nike, Child Labour, and Pakistan's Soccer Ball Industry. *Journal of Small Business & Entrepreneurship, 22*(1), 9–24. https://doi.org/10.1080/08276331.2009.10593439

Boyden, J., & Levison, D. (2000). *Children as Social and Economic Actors in the Development Process*. Working Paper 2000: 1, Expert Group on Development Issues. Stockholm, Sweden: Ministry of Foreign Affairs.

Castells, M. (2010). *The Information Age. Economy, Society, and Culture. Vol. I: The Rise of the Net-work Society*. Oxford: Wiley-Blackwell.

Harrison, L. E., & Huntington, S. P. (2000). *Culture Matters. How Values Shape Human Progress*. New York: Basic Books.

Hodgson, G. M. (2000). What Is the Essence of Institutional Economics? *Journal of Economic Issues, 34*(2), 317–329.

Hodgson, G. M. (2001). *How Economics Forget History*. New York: Routledge.

ILO. (2011). Employers and Workers: Handbook on Hazardous Child Labour. Geneva, Switzerland. Retrieved from http://www.ilo.org/public/english/dialogue/actemp/downloads/projects/cl_handbook.pdf

Khan, A. (2010). Discourses on Childhood: Policy- Making with Regard to Child Labour in the Context of Competing Cultural and Economic Preceptions. *History and Anthropology, 21*(2), 110–119.
Medema, S. G. (2019). *The Economics Book: From Xenophon to Cryptocurrency, 250 Milestones in the History of Economics.* New York: Sterling.
Milanović, B. (2016). *Global Inequality: A New Approach for the Age of Globalization.* Cambridge: Harvard University Press.
Milanović, B. (2019). *Capitalism, Alone. The Future of the System that Rules the World.* Cambridge: Belknap Press at Harvard University Press.
Naz, F., & Bögenhold, D. (2020). Understanding Labour Processes in Global Production Networks: A Case Study of the Football Industry in Pakistan. *Globalizations, 17*(1), 1–18.
North, D. C. (1990). *Institutions, Institutional Change and Economic Performance.* Cambridge: Cambridge University Press.
Örtenblad, A. (Ed.). (2020). *Against Entrepreneurship. A Critical Examination.* London: Palgrave.
Pressman, S., & Summerfield, G. (2000). The Economic Contributions of Amartya Sen. *Review of Political Economy, 12*(1), 89–113.
Raworth, K. (2018). *Doughnut Economics. Seven Ways to Think Like a 21st-Century Economist.* London: Random House Business Books.
Schumpeter, J. A. (2000). *Capitalism, Socialism and Democracy.* London and New York: Routledge.
Sen, A. (1983). Development: Which Way Now? *The Economic Journal, 93*, 745–776.
Sen, A. (1987). *On Ethics and Economics.* Oxford: Basil Blackwell.
Sen, A. (1990). Gender and Cooperative Conflict. In I. Tinker (Ed.), *Persistent Inequalities* (pp. 123–149). New York, NY: Oxford University Press.
Sen, A. (1992). *Inequality Reexamined.* Oxford, UK: Oxford University Press.
Sen, A. (1993). Capability and Wellbeing. In M. Nussbaum & A. K. Sen (Eds.), *The Quality of Life* (pp. 30–53). Oxford: Oxford University Press.
Stiglitz, J. (2002). *Globalization and Its Discontents.* New York: W. W. Norton.
Stiglitz, J. (2006). *Making Globalization Work.* New York: W. W. Norton.

Index[1]

A

Agency, 10, 28, 34–38, 62, 113, 147, 150, 158, 159, 170, 175, 182, 189

Apprenticeships, 142

B

Bourgeoisie, 4

Buyer-driven, 54, 83, 87

C

Capitalism, 2, 5, 6, 8, 11–14, 21, 36, 53, 69, 76, 145, 146, 182, 183, 185–187

Childhood, 36, 161, 174, 189

Child labour, 65, 88, 90, 97, 104–107, 109, 110, 112, 114–119, 126, 128, 133, 134, 142, 189

Citizenship premium, 6

Classical liberalism, 12, 21

Consumer behaviour, 3

Cultural globalization, 8

D

Death of distance, 24

Debt bondage, 55, 136, 145, 152

De-middledization, 3

Deregulation, 12, 22, 23, 25, 47, 58, 68, 70, 123, 186

Discrimination, 32, 34, 39, 62, 88, 112, 130, 135

E

Economic globalization, 2, 8, 9, 11–14, 21–23, 25, 26, 28, 34–35, 77, 107

Economic liberalism, 21, 22

Empowerment, 28, 35–38, 58, 175, 176

[1] Note: Page numbers followed by 'n' refer to notes.

F. Naz, D. Bögenhold, *Unheard Voices*,
https://doi.org/10.1007/978-3-030-54363-1

Ethical dilemmas, 107, 114–118, 189
Ethical sanctuaries, 75
Exponential growth, 76

F
Feminization, 20, 27, 29, 35, 39
Flexibilization, 58–61
Forced sterilization, 36
Free market, 7–12, 21, 22, 190

G
Gemeinschaft, 75
Gender, 6, 19–39, 56, 58, 61, 62, 64–66, 68, 70, 84, 99, 111–113, 130, 135, 136, 139, 140, 142, 143, 146–149, 151, 152, 157, 160, 167, 173–175, 181, 188
Gesellschaft, 75
Global capitalism, 2, 58, 186
Global interdependence, 23
Globalizations, 1–14, 21, 23–26, 28–36, 38, 70, 81, 101, 107, 124, 157–177, 183, 184, 188
Global manufacturing, 54, 102
Global production networks (GPN), 20, 61, 69, 79, 80, 82–91, 97, 98, 102, 103, 118, 119, 126
Global production organization, 20, 24, 26, 83, 85, 138, 147, 177, 191
Globaphilia, 8
Globaphobia, 8
Governance, 11, 77, 83, 87, 97, 98, 118, 126

H
Home-based work, 29–35, 39, 47, 59, 60, 63, 65, 75–91, 102–104, 111, 118, 119, 123–153, 169, 173, 174, 177, 184–191
Homeworkers, 14, 30–32, 39, 45–70, 77, 85, 87–91, 98, 102, 104, 107–114, 119, 127–128, 133, 134, 136, 139, 140, 142, 144, 146, 147, 149–153, 158, 160, 165, 168–177, 184, 188–193
Horizontal linkages, 128
Human capital, 28, 34, 37, 57, 190, 193
Human rights, 66, 97, 104, 105, 177

I
Industrial outwork, Industrial relations, 4, 30–32, 181, 183
Industrial restructuring, 53
Inequality, 1–7, 20, 29, 34, 35, 59, 60, 76, 89, 157, 158, 181, 185, 188, 190
Inflation, 22
Informalization, 57–59, 138
Informational societies, 123
Institutionalization, 127
Instrumental value, 159
International communication, 23
Internationalization, 2
International trade, 23, 81

L
Labour force, 6, 20, 23, 25–30, 34, 35, 39, 52, 53, 59–61, 66, 101, 103, 110–112, 115, 126, 130–138, 145, 146
Labour market, 4, 13, 19–39, 57–58, 60, 63, 67, 111, 124, 145–147, 149, 152, 172, 175, 182, 183
Labour rights, 24, 33, 54, 58, 60, 89, 106, 113, 173, 192
Laissez-faire economic, 21
Liberalism, 12, 21
Liberalization, 12, 19, 22–26, 28, 35, 38

Life stories, 14, 158, 160, 161, 170, 173, 176, 177, 186
Livelihood, 11, 47, 55, 56, 63, 101, 107, 114, 115, 125, 132, 135, 137, 176, 188–190

M
Market fundamentalism, 12, 21
McDonaldization, 5
Merchandise, 99
Modern liberalism, 21
Multidimensionality, 158

N
Neoliberal globalization, 10, 12–14, 22–26, 28, 89
Neoliberalism, 10, 12, 13, 21–23

O
Organized labour, 24

P
Paradigmatic shift, 20, 38, 82
Patriarchy, 30, 37, 38, 69, 146–148
Political development, 21, 183
Political economy, 1–14, 32, 75, 85, 98, 111, 123–153, 158, 181–182, 184–192
Political globalization, 8
Poverty, 3, 5–7, 9, 23, 37, 54, 59, 64–66, 68, 107, 113–116, 136, 141, 149, 183, 190
Precarious employment, 14, 22
Privatization, 12, 22, 23, 27, 123, 186
Proletarians, 4

S
Segmented labour, 146
Social justice, 6
Social mobility, 3
Social protection, 54, 60, 65–68, 163, 164, 175, 177, 191
Social reproduction, 56, 63, 64, 111–114, 145–153, 166
Social stratification, 3, 5
Stratification, 3, 4
Structural adjustment, 22
Subcontractors, 32, 52, 55, 57, 58, 61, 65, 66, 102, 109–113, 115, 126–128, 133–136, 138–140, 142–144, 148, 163, 165, 167–170, 174, 175, 188
Supply chain, 53, 54, 57, 59, 65, 67, 78, 79, 83, 87, 88, 98, 99, 101–107, 112, 124–128, 130–137, 140, 141, 144, 147, 152, 158, 173, 176, 188, 189
Surplus labour, 54

T
Trade liberalization, 2, 22, 23, 25, 26
Transnational corporations, 19
Triangulation, 98, 124

The manufacturer's authorised representative in the EU is Springer Nature Customer Service Centre GmbH, Europaplatz 3, 69115 Heidelberg, Germany. If you have any concerns regarding our products, please contact ProductSafety@springernature.com

Printed and bound by CPI Group (UK) Ltd, Croydon, CR0 4YY
30/09/2026
02225698-0003